The
Art of
Jewish Prayer

The Art of Jewish Prayer

By Rabbi Yitzchok Kirzner

with Lisa Aiken, Ph.D.

Jason Aronson Inc.
Northvale, New Jersey
London

Production Editor: *Adelle Krauser*
Interior Designer: *Arthur Hamperian*
Editorial Director: *Muriel Jorgensen*

This book was set in 11/13 Palatino by The Coghill Composition Company of Richmond, Virginia, and printed and bound by Haddon Craftsmen of Scranton, Pennsylvania.

Library of Congress Cataloging-in-Publication Data

Kirzner, Yitzchok.
   The art of Jewish prayer / written by
Yitzchok Kirzner with Lisa Aiken.
     p. cm.
   Includes bibliographical references and index.
    ISBN 0-87668-652-8 (hardcover)
    ISBN 0-87668-220-4 (softcover)
    1. Amidah. 2. Judaism—Liturgy—Texts—History and criticism.
3. Prayer—Judaism. I. Aiken, Lisa. II. Title.
BM670.S5K57   1991
296.7'2—dc20
                                       90-21385

Manufactured in the United States of America. Jason Aronson Inc. offers books and cassettes. For information and catalog write to Jason Aronson Inc., 230 Livingston Street, Northvale, New Jersey 07647.

This work is dedicated
to Rabbi and Rebbetzin Michel Twerski
of Milwaukee, Wisconsin—
two outstanding individuals
who have touched the lives of thousands of Jews,
including those of the authors,
with their wisdom, understanding,
warmth, and friendship.
Their unique qualities
have brought a true dignity and vibrancy
to the lives of those whom they have touched.

Contents

Foreword

The meaning and sanctity of prayer and its application to man's ongoing relationship with G-d stand at the very core of Judaism. A Torah perspective—an exposition that will enlighten the modern-day reader to the insights and depth of our prayers—is thus of vital importance in these times.

Rabbi Yitzchok Kirzner, who is renowned as a very effective exponent of Torah philosophy and whose personal involvement and concern have impacted on many hundreds, has now contributed a written work, which I have had the pleasure to read, that conveys the basic truths and challenges inherent in the daily Shemoneh Esrai. This is a work that will enhance and deepen the obligation of Divine service to the seeking and thoughtful Jew, both the newcomer and the regular *davener*.

Rabbi Yaakov Perlow

Preface

Prayer has traditionally been a major focus of Jewish life. The edifices with which Judaism is so often associated—the Sanctuary of the Israelites, the holy Temple, the synagogue—were primarily houses of worship. In fact, the association between being Jewish and prayer is so strong that one's Jewish affiliation is often described according to where one prays.

Unfortunately, even those Jews who have been raised with the benefits of a strong Jewish education have rarely studied Jewish prayer in a relevant or meaningful way. The greatest link many Jews have to their religion is through prayer services. Yet many leave the services feeling no more inspired or spiritually aware than they were before they prayed.

The purpose of this book is to make Jewish prayer comprehensible and relevant to all Jews, whether they come from traditional Jewish backgrounds or have no formal Jewish education. This is one of the most comprehensive explanations in English of the Shemoneh Esrai prayer that has ever been written.

The Shemoneh Esrai is the most central of Jewish prayers, and its centrality is the reason for its selection as the focus of this book. Many of the commentaries that are presented here have never before been available to an English-speaking audience. Rather than simply limiting itself to explaining the Shemoneh Esrai, this book uses the Shemoneh Esrai as a vehicle through which the beauty and depth of Jewish philosophy and religion can be understood and appreciated. In so doing, it translates lofty spiritual concepts into ideas that are meaningful to the contemporary Jewish man and woman.

This book is based on lectures given by Rabbi Yitzchok Kirzner to students of his "Prayer" class. Dr. Lisa Aiken's role in writing this book was to convey Rabbi Kirzner's philosophical and psychological insights as faithfully as possible. Each chapter, from Chapter 4 through Chapter 22, discusses one of the nineteen prayers of the Shemoneh Esrai, according to its order there; each of these chapters begins with the text of its prayer, gives the historical background, and discusses the meanings of the Hebrew words. In most chapters, the rationale for that paragraph's order in the Shemoneh Esrai is also presented, along with a detailed explanation of each prayer's theme. The chapter concludes with a discussion of how the message of that prayer can be applied to improving human relationships.

For simplicity's sake, all of the Hebrew words from the Shemoneh Esrai have been translated into English, and in some cases they have been transliterated as well.

It is our hope that this book will transform the experience of praying into one that is meaningful and uplifting.

We would like to express our appreciation to Rabbi Moshe Kirzner for his assistance in supplying the footnotes for this book, and to Mrs. Shana Kramer for her invaluable help in proofreading.

May it be the will of God that, in the merit of revealing the Jewish art of prayer, the authors be granted the strength and inspiration to pray meaningfully before God, and be worthy of long lives in the service of the Almighty and His great people.

Rabbi Yitzchok Kirzner
Lisa Aiken, Ph.D.

Iyar 5751

The
Art of
Jewish Prayer

CHAPTER 1

The Relevance of Jewish Prayer

Many of us shy away from praying because of limitations in how we view God, and also due to our expectations of how He should act. We often feel motivated to pray for very specific reasons, and there are specific things that we expect as a result of praying. For many of us, it is the lack of things that we need, or think we need, that motivates us to pray. For one person, the need may be to have a good job. For another person, it might be to find a spouse. For a third person, it might be to have children. For a fourth person, the need might be for good health.

Since we want to directly express our words when we pray, instead of having God read our minds, we often enclose a description of our desires that resembles a shopping list. We then feel rejected or ignored if our wishes are not fulfilled, preferably by that same afternoon. One of our expectations of God is that He should make us happy by giving us what we want, when we want, and how we want it. Frequently, we see prayer as a vehicle to acquiring those desired objects.

Prayer should be more than simply a vehicle by which we acquire things that we want. However, it can be more than that only if we are prepared to be active participants in a challenging task. That task begins with our seeing God in a more mature way.

Imagine that you are a 3-year-old child and you want a piece of cake. In fact, not only do you want a piece of cake, but you want to eat the whole cake! Your considerations as a 3-year-old are, "If I want cake, then I am entitled to it, and I must have it." From the viewpoint of a young child, the major function of

3

parents is to gratify the child's wishes. When they don't, the child feels angry and deprived.

Now imagine yourself in the place of the parent of the child who wants the cake. You happen to know that if the child were to eat the cake, he would get sick, or would lose his appetite for nutritious food for the rest of the day. From the parent's perspective, how would you feel declining the child's request? How great is the difference between the child's feeling and that of the parent in the same situation!

Imagine a second vignette involving the difference in perspective between a child and a parent. If someone were to ask a 6-year-old what his housewife/mother does all day, what might he say? There is a good chance that the child would say, "Nothing." If the mother were then asked what she does, her reply might be something like: "I got up at 6:30 and made breakfast for the children. Then I made lunch for them to take to school. One of the children forgot to show me his homework from the night before, so I had to go over it with him. Next, I did a load of laundry. . . ." In the same situation, people can have very different perspectives about what is occurring and *why* it is occurring.

Now imagine a third scenario. You see a cadre of men stabbing a person with knives. They proceed to knock the victim unconscious, saw open his chest, and suction out his blood. . . . How do you feel upon witnessing such a scene? When you are told that you are witnessing a man undergoing open-heart surgery, how do your feelings change?

One of the fundamental differences between how children and adults view the world is that children filter the world primarily through their emotions whereas adults can rely more on their intellect to make sense of their experiences. Our emotional view of God is often that of the child who wants, and whose perception of a totality of a picture is lacking. We often feel angry at God for hurting, frustrating, or ignoring us. We have to realize that these feelings are reactions to our perceptions of God, not to the reality of how God acts with us. We can never get total knowledge about God's motivations in how He acts with us. Therefore, when we react to God's denying us what we want, we must rely, at least in part, on our intellectual understanding of His behavior, and also in part on trust.

Trust

Trust between two people is built primarily in three ways: First, it is an outgrowth of the history of a relationship. If a wife has found her husband to be generally caring and loving over a variety of situations and over a long period of time, then she learns to trust him. Second, the more one does for the other, the more the recipient learns to trust the giver. Third, trust is furthered through communication. The more two people share their inner thoughts and feelings with each other, the more trust is fostered between them. Just as these three elements foster trust between people, they are factors in how we learn to trust God.

The manner in which we were created was designed to maximize our ability to trust God. In addition, our prayers were designed to foster trust by focusing us on how God provides for us in the same way that a trustworthy husband provides for his beloved wife.

One of the ways in which our lives were set up to teach us to trust God was through our having parents. Parents were created to serve as partial models of God. We learn to trust our parents, and their intentions, through their constant demonstrations of love. We learn to accept authority when we obey our parents, even when their rules seem unreasonable, because we learn to trust that they know certain things that we don't. Moreover, we learn to accept disappointment and to continue feeling attached to our parents even when our desires aren't gratified. We can do this because the closeness with our parents is inherently gratifying.

We can graciously accept disappointment only if it is in the context of a loving relationship. Once we don't feel that our parents love us, we feel manipulated and controlled if they continue to affect our lives. When we feel that God loves us, then we can accept His disappointing us. When we feel that He doesn't love us, then pain and disappointment make us feel as if God is exercising punitive power over us.

When the parental relationship is loving, we learn to accept situations that are emotionally disappointing, because we know that they are ultimately for our benefit. In the same way, we are then able to accept that God's love can be given in ways that we can't fully appreciate, and that we may not always experience as immediately gratifying.

Relating to God

In order to grow spiritually, we have to generate for ourselves a sense of the presence of God, and then we have to be able to relate to it. Although God may seem to be quite hidden at times, He makes us feel His presence when we seek Him. Prayer reaches into the highest realms of heaven, even when we ask for mundane things, because prayer addresses God directly. When we start the day having an encounter with God through prayer, we create a spiritual base on which our entire day rests.

We prepare ourselves for prayer by imagining that God is in front of us and that He is listening to our prayers. As a result, we try to pray in such a way that the Godly presence will hear us. Maimonides (Rambam) says that creating the mind-set that we are in the presence of God is a prerequisite for our words to be considered prayer. This is an essential part of what is referred to as *kavanah* (concentration) in prayer.[1] If we simply mouth the words of prayer without having the feeling that we are addressing God, our words are nothing more than a monologue. In order for words to be considered prayer, we should have at least minimal concentration and awareness as to the meanings of the words we say.

Historical Background of the Need to Communicate with God

God created us with the need to pray so that we would have a vehicle through which we could forge an ongoing relationship with Him. We see this from the story of Adam and Eve in the Garden of Eden.[2] In the beginning of the Bible, we read the account of the serpent enticing Eve to eat of the prohibited fruit of the Tree of Knowledge. She, in turn, gives Adam the forbidden fruit to eat. God responds by punishing Adam, Eve, and the serpent. Adam and Eve are expelled from the Garden of Eden and are punished with other curses. God curses the serpent by telling him that from that point on, his food will be the dust of the earth.

The dust of the earth is ubiquitous. It seems baffling that God considered it a curse to tell the serpent that no matter where he might find himself, he would always have plenty of food. How was it a curse to tell the serpent that he would eat dust for the rest of his life?

The reason this was such a curse is that dust is so plentiful that the serpent would never have to turn to his Creator in order to get his food. God was so disgusted with what the serpent did that He wanted to have as little connection as possible with it. By cursing the serpent with self-sufficiency, God would have no need to be involved with him.

In contrast to God's reaction to the serpent was God's wish that people would always turn to Him to get what they needed. As with the serpent, however, it is frequently the case that the more self-sufficient people feel, the less contact they feel compelled to have with God. The more people's needs are met without their turning to God, the less motivated they often feel to be involved with Him.

The Reasons for People's Physical Limitations

God could have created human beings without physical limitations. After all, angels have no physical or material needs. The Talmud says that God specifically set up our lives in such a way that we have to turn to Him three times a day in order to get what we need. We have to ask Him on a regular basis to provide us with knowledge, food, health, shelter, as well as with spiritual awareness. We are supposed to be motivated to maintain a relationship with God through needing to turn to Him for our daily requirements.

This concept is illustrated by a parable in the Talmud, in which a king gives his children their monetary allowances every day.[3] Even though the king could have given them their allowances in a lump sum once or twice a year, he knew that his system would ensure that he saw his children on a daily basis.

God specifically created human beings with physical limitations so that we would not be self-sufficient. He created us with the necessity of praying for our physical and material needs. However, the acquisition of material needs is not supposed to be the only thing that happens when we pray. Prayer has two essential purposes: First, it is to be a vehicle through which we can forge a relationship with God and make Him a reality in our lives rather than an abstract concept. The second purpose of prayer is for us to transform ourselves into more developed people through having to ask God to fulfill our physical and material needs.

Throughout Jewish history God created, and will always create, situations in which Jews lack something critical. When He creates a situation of need for us, it is His hope that we will turn to Him and pray for what we need. For example, most of our Matriarchs were barren when they got married because God desired their prayers. Without God's having created a situation of lack for them, they might not have prayed to God with the same intensity and introspection with which they ultimately prayed to have children.

God frequently holds back from giving that which someone wants so that the supplicant will introspect about his or her true reasons for wanting it. It is hoped that, through introspection, the person will develop a more authentic and meaningful motivation in asking for whatever he or she requests, and that, when the gift is finally granted, the person will then use it in a spiritually meaningful way.

The Purpose of Prayer

The task in prayer is not to get God to change. God doesn't change. The task is for us to become better and more developed through our encounter with God. We can become better people through lacking something and then having to ask ourselves if we should really want what is missing. If we decide that we should want it, and we do get it, this process reinforces to us that we should use that gift in a way that God intended in order to elevate us spiritually. Otherwise, we might simply use it to satisfy our physical or material desires.

Reasons for Standardized Times for Prayer

Our Sages ordained that we are supposed to pray three times a day—in the morning, in the afternoon, and in the evening.[4] The reason is that we need to include God in our lives at different times throughout the day. When we arise in the morning, we need to go into the day knowing that each day is a gift which God graciously gave us. This awareness results in our relating better to people during the course of the day. It sets the stage for our being ethical in our business and personal dealings, and for our being appreciative of what we have. Once we realize that everything we have is a gift from God, we want to dedicate our resources to developing spiritual goals rather than to misusing our resources. The whole experience of the day thereby becomes one in which God is actively involved.

In the middle of the day, it is easy to get so caught up in our ability to create and to control the world that there is a danger that we will forget there is also a God. While we're busy working, it's easy for us to feel that everything we accomplish is due to our efforts alone. We are therefore required to pray the afternoon service at a time when we have to drop everything we're doing in order to pray. Doing this makes a powerful statement that even in the midst of our creativity, we recognize that our success and creative abilities are also blessings from God.

The evening prayer teaches us the concept of faith and belief. Even if we haven't accomplished everything we wished to do today, there will be new opportunities for accomplishment tomorrow.

These three critical elements—the opportunity of the day, recognition that our creativity and power are blessings from God, and faith—help us share our life experiences with God.

If we prayed only when we felt like it, there would be times when we would be far removed from prayer, and we would not make the necessary effort to recognize God's involvement in our lives.

The lack of motivation to pray should not be taken as a sign that we shouldn't bother with it. Rather, it should serve as a sign that we need to make a greater effort to let the words of the prayers affect us as they can and should. The amount of time we take to pray is not as important as the feelings of our hearts which we bring to prayer.

Another reason for having standardized times for daily prayer is that there are special times every day when God waits to hear our prayers. This is analogous to the way that one expects one's spouse to be home at a certain time every day, and to connect with him or her at that time. Imagine what would happen to a marriage if the husband and wife spoke to each other only a few times a year—about as often as many people feel motivated to pray with feeling!

When the men of the Great Assembly redacted the prayers of the Shemoneh Esrai, they did so with prophetic knowledge and divine wisdom. This granted them the ability to see what would happen to the Jewish people throughout history, until the time when the Messiah would come. This foreknowledge allowed them to compose the prayers that Jews would need to say in all future generations in order to maintain their vital connection with God, both individually and as a nation. They were able to discern, in ways that we frequently are not, what Jews in every generation would require in order to flourish emotionally, intellectually, materially and spiritually.

The Work of Prayer

The Hebrew words for prayer tell us something about what is supposed to happen when we pray. The Hebrew word *lihitpallel* is usually translated as "to pray," but *lihitpallel* also means "to judge oneself." Prayer is supposed to be a process by which we preface any words that we might say to God by first taking a long, hard look at who we are spiritually. Before we pray we have to ask ourselves: "What am I doing with my life? What are my material, intellectual, and emotional assets? How am I using them to further my spiritual growth?"

Another Hebrew term for prayer is *avodah shebelev*, "work of the heart."[5] The work of prayer is the transformation that we undergo in confronting the real reasons that we are asking for what we want. In meaningful prayer, we work on ourselves to ask for that which will enable us to serve God better, not simply service our own egos.

Many people, in asking God to give them things, have the attitude that "If I want it, then I should have it." They wouldn't find these types of requests legitimate coming from their own children, let alone from other adults, so why should God find them legitimate? If we pray to God primarily for the purpose of His giving to us, just so that we can have more of what we want, this is glorified narcissism, not prayer. If we pray for the sole purpose of controlling the Master of the World so that He will do our will, this is not prayer.

The Need to Verbalize Prayer

One of the tenets of Jewish prayer is that it is not enough simply to "think" a prayer, or to have a certain feeling in one's heart toward God. Jewish prayer requires that people actually say the words that they think or feel.[6] Why do we have to verbalize prayer? Why can't we just feel something in our hearts and communicate it to God through our thoughts?

When two people have a relationship with each other, one of the greatest challenges of the relationship is in communicating effectively with each other. Many married couples love each other but cannot communicate that love. Love and communication are not synonymous. For example, ask any woman if she would rather have her husband tell her that he loves her or have him only feel it in his heart. If a husband can't express his love to his wife, or vice versa, the love may ultimately be eroded and eventually be replaced by anger and resentment.

In the same vein, it's not enough for us to worship God in our hearts. We must also communicate our thoughts and feelings verbally, or they cannot enable us to develop a deeper relationship with God. When we say what we feel, God becomes more of a reality for us, and we show a deeper level of sincerity about the relationship. No normal person speaks out loud unless someone is listening. Our verbalization concretizes for us that God really hears what we say. In addition, once we verbalize our feelings, they attain a reality that is much stronger for us than had we not committed these feelings to words.

We can't get as excited about someone by simply thinking about them as we can by verbalizing our feelings about them, and to them. When we say something, the power of our words crystallizes our feelings in a way that demands inner clarification. Until something has been committed to words, it can remain a nebulous feeling. Our relationship to God requires that our inner feelings become clear to us and that we use words to express our feelings to connect with Him.

Fulfilling the Purpose of Creation of the World

Our standardized prayers are structured so as to develop our relationship with God. Part of the vehicle by which we do this is our appreciation of all of the good things God does for us. Our relationship with God begins when we express this appreciation verbally through prayer, and when we recognize it behaviorally by observing the commandments of the Torah. This also makes us worthy recipients of that which God wants to give to us.

God has put each of us in the world in order for us to experience His presence. That is the ultimate way in which a person can receive goodness from the Almighty. No two people have the exact same life experiences that bring them to the realization of God's presence. God's master plan is for all of us to develop ourselves individually, such that God's presence in the world is obvious to us in every facet of our lives. God created the world in such a way that His presence in it would be hidden, but would still be detectable should we wish only to look for Him. When we see that everything God has given us—physically, materially, intellectually, and emotionally—has a spiritual purpose, and when we use these gifts to serve Him, then we have brought to fruition God's plan in creating the universe.

Notes

1. Maimonides, *Yad HaChazakah*, Laws of Prayer 4:15,16.
2. Genesis 3:6.
3. Talmud *Bavli*, *Yoma* 76a.
4. Maimonides, *Yad HaChazakah*, Laws of Prayer 1:5,6,8.
5. Talmud *Bavli*, *Taanit* 2a.
6. Maimonides, *Yad HaChazakah*, Laws of Prayer 1:5,6.

CHAPTER 2

Prayer as Intimate Communication

I t is very difficult for most contemporary people to relate to
prayer. It is rare for us to pray in the meaningful ways in
which prayers were designed to be said. It is so easy to become
distracted as soon as we open our prayerbooks. We think about
our latest business deal or investment, about what we are
going to say to our friends once we finish praying, about what
we will eat once prayer is out of the way, and so on. Frequently,
the ways in which we set ourselves up to pray are guaranteed
to fail.

Even if we intellectually appreciate the need to pray in a
standardized and regimented way, that knowledge does not
ensure that we will pray in a meaningful manner. Many Jews
know that they should pray, yet they don't want to discipline
themselves in order to pray successfully.

Thus, we come to prayer with many barriers. Most of these
barriers are rooted in questions that develop, some of which
generate negative attitudes. The most important change we
can make in our attitude about Judaism, and about prayer, is
to realize that whatever small changes we can make are worthwhile. Any small steps, any attempts to make positive changes
in the ways that we pray, are valuable.

The Hebrew word *kol* (or *chol*) has two meanings. Sometimes
it means "everything," and other times it means "any part of
the whole thing." When the Torah speaks about prayer, it says
that the Jews should worship God *bichol levavchem*.[1] This can be
translated as "with your whole heart," or "with any little piece

of your heart" that one cares to devote to serving God and praying to Him. When we pray, we need to know that it is not an all-or-nothing phenomenon. Even if we spend an hour reading from the prayerbook, if we can dedicate just three minutes of that hour to intense worship, that is significant. Those three minutes are a good start. We can try to discipline ourselves to concentrate a few minutes longer the next time, and the next. True concentration in prayer starts with a single step, not with an iron mind and a genius' brain.

Levels of Spiritual Development

Most of us believe that there are certain absolute truths and that we possess them; we feel others may be entitled to their opinions, but most people believe the truth is whatever they personally believe. Judaism believes that there are different levels of truth, depending upon the individual's level of spiritual development.

Let's say that two people trust God. There may be vast differences between the degree to which one person trusts God's ability to take care of him and the extent to which the other person trusts Him. One person may trust in God only when he is in a crisis and all else fails. This person believes that God involves Himself in people's lives only when they cannot take care of things themselves. In such a person's reality, God does not involve Himself in people's lives when there is no crisis.

A person who is more spiritually developed can see that whatever he does will not be successful unless God wants it to be successful. This is a higher level of reality and truth than the former "truth."

When we want to grow spiritually, we must develop a heightened sense of reality for ourselves. Growth is the ability to see and understand reality more fully and to be more involved in realizing our potentials.

How do we expand our sense of reality? How do we make not only quantitative changes, but qualitative leaps in our understanding of reality?

One way in which we can grow to a higher level of reality is through our actions. Someone may study a spiritual concept and want to internalize that higher level of reality. However, studying and wishing alone will not make that reality a true part of him. The person has to try to behave in a manner consistent with the higher level of reality. When this reality is concretized by a certain behavior, the person develops an infinitely higher spirituality than if he simply thinks and hopes about where he should be.

For instance, let's say that someone believes in God and is presented with a lucrative business deal. Unfortunately, the deal is dishonest. If the person truly believes in God's abilities, he will realize that just as God presented him with a dishonest deal, He also has the ability to present him with an honest one. Even though the person cannot fathom at that moment how God can give him as good a deal in the future, he backs away from the dubious venture. Despite his disbelief, his actions make his belief in God stronger, because he concretizes his belief with deed. Thus, one way of growing from one level of reality to another is to do something to concretize a higher level of belief. People invest more in what they do than in what they simply feel or think.

Praying to the Essence of God

A second form of growth comes about through prayer. Jewish philosophy speaks about the distinction between the essence of God and a definition of the characteristics of God. The essence of God has to do with limitlessness and lack of boundaries. These concepts are beyond our comprehension, since we are rooted in the physical world. Inasmuch as we can't meaningfully talk about the essence of God, we speak about His actions. An act of God may seem to us to be compassionate, or just, or powerful. Thus, we can define God's actions and attributes, but not His essence.

When we pray, do we communicate with the essence of God or with an attribute of God? We don't pray to the attributes of God, or to symbols of Him. We don't pray to the Holy Ark, to a Star of David, or to angels. We pray to God directly, and we ask Him to assist us in various ways through His actions.

This presents a very interesting paradox. On the one hand, we don't pray to God's attributes. This means that we pray by speaking to a God that we cannot even define! Whom, then, are we addressing when we pray? It is very difficult for us to relate to a Being who presents us with no physical reality. When we pray, we must somehow imagine that we are standing in front of a Being who listens to our every word and yet who gives no instantaneous feedback. The mind-set of prayer requires making a leap from our limitations in defining God, to making Him a concrete reality for ourselves without being able to see or touch Him.

Since we can't understand God, how can we go through the motions of trying to reach Him?

The answer is very simple. While our intellects cannot understand God, our emotions and hearts can comprehend and feel God. Were prayer a function only of our brains, then we would never be able to pray. The brain would never be able to transcend its physical limitations to truly comprehend God. Our hearts have the capacity to reach where our intellects can't. A heart can sometimes understand how to reach another human being where the mind cannot fathom how to do so. Our minds might *believe* that God exists, but our hearts can *feel* and know how God exists.

As much as we yearn to reach a God who at times seems inaccessible, God yearns, as it were, to respond to our strivings. Were our entire task in prayer to try to engage our hearts to talk to God, we might not succeed. However, the process of prayer is not a one-way street. Once we start talking to God, we demonstrate that we are trying to access Him. That act on our parts is very touching, so to speak, to Him. He desires the relationship with us as much as we need the relationship with Him. When we attempt to come closer to God, He responds by narrowing the gap. If we sincerely want to talk to God, then our prayers never go unanswered.

If this is so, how is it possible for us to pray with sincerity and yet not get that for which we prayed?

The Goal of Prayer

The major goal of prayer is not simply to get the "thing" we request. It is to create a relationship through the object we desire. For this reason, we should never feel that if we pray for something and we don't get it, then we have wasted our time.

There are many reasons why God may not give us what we request, and some of these will be addressed later. When we feel that our prayers accomplished nothing because our requests were declined, we miss the most essential purpose of prayer. The primary goal of prayer is to elevate us through communication with God. This is always accomplished when we pray with sincerity.

When we try to grow spiritually, we should want only things that will further our spiritual development. Let's say that we want to make a good living, and we ask God to grant it to us. If we were to make the same request of a human being, we would have to make a case as to why our request should be granted. If we imagine that we are talking to God when we pray, then we also have to imagine that He is listening to us. What does it sound like to God if we tell Him that we need to make $100,000 next year so that we can have a new car and a fancier house? If we made that same request of a friend— expecting him to give us money for the same reason—would he find it legitimate?

When we try to imagine speaking to God, we must consider what our requests sound like to Him. The more we can construct a way for God to relate to what we say, the better we are communicating with Him. In true communication, it is not enough simply to tell others what you feel. You try to make them feel what you yourself feel, by describing your feelings in terms to which they can relate. Similarly, when we communicate with God, we ask, "Have I just communicated something to God that will sound meaningful enough for Him to respond to my request?"

There may be numerous reasons for God's rejecting our requests. There are times when we should assume that our requests were not legitimate, or that they will not be granted unless we plan to use them for positive purposes. For instance, if a man asks God to help him find a wife, or grant him good health, or children, or a good income, the ultimate reason for this should be not only so that he can be happier. Ultimately, he should want these things so that he can lead a better Jewish life.

When we pray, we should communicate to God that if He grants our requests, they will be used to help others and they will improve us spiritually. Doing this reorients us into taking stock of why we should ask for what we are requesting.

Whether or not we get our requests should not impede our ability to create a bond with God. Any time we create an authentic connection with God, we are engaging in a type of prayer. If we are in a crisis and we ask God in the space of thirty seconds to help us out of the situation, that is prayer.

When someone prays the standard prayers only because it is the right time of day to do so, he is going through the motions of prayer but has no desire to make a true connection with God. The standard times and the standard words of the prayers may or may not be connections to God, depending upon how we each determine what we want to happen when we pray. If we are not interested in expressing what we feel in our hearts, nor in having God connect to us, then the words are lip service, not prayer. True prayer requires that we ask God to be close to us.

The Obligation to Pray

One of the 613 commandments of the Torah is the require-ment to pray. The Torah tells us in Deuteronomy that every Jew is required to "serve God with his whole heart and with his whole soul."[2] The Talmud asks, "What is meant by *serving God with one's heart?*" It concludes that this verse means we are required to pray.[3] This is one of the two sources of the Jews' obligation to pray.

The second source comes from the Prophets.[4] It refers to our obligation to pray after we have sinned as a means of spiritual growth. This second source refers to our having turned away from God, and our asking God to help us return. We can always ask God to assist us in our spiritual growth, even when by straying we have removed ourselves from our spiritual roots.

We can only call out to God truthfully if we are ready for spiritual elevation and personality modification. We must have a certain humility, and recognition of God's power, in order to be able to relate to Him. A relationship with God requires many of the same elements that a relationship between two people requires. They both require communication of feelings from one person to the other, and the desire for one person to ask the other for help at times. When we open ourselves up in any relationship, not only do we become closer to the second person, but the second person becomes closer to us as well. Similarly, the more we share what is in our hearts with God, the closer He can be to us.

Conversely, the more we hide ourselves from God and keep our feelings private, the more distance we maintain between ourselves and Him. If we hold back, we prevent God from being close to us. The reality of God for us is created by our willingness to share our inner selves with Him. The more we share our thoughts and feelings with God, and the more we develop ourselves to make these thoughts and feelings acceptable to Him, the more we deepen our relationship with Him.

"God is close to those who call Him."[5] We try to create a bond with God, and He meets us halfway. This means that when we begin to pray, we often find it difficult to imagine having a relationship with God, but as soon as we begin sharing our feelings with Him, He quickly responds by allowing us to feel His nearness and His reality. The more we allow ourselves to let go of our privacy and share our innermost selves with God, the more we overcome the distance that we feel between ourselves and Him.

Many times in life we busy ourselves because we are afraid to look at ourselves. We do the same thing when it comes to connecting ourselves to God. We are afraid to let go of what we feel is our ultimate control over ourselves. We distract ourselves so that we can run away from God and not face who we are and who we should be. If we would only start to express our feelings and emotions when we pray to God, His "abstractness" would quickly be replaced by a sense of His immanence and reality.

A Mystical Concept of Prayer

When we open up and pray to God, we bring to bear our feelings about human relationships. For example, a married man may want the attention, love, and devotion of his wife, but he may believe that she is not really interested in him. As long as he feels that way, he will not be able to open himself up to her nor to express his deepest emotions and concerns. No one reveals his or her innermost self to someone they don't believe cares about them.

In a similar manner, we cannot open ourselves up to God without knowing what His true "feelings" are about us. What does God think about us, and what does He want us to be? If deep in our hearts we believe that God doesn't care about us, or He dislikes us, then there is no way we can pray to Him. When we talk to someone we believe isn't interested in us, even if the person truly is, we will not share ourselves with that person.

In all of our prayers, we refer to God in an absolute sense as well as a relative sense. We begin most blessings with the words, *Baruch atah A-do-nay Elo-heinu Melech haolam*—"Blessed are You, God, King of the universe." The word *baruch* ("blessed") means that God is the Source of all blessing which comes into this world. We refer to God by various names, each of which expresses some aspect of this essence, or conduct in the world. The name Y-H-V-H, which we now pronounce A-do-nay, is known as the Tetragrammaton. It can refer to God in an absolute sense, as He exists even without a world. In this description, He is not defined in terms of His relationship with anything or anyone else.

It is fairly common in our prayers that when we refer to God by His absolute Name, we follow it by calling Him *Elo-heinu Melech haolam*, "our God, who rules the world." The moment we refer to God as an abstract God, we immediately follow it with the realization that God has bound Himself up in our world and is interested in a relationship with us. *Elo-heinu* means that God wants to be our God, He wants to be connected to us. *Melech haolam* ("King of the universe") means that God wanted to create a world in which He could give of His love and could show His concern for His creatures.

How Should We Relate to God's Withholding What We Want?

Judaism says that everything God does is for the ultimate benefit of the person who is being affected. If this is so, why can a sick person pray to have sickness taken away from him? Isn't that tantamount to asking God to take away something that is beneficial?

There are many answers to this question, and the following is only one response. God, more than anything else, wants us not to have to be in pain. Had God only been interested in making people suffer, and were He not interested in giving to us, He would not have created us, nor the world. God created human beings because He wanted to give. The ultimate concern on God's part is to be able to give, but the world was constructed in such a way that we need to learn how to receive.

Imagine for a moment that a man has a family heirloom worth thousands of dollars and he wishes to give it to his son. The son happens to be very clumsy and careless, and it is obvious that if he gets the heirloom, it will be shattered within moments. Nevertheless, it would be very painful for the father to be deprived of the opportunity to give the gift to his son. Thus the father wants to train his son to be able to receive the heirloom.

When we go through situations in which we don't receive from God, we should wonder if we haven't prepared ourselves to receive, or if we have in some way damaged our ability to receive. (There are many reasons for people's suffering, and some have nothing to do with their being unable to receive.) Nevertheless, as a starting point, we should be aware that God wants to give and at that moment He is not giving. Therefore, even though it hurts us that we are not receiving, we should be aware that God must also be hurting. God's desire to give is at least as strong, if not stronger, than our desire to receive.

Yet, He wants us to receive in a deserving way. This means that He can give only when we have done what we must in order to be able to receive properly.

When God is not giving, it may be that we have not done what would make it appropriate for Him to give to us. If that is the case, then we should work on improving ourselves so that we can be appropriate recipients of whatever God wishes to give us. Moreover, when God does not give to us, we need to generate a sense of the disappointment that God "feels." After all, He is being deprived, so to speak, of that which He most wants to do. When we can empathize with His disappointment, we will have generated a very deep feeling in our relationship with Him. The moment that we begin to empathize with someone else's feelings, we inevitably open ourselves up to the other person. This process automatically reinstates us as "receivers" of God's giving, because it restores our relationship with Him.

Prayer is more than our search to acquire objects. We seek the individual who gives us the objects. In order to find the Being who is behind all giving, we have to be willing to share our feelings with Him, and appreciate the importance of having a relationship with Him. In so doing, we recognize how important our relationship with God is to Him. When we feel God's pain of disappointment in us, we take an important step in deepening our relationship with Him. Prayer is the vehicle through which this relationship is expressed and nurtured.

Implications of Human Interaction for Prayer

Our ability to pray can be only as developed as our ability to communicate with other people. The difficulties a person has relating to others will also manifest themselves in his or her relationship with God. Each prayer in the Shemoneh Esrai contains information that helps us relate to God. Each also tells us what we need to develop in our human relationships in order for them to flourish, even though the prayers were not composed for this purpose. When we develop these qualities vis-à-vis others, we simultaneously establish the foundation for a relationship with our Creator. The forum for expressing the qualities that establish and maintain a relationship with God is prayer.

Notes

1. Deuteronomy 11:13; *Nefesh HaChaim*, treatise 2, chapter 15.
2. Deuteronomy 11:13.
3. Talmud *Bavli*, *Taanit* 2a.
4. Gates of Repentance 1:15.
5. Psalms 145:18.

CHAPTER 3

Standing in God's Presence

אֲדֹנָי שְׂפָתַי תִּפְתָּח, וּפִי יַגִּיד תְּהִלָּתֶךָ.

My Lord, open my lips and my mouth
will tell Your praise.

Theme of the Prayer

The most central prayer of every Jewish service is the Shemoneh Esrai ("eighteen blessings"). It is also known as the Amidah, which means "standing" in Hebrew. It has been given this appellation because it is the only part of the prayers for which we must stand, provided that we are able to do so.

The Shemoneh Esrai was composed by the 120 men of the Great Assembly, with divine inspiration. It was designed to create a format for the spiritual growth of the person praying. If someone has time to say only one prayer every day, he or she should say the Shemoneh Esrai, because it encompasses within it all of the elements of prayer. It focuses in on our needs in the most personal way of any of the prayers. Anyone should be able to find within it all of his or her hopes, aspirations, and goals for living. At first glance, the themes of the Shemoneh Esrai prayers may seem to be archaic and not relevant to our needs in the twentieth century. With proper understanding, however, the relevance of these prayers today can readily be seen.

Structure of the Amidah

Even though this prayer is known as the "eighteen blessings," the Amidah now consists of nineteen prayers, each of which ends with a blessing. The Amidah did originally contain just eighteen prayers, but a nineteenth was added in talmudic times. There are three prayers of praise at the beginning of the Shemoneh Esrai, three prayers of thanks at the end, and thirteen prayers of personal request in the middle. Each of the prayers is based on an event that occurred during early Jewish history. The blessing that concludes each prayer was originally recited by angels to God when that historical event occurred.

How One Says the Shemoneh Esrai

We derive many of the laws about how the Shemoneh Esrai is to be prayed from the conduct of a woman named Chana. Chana was married to a prophet. Despite their many prayers over the course of their marriage, Chana remained barren. One Rosh Hashanah she went to the Holy Temple and fervently prayed to have a child. Her prayers were answered, and she gave birth to the prophet Samuel. Since her prayers were an example of the sincerest devotion in prayer that one might have, we try to emulate her when we pray. Two examples of how we emulate her are, first, that just as Chana said her prayers silently, moving only her lips, so do we say the Amidah to ourselves instead of aloud. Second, just as Chana prayed standing, so do we.

When we pray the Shemoneh Esrai, we begin by standing with our feet together, facing Jerusalem. Generally, this means facing east, although theoretically it could mean any of the four directions, depending upon where we are. Next, we take three steps backward, followed by three steps forward, returning to our original place. Doing this gets us into the mind-set that we are about to address a King and we are humbly presenting our petitions to Him.

Redemption as a Prelude to Prayer

Before we say the Shemoneh Esrai in the morning prayer service, we say a sequence of prayers. These begin with the morning blessings and verses of praise to God. Following these, we say the Shema, a fundamental prayer that affirms our belief in one God and our acceptance of His command-ments. Then we speak about how God took us out of Egypt; this is referred to as our redemption (*Geulah*).

It is significant that we discuss God's having redeemed us from Egypt immediately before we say the Amidah. The Zohar says that when the Jews were in exile in Egypt, their power of speech was also "in exile."[1] This means that the Jews could not express themselves while they were in Egypt because their spiritual sensitivities had become dulled. As long as this was the case, the Jews' ability to pray was hampered. When they were redeemed from Egypt, their power of speech was redeemed with them, and they were again able to pray. This is vividly seen by the fact that they sang the Song of the Sea to God shortly after their redemption.[2]

True redemption is the revelation of qualities that are hidden within a person. Prior to the Jews' redemption from Egypt, their deepest essences were hidden within themselves, and they had lost their ability to communicate their deepest feelings. When the Jews were freed from Egypt, they were once again enabled to express their deepest yearnings, longings, and emotions. It is for this reason that the primary commemorative event of the Exodus is the Passover seder. The hallmark of the seder is the recitation of the Haggadah—literally, our recounting of the redemption of the Jews from Egypt. Passover in this way celebrates the redemption of the Jews' speech by using the faculty of verbal expression.

The process of prayer is learning the techniques of self-expression to God. Redemption, which must immediately precede prayer, is the process of discovering our innermost feelings so that they can then be communicated to God.

There is another reason why prayer, par excellence, directly follows redemption. When we yearn for redemption, we want to capitalize on that feeling. Once we feel a spiritual awakening brought about through reliving God's past redemption of us, we pray to Him to redeem us again. Therefore we connect past redemption in the *Geulah* prayer to present and future redemption in the Shemoneh Esrai prayers. We don't interrupt between the prayer of past redemption, which immediately precedes the Amidah, and the Amidah prayers themselves.

"My Lord, Open My Lips"

We preface the Amidah prayer with the words, "My Lord, open my lips and my mouth will tell Your praise."[3] This verse is technically not part of the Amidah itself. As was just noted, we are not allowed to interrupt between the prayer for redemption and the Amidah itself. Why, then, is this verse from

Psalms recited, as an apparent interruption, between the Redemption prayer and the beginning of the Amidah proper?

The verse in question is found in a psalm of repentance, in which King David reflects about how he can return to God after having behaved inappropriately with Batsheva.[4] After being reprimanded for his actions, David wished to reestablish a relationship with God. His actions serve as a model for how we, as individuals, are supposed to repent when we sin.

In the process of David's repentance, he was overcome by certain emotions. Primarily, he felt inadequate. Had his actions only been accidental, he could have expiated his sin via an animal offering, combined with repentance. When a person sins, he distances himself from God. Through the process of offering an animal as a "sacrifice," the sinner brought himself back to God; he did this by recognizing the enormity of the distance that the sin put between himself and God, and he underwent a process that closed that gap. However, offerings atone only for unintentional mistakes. David's behavior had been deliberate, and there are no animal offerings that expiate deliberate sins. David did not know how he could close the chasm that he felt kept him apart from God.

David realized that under the circumstances, God wasn't interested in the sacrifice of an animal. He wanted David to return to Him. David then realized that he could bring himself back to God through prayer. Nevertheless, he felt so embarrassed about what he had done that he couldn't engage his mouth to start speaking. He felt that he had erred so badly that he didn't even have the right to ask God for an audience with Him. Therefore, having trouble opening up his mouth, David asked God to help him. He turned to God and said: "My personal God, the God who has always been my God and who has never moved away from me, give me the ability to open up my mouth. Help me start to rebuild our relationship, since I am the one who went away from You. Once I can communicate with You again, and You grant me an audience, I will be able to praise You again."

David's situation has tremendous significance for us today. The Talmud tells us that after the destruction of the Second Temple, the Jewish people said to God, "We are a terribly impoverished people. We no longer have a Temple in which we can bring sacrifices to You. We no longer have a format through which we can come close to You when we do something wrong."[5]

God's response to their poignant plea was: "I want words. Bring forms of communication, bring your feelings, bring your heartfelt emotions to Me. Allow yourselves to cry and pray to Me, and I will accept you in the same way that I always accepted what was done in the Temple." This is what God meant when He said: "I am not interested in your sacrifices and offerings. Rather, I want to hear your words of emotion. Bring yourselves to Me."[6]

During the time when the Temple stood, there was a scarlet thread on top of the Holy Ark.[7] If God granted the Jewish people forgiveness every year on the Day of Atonement, the red strand turned white. When this sign of forgiveness occurred, the entire Jewish people rejoiced. In the Song of Songs (a book that describes the love God feels for the Jewish people), God says to the Jews, "Your lips are like a scarlet thread."[8] This verse means, "The lips of Jews communicating their feelings to Me are as significant as was the scarlet thread in the times of the Temple."[9] Forgiveness is not tied to the Temple, nor to a scarlet thread. It depends upon the words and feelings that the Jewish people bring to their relationship with God.

In a relationship between two people, one of them may hurt the other and create a distance from the friend. Sometimes the one who created the gap recognizes that he or she was wrong and wants to heal the relationship. When this occurs, there is nothing wrong with the injured party's helping the person who made the error. The injured one could also make known to the one who inflicted the hurt how much he or she appreciates hearing the friend's sentiments. At the same time, the one in error can try to rebuild the relationship by telling the friend: "You know, I have trouble saying things. Try to understand what I want to say, because it's not easy for me to open up to you. Please help me."

When we pray in contemporary times, we have no Temple. We might feel very inadequate talking to God, or think that He is not really listening to us. Some people think that God has better things to do than listen to us when we pray. When we feel inadequate coming before God with our prayers, we have to keep in mind that it is precisely our innermost feelings, thoughts, and words that God truly desires. When we feel far away from God, and as if we have nothing to say to Him, we remind ourselves of King David's approach to God after a gap was created between the two of them. We begin by asking God to help us open up and communicate by requesting, "My Lord, open my lips."

Implications for Us of "Open My Lips . . ."

The problem that King David had in feeling too embarrassed, or too inadequate, to speak to God also occurs between two people. Relationships between people can easily be destroyed when one party makes a mistake and is too ashamed or afraid to approach the other. He or she may be afraid of being ridiculed or rejected by the partner. Sometimes, the outcome of this situation is that the first person shuts down emotionally and remains silent rather than facing the humiliation of acknowledging that he or she erred. Such withdrawal will eventually erode the relationship, and the silence will soon be replaced by resentment.

The more times that partners in a relationship refrain from communicating, the less possible it becomes for them to acknowledge the positive points about one another. One of the worst things for someone to do is to convince him or herself that when the partner demonstrates one bad quality, there are no good qualities remaining. In a relationship, each person must understand the importance of always trying to recognize and acknowledge the partner's positive qualities. It is essential always to keep the lines of communication open in order for a relationship to thrive.

". . . And My Mouth Will Tell Your Praise"

The second part of "My Lord, open my lips and my mouth will tell Your praise" seems a bit strange. If David wanted a renewed relationship with God after feeling distant from Him, then it would seem more logical for him to say, "My Lord, open my lips, and then we will be back together again." Why is "and then I will tell God's praise" the logical consequence of David's opening his mouth to God?

When two people don't get along and there is a lack of communication, this lack of communication creates even more distance between them. If this cycle continues, allowing a build-up of anger, they will get to a point that each will deny even what is true about the other. The last thing an angry person wants to do is praise someone who infuriated him. This same cycle happens in our relationship with God. When we feel distant from God, we aren't able to open our mouths and praise any of God's virtues. It is incongruent with our natures to praise people as long as we feel a tension about them. In order for us to legitimize our lack of communication with others, we deny enough of their good qualities to justify our position.

We do this with God as well. When people have a certain complaint against God, they don't want to hear anything good about Him. If they feel that He didn't deal with them fairly in some way, they don't want to acknowledge any of the good things that He did for them. They have to protect their position of feeling wronged. Such an attitude makes it almost impossible to establish communication with God.

When David said "Open my lips," he was asking for God's help in communicating with Him. Once communication resumed, David would then again be able to see the positive attributes of God. He would be able to let his mouth "tell God's praise."

When we pray, the more we want to communicate with God, the less threatening the idea of prayer becomes. Moreover, the communication itself causes us to open ourselves up more and more to God.

Implications for Us of "Telling Your Praise"

One reason we begin the Amidah by praising God is so that we can remind ourselves of all the wonderful things that He has done for us. In order for us to nurture our human relationships, we must likewise acknowledge that we receive wonderful and beautiful gifts from others. If these feelings remain unverbalized and unexpressed, they cannot nourish the relationships with those who give to us. Every relationship requires moments when each partner says positive things about the other. When either party feels that he or she is never praised and is never the central concern in the partner's heart or mind, that relationship cannot be a good one.

Understanding God through His Praise

There is a concept that when we are attracted to God by a deeper understanding of Him, the energy of that attraction helps bring us closer to Him. The more we understand someone, the more intimate that relationship becomes. For this reason, the most intimate relationships in the Bible are referred to as one person "knowing" another person (*daat*), as when Adam "knew" his wife.[10] A relationship built on knowledge is deeper than any other type of relationship. Understanding leads to true and lasting appreciation of another person.

When we say that we "praise" God, we mean that we attempt to understand Him and to be enthralled by who He is. We praise God for our benefit, not because God needs it. There is a verse in Proverbs that says, "Someone can know the value of a person by how that person is praised."[11] Rabbenu Yonah says that this verse does not mean that one can tell the value of a person by what others say about him, because it is easy for people to put up facades.[12] Rather, it means that one can tell the value of a person by what that person praises. No matter who a person is, and what he has or hasn't accomplished, a person can be judged by what he aspires to in life, and by what he praises. Even if his aspirations are not totally realized, they are usually a good indication of where his heart is and what his values are. Thus, accomplishments alone are not as important in assessing a person as are the person's motives and goals.

Once we can say that someone else is great, which may in itself be a difficult thing to do, our ability to compliment and appreciate his or her qualities helps us become greater. If we can be only critical, and can never fully appreciate the greatness in anything else, we have nowhere to aspire to grow within our own lives. We must admire something enough to commit our energies behind it in order to foster our own growth. Therefore, when we say that we praise God, we are referring to allowing ourselves to be excited enough about God's attributes that we want to emulate Him. The more we look up to God, the more we want to know Him, emulate Him, and serve Him.

Finding Meaning in Life through Appreciating God

There is a verse that says, "Everything was created for God's honor."[13] This does not mean that the world was created for God's ego satisfaction. It means that all things in the world should strive to appreciate God's attributes so that they have something meaningful toward which to direct themselves. The more we strive toward ultimate meaning, the happier we become.

A person who is depressed loses his or her aspirations. Nothing seems important; the individual has no one to look up to and nothing toward which to strive. Someone who loses his focus in life must reorient himself toward finding something important in order for life to be meaningful.

When David asked God to help him communicate so that he could say God's praises, he meant that in distancing himself from God, he had lost his sense of striving. He had lost his sense of appreciation of true meaning in life. Later, when David yearned to return to the closeness of a relationship with God, he wanted to be able to strive once again. He wanted to be able to appreciate God's virtues and to try to refine himself to emulate those characteristics.

The challenge of praising God is a personal one. The word for "thanks" in Hebrew is *todah*, and the root of this word also means "admission." When we truly thank someone, or truly thank God, it is always an admission—an admission that we have received, have appreciated, and have acknowledged that someone has given to us and we have benefited from that giving. Once we are willing to admit the greatness and goodness of God in His actions with us, that admission becomes a major factor in our ability to communicate with Him. Once we can acknowledge God as the source of everything, we recognize that there is no need to go anywhere else but to Him for what we need. Moreover, once we recognize that God has already given, we understand that He will give again. Through this admission, we realize that God gives to us only because He cares for us. If He cares so much about being involved with us, then we should want to respond to His caring by reciprocating and involving ourselves with Him.

Thus, even though it is forbidden to speak between the prayers of Redemption and the Shemoneh Esrai, we are required to add the words, "My Lord, open my lips and my mouth will tell Your praise." Without this mind-set of wanting to connect ourselves to God, to appreciate who He is, and to strive in our own lives to be better, the prayers that follow have no meaning. This preface is considered vital to our efforts to communicate meaningfully with God.

Implications of Bowing at the Start of the Amidah

After saying "Open my lips and my mouth will tell Your praise," we begin the first paragraph of the Shemoneh Esrai by bowing. Bowing symbolizes a sense of humility, which is a required component of any relationship. Arrogance and egocentrism are barriers to two people becoming one. True humility means that people are able to defer their desires and to temper their sense of entitlement. It means being able to forego what they want in order to compromise with another. It means being able to listen empathically instead of being interested only in expressing themselves. Two people can't bond together without both having some sense of humility.

The art of prayer requires that we let go of our inner stubbornness that cries out, "I don't need God." We cannot bond with God unless we are able to acknowledge that we do need Him. Similarly, when people maintain that they are totally self-sufficient and need no one, they remain single.

Bowing at the beginning of the Amidah expresses the recognition that we can want, and that we can depend upon God to give. When He does give, we can be gracious recipients as long as we maintain our humility.

It is common for people to dislike admitting that they have received something. It makes them feel inadequate. If a person is not capable of receiving, he or she can't possibly have a relationship with any other person, nor with God. By the same token, it is important for a person to recognize that sometimes his or her partner needs to give, even if at that moment the first person feels no need to receive. Being a gracious recipient encourages a partner's self-esteem and sense of accomplishment and deepens the bond between the giver and the receiver.

Notes

1. *Zohar Chadash* II 25:2; Introduction to *Reb Zadok Haggadah* #108.
2. Exodus 14:30–15:19.
3. Psalms 51:17.
4. Psalms 51:3,4,9–15.
5. *Bamidbar Rabbah* 18:21; *Shemot Rabbah* 38:4.
6. Hosea 14:3.
7. Talmud *Bavli, Yoma* 67a.
8. Song of Songs 4:3.
9. *Shir HaShirim Rabbah* 4:3.
10. Genesis 4:1.
11. Proverbs 27:21.
12. Gates of Repentance 3:148.
13. Isaiah 43:7.

CHAPTER 4

Shield of Abraham

בָּרוּךְ אַתָּה יהוה אֱלֹהֵינוּ וֵאלֹהֵי אֲבוֹתֵינוּ, אֱלֹהֵי אַבְרָהָם,
אֱלֹהֵי יִצְחָק, וֵאלֹהֵי יַעֲקֹב, הָאֵל הַגָּדוֹל הַגִּבּוֹר
וְהַנּוֹרָא, אֵל עֶלְיוֹן, גּוֹמֵל חֲסָדִים טוֹבִים וְקוֹנֵה הַכֹּל, וְזוֹכֵר
חַסְדֵי אָבוֹת, וּמֵבִיא גוֹאֵל לִבְנֵי בְנֵיהֶם, לְמַעַן שְׁמוֹ בְּאַהֲבָה.
מֶלֶךְ עוֹזֵר וּמוֹשִׁיעַ וּמָגֵן. בָּרוּךְ אַתָּה יהוה, מָגֵן אַבְרָהָם.

❖❖❖❖❖❖❖❖❖❖❖❖❖❖

Blessed are You, Lord, our God, and the God of our forefathers, God of Abraham, God of Isaac, and God of
Jacob. The God, the Great, the Powerful, and the Awesome,
most high God, who does good deeds of lovingkindness, and
is the Creator of everything, and remembers the deeds of
lovingkindness of our forefathers, and who brings a redeemer
to their children's children, for the sake of His name, with
love. King, Helper, and Savior, and Shield. Blessed are You,
God, Shield of Abraham.

Theme of the Prayer

This is the first of the paragraphs of the Shemoneh Esrai, and it is referred to as the prayer of *Avot* (Forefathers). It discusses the relationships our forefathers created with God, and how we benefit from them.

In order for us to fulfill our obligation to pray the Amidah every day, we must understand and be conscious of the definitions of the words of at least this first paragraph.[1] This paragraph is the first of the three prayers in the Amidah that praise God. Although each Amidah prayer ends with a blessing, this is the sole paragraph that also begins with the words, "Blessed are You, God" (*Baruch Atah HaShem*).

There is a verse in the Song of Songs that says, "We have a little sister. . . . If she becomes a wall, silver pillars will come from her."[2] This verse alludes to Abraham. The word in Hebrew for "silver" (*kesef*) comes from the word meaning "yearning" (*lichsof*). Thus, the "silver pillars" in the above verse are homiletically interpreted to mean that "pillars of yearning" would emanate from Abraham. These would be his descendants who would always yearn for God. Abraham was willing to defend God's existence and honor against Nimrod and the four kings. This manifestation of Abraham's love for God subsequently became an innate part of Jews for all generations, never to be uprooted from them.

How does God protect the love that the Jews have for Him, to ensure that it will never die? God promised Abraham that since he loved God so much, God would always love his Jewish descendants. When we feel God's love for us, then we will also feel love for God. Through this mirror-like process, God protects the love. The Song of Songs says, "Many waters cannot quench love, neither can the floods drown it."[3] No matter what the Jews absorb from the nations of the world that causes them to forsake the Torah, they will not be able to extinguish the love of God for His people and hence the Jew's love of God. This everlasting love always has the potential to draw us back to Him, regardless of how far away we have strayed. This idea is what is referred to in Yiddish as the "pintele Yid"—the indestructible love that deep down we feel for God.

Historical Background

Each of the prayers of the Shemoneh Esrai is identified with a particular historical event. In the case of the *Avot* prayer, the event was Abraham being condemned to death by King Nimrod. Nimrod wanted to punish Abraham for insisting that idol worship was folly and for promoting the belief in God. Nimrod threw Abraham into a fiery furnace, telling him that he should rely on his deity to save him.[4] God came to Abraham's rescue by sending an angel who saved Abraham from the inferno. This first paragraph of the Shemoneh Esrai ends with the words, "Blessed are You, God, Shield of Abraham." The angels said this blessing in praise to God when He saved Abraham for refusing to bow down to idols.

There is a second version as to the historical background of this prayer. In Genesis, a story is told about five kings who rebelled against four kings but were defeated by them. The four kings then kidnapped Lot, who lived in the region of the five kings.[5] Their reason for abducting Lot was to force Abraham, Lot's uncle, to come to Lot's rescue and fight against them. Abraham came to save Lot, and then conquered the four kings in order to accomplish his mission.

In this version, the kings hoped to accomplish the same thing Nimrod hoped to do: Eradicate Abraham and everything he stood for. Abraham felt his life's work was to promulgate a belief in one God. Nimrod and the four kings made it their mission to try to keep this ideology from gaining adherents. In both situations, God shielded Abraham so that he could convey his belief in one God to others. When the angels saw this, they exclaimed, "Blessed are You, God, Shield of Abraham."[6]

The Concept of Blessing

What does it mean to say that God is "blessed" (*baruch*)? Rabbi Chaim Volozhin says that the Hebrew word *brachah* (blessing) comes from the Hebrew word *braichah*, meaning "to gush" or "to flow."[7] When God created the world, He wanted to be the source that flows into and that nurtures the world. When we say that God is "blessed," we are asking God to let His blessing and energy flow into and nourish the world.

There is a talmudic story in which God turns to Rabbi Yishmael ben Abuyah and says to him, "Bless Me, My son." Rabbi Yishmael responds by saying, "May Your attribute of mercy overcome Your attribute of judgment."[8] When Rabbi Yishmael "blesses" God, he asks God to allow His attribute of giving to flow into the world and not to be withheld through His attribute of justice. However, God has set up the world in such a way that His ability to flow depends upon people's actions. We must make ourselves capable and worthy of receiving God's flow in order for God to act as a gushing source of blessing. The Source is always ready to give, but we must be ready to receive. We must be appropriate channels or conduits for the blessing. God allows His continuous blessing to flow only if the blessing will be used constructively, not if it will be channeled into destructive behavior. Thus, God is bursting to gush with His nourishing flow, but we can figuratively tie God's hands by making ourselves unworthy of receiving.

When we make it impossible for God to allow Himself to give to us, God gets "upset" that He can't give. (Obviously, this is an anthropomorphism, but this is the best way to describe God's reactions in terms that we can understand.) This means that each negative act we do has two negative consequences. First are the consequences of the act itself. Second, a negative act frustrates God's desire and ability to give to us. If we do the right things, then God can give to us and thereby fulfill His purpose in creating the world. If we do the wrong things, then God must withhold from giving and thereby keep His purpose in creating the world from being fulfilled.

Meaning of the Words

"Blessed Are You, Lord, Our God"

When we refer to God as "blessed," we acknowledge His role as the source of all blessing and thereby enable His flowing into the world. By saying these words, we ask God not to "forget" His commitment to give to the world, and we promise that we will do what is necessary in order for Him to give. Through this process, we transform ourselves into recipients of God's blessing. Beginning a prayer with the words, "Blessed are You, God" (*Baruch Atah HaShem*) is a logical opening to prayer. We must establish a bond of communication with God before we can ask Him to respond to us, and this is the manner in which we do it.

After we say that God is blessed, we refer to Him as "our God" (*Elokeinu*). By calling Him "our God," we are saying that each individual has the potential to establish a relationship with God in a unique way. We thereby each "own" our special relationship with our Creator.

We follow this by saying that God is the "God of our forefathers." This means that each forefather developed an individual relationship with God that was a reflection of that forefather's unique personality.

"Our Forefathers"—The Uniqueness of the Patriarchs

Jews have three Patriarchs—Abraham, Isaac, and Jacob. Abraham's main character trait was that of lovingkindness. It led Abraham to find God by appreciating and recognizing how God gave of His own lovingkindness into the world. Abraham saw this lovingkindness manifested in the world as testimony to God's existence, and Abraham himself served God through his own trait of lovingkindness. When a person has a certain positive trait, he will tend to see it also as it appears in other people, and as it is manifested in other places.

Isaac did not rely solely on his father, Abraham, to teach him about God. Rather, he found God through his own character traits of discipline and self-control. Through this attribute of *gevurah* (self-discipline), Isaac was able to see the clarity of God's spiritual manifestations in the world.

Abraham was tested by God with ten tests, all of which challenged Abraham's view of God as all-loving and all-giving. (Although God is all-loving, discipline plays a role in how He demonstrates this love.) Isaac was able to relate to God's aspect of discipline and judgment—His holding back of giving.

Jacob's attributes of truth and beauty (*tiferet*) were the paths through which he found, served, and related to God. He was able to reconcile the seeming contradictions between God's giving to the world and His holding back from giving, or punishing people. Thus, Jacob drew on his grandfather's lovingkindness and his father's self-control, and integrated the two into his own personality. Like his father and grandfather, he then applied his trait of truth to his perceptions of how God acts in the world.

In this prayer, we repeat the word "God" with the name of each Patriarch. The text could have said that God is the "God of Abraham, Isaac, and Jacob." Instead, it says that He is the "God of Abraham, God of Isaac, and God of Jacob," thereby emphasizing how each Patriarch forged his own relationship with God based on his unique character attributes. It is similarly the task of every Jew to discover, relate to, and serve God according to his or her own primary nature.

The spectrum of all character types of Jews are reflected in the three characters of the forefathers. Every Jew can tap into the spiritual pools of the forefathers in order to learn how to relate to God according to his or her individual nature or circumstances. The Patriarchs serve as models from whom we each can discover our true nature and our way of serving God. This idea of spiritual heritage forms the core of the first blessing of the Amidah, in which we praise God that He has given us a spiritual heritage through which we can always relate to Him.

We start the first prayer of the Amidah, then, by recognizing that God is "our God" and then mentioning that He was God to our forefathers. This shows that each of us should strive to find a personal relationship with God when we pray. Only after finding our own personal connection with God should we draw on the historical relationship between the forefathers and God that also enables us to connect with Him.

In the Torah, Moses says that the "Egyptians were evil to us and to our forefathers."[9] This tells us that no individual has such a unique life circumstance that a road to God wasn't previously paved by an ancestor in a similar situation. Nevertheless, when we pray, we must first call out to God in recognition of what He has personally done for us, before we focus on how He provided for previous generations. Sometimes Jews whose parents or grandparents were far removed from Judaism wonder how they can find a model of someone who has a personal relationship with God. This prayer teaches us that no matter how far removed a Jew's personal ancestors were from God, our past history always has strong links to Him. It also teaches us that as individuals, we have the capacity to forge a personal relationship with God.

"Great, Powerful, and Awesome," and "Most High"

The *Avot* prayer next refers to God as "Great, Powerful, and Awesome" (*gadol, gibbor, vehanorah*). The Zohar defines "great" (*gadol*) as meaning that God manifests His greatness by doing deeds of lovingkindness.[10] "Powerful" (*gibbor*) means that God relates to the world through acts of justice, and "Awesome" (*norah*) means that God manifests His Presence through truth and beauty. These are the same characteristics through which Abraham (lovingkindness), Isaac (power, through self-control), and Jacob (truth and beauty) related to God. Because our forefathers related to God in this way, we now can relate to these manifestations of God as well.

Of all of the possible ways we could describe God, we use the above three adjectives, because these are the same words used by Moses to describe Him.[11] Were we to extol God's greatness using other terms, people might think that those descriptions defined the limits of God's abilities. Were it not for the fact that the words we use in prayer have historical precedent in our Bible, we would not be able to use these words at all to describe God.

At the time of the destruction of the First Temple, the prophets Jeremiah and Daniel did not want to use even these adjectives to describe God. When the Jews were exiled from the land of Israel and their Temple destroyed for the first time, these prophets wanted to remove the words *gibbor vehanorah* (strong and awesome) from this prayer. As long as the Jews were not in their land, and the primary place of God's splendor lay in ruins, they felt that God's attributes of strength and awesomeness were no longer manifest.

Seventy years later, at the end of the Babylonian exile and

just prior to the rebuilding of the Temple, the men of the Great Assembly restored these words to the prayers. Although it seemed that the destruction and exile denied the strength and self-control of God, the men of the Great Assembly disagreed with this idea. The Talmud says that God's holding Himself back from giving, given His tremendous love for the Jewish people, and His being able to punish them for their own benefit, was precisely a manifestation of His discipline and self-control.[12] He displayed His strength and awesomeness by doing what needed to be done for the benefit of the Jewish people, despite the pain of having to hold back from showing His love.

God has an ultimate plan for us. Sometimes it requires that He hold back from giving, so that we can develop in the directions that we need. God's awesomeness has been manifested by the fact that the Jewish people have survived throughout history despite being surrounded by their enemies. God's ability to personify the highest forms of love, while simultaneously executing certain forms of severity and judgment, are evidence of His power.

Most human beings who possess a strong trait are overtaken by their characteristic emotion when certain situations arise. People frequently find it impossible to possess two contradictory emotions simultaneously. God does not have a problem doing this, because no contradiction of traits exists within His Oneness. He can have an overriding love for the Jewish people while still recognizing that He must sometimes hold back His love in ways that are very painful, so to speak, to Him. He does this for the ultimate good of His children. He is neither overtaken by "anger" when we act in destructive ways, nor inappropriately overwhelmed by His love for us.

After using these three adjectives—great, powerful, and awesome—the *Avot* prayer then refers to God as "Most High." When we say this, we mean that God is greater than all other powers. It also means that any understandings that we have about who God is must necessarily be inadequate to truly comprehend God in all of His greatness. God is ultimately above all human comprehension.

*"Who Does Good Deeds of Lovingkindness . . . the Creator of
Everything"*

We are next told that God "does good deeds of lovingkindness." It might be thought that because God is "great, powerful, and awesome," He is aloof from the world and has better
things to do than occupy Himself with the affairs of humans.
This verse tells us that part of God's greatness is that He is
constantly involved in doing acts of lovingkindness for human
beings.

It states that God does "good" deeds of lovingkindness
because not all acts of lovingkindness are good. A person can
do an act of lovingkindness for another with the best of
intentions, but the effects can be negative. The act could make
a cripple out of the recipient, it could spoil him, it could make
him feel arrogant, or it could make him feel demeaned or
degraded. Our kind acts do not always have positive consequences for the recipients, but when God does kind deeds, He
can guarantee that the act will ultimately be good for the
person. God understands exactly what we need at every moment in time, and He acts according to His knowledge of what
will truly be good.

This prayer next says that God is "the Creator of everything."
As a result, there is no act of lovingkindness that is beyond
His power to do, should He deem it appropriate. People may
have the desire to do certain acts of lovingkindness but may
lack the capability. Since God created everything, His resources
and abilities have no limits. When we realize that He has the
power to do anything, we should pray to Him whenever we
need help accomplishing something.

Another interpretation of "God does good deeds of lovingkindness and is the "Creator of everything" has the latter half
of the verse explaining the former half. In other words, how
does man know that God acts in lovingkind ways? The greatest
proof is that God created the world. Rabbi Moshe Chaim
Luzzatto tells us that God created the world because He wanted
to give of Himself to people.[13] The creation of people, and of
the world, were done as acts of lovingkindness to benefit us.
Once the world was created, every act that God has done to

sustain the world and the people within it is evidence of His lovingkindness.

If we have the attitude that we received a gift of life from God when we were born, and every day God gives us more gifts, we will want to reciprocate.[14] We come into the world and receive so many things without having done anything to deserve them. The way we can reciprocate is to be sensitive to God's will and to strive to do what God wants. We should feel obligated to show our appreciation to God by doing what He wants.

One example of God's many kindnesses is His having designed people in such a way that we must eat. God could have given all food the same taste, texture, color, and scent—but He didn't. Instead of making food simply nutritious, He also made it provide multiple pleasures for us. There are many other examples of this type of kindness. We could begin to appreciate some of these pleasures by simply observing the world around us and noticing how God made it in a way that enhances our enjoyment.

The Concept of "Merit of Our Forefathers"

The phrase "remembers the deeds of lovingkindness of our forefathers" refers to a concept known as "the merit of our forefathers" (*zechut avot*). We sometimes ask God to be compassionate to us based on the merit of our forefathers. This doesn't mean that regardless of our own personal behavior and beliefs, we can call on our lineage to make God grant us something that we would not ordinarily merit. Such an idea doesn't reflect Jewish belief. Rather, each individual stands on his or her own personal merit. Having the right connections, in and of itself, does not pull strings with God.

Throughout Jewish history, Jews of the highest spiritual caliber have sinned. God does not expect mortals never to make mistakes. He does, however, expect that when we do sin, we acknowledge our shortcomings and be honest about where we need to improve ourselves. Throughout the wanderings of the Jews in the desert after the Exodus, the Jews sinned. At each juncture, Moses prayed to God on their behalf, and each time he invoked the merit of the forefathers, asking God to forgive the Jewish people in the memory of the Patriarchs. There is, however, one time that Moses prayed for God to forgive the Jewish people but did not ask Him to do so in the merit of the forefathers.

Nachmanides, a biblical commentator, notes this omission.[15] He explains that one can pray to God in the merit of one's forefathers only if the descendant adores what the forefathers stood for. The person praying does not have to be the spiritual equal of his forefathers; however, the spiritual values of the forefathers can serve as goals which the descendant strives to reach, in his or her own way.

One of the fundamental yearnings of our forefathers was to be granted the opportunity to live in, and inherit, the land of Israel. Israel was their dearest possession. They felt that God's enabling them to take possession of this land was one of the most supreme blessings He gave them. The Israelites in the desert sent out spies to evaluate whether or not they should take possession of the land which God wanted to give them. The spies came back with an evil report, and the Israelites accepted this report, thereby showing their disdain for the land. Because of their rejection of the land, Moses could not ask God to forgive them for this sin in the merit of their forefathers. The Israelites had categorically rejected one of the most sublime values which their forefathers held most dear— the importance of living in the land of Israel. It would have been a contradiction in terms for Moses to ask God to forgive His people in the merit of their forefathers for spurning the land. If the forefathers had loved the land so much, their desire should have been implanted in their descendants. Had Moses even mentioned the Patriarchs when he asked God to forgive this sin, he would have reinforced how unworthy the Jews were of being forgiven for their rejection of their forefathers' values.

Nachmanides' commentary on this event teaches us two principles. First, we have the potential to do what our forefathers did in terms of our own spiritual development, because they blazed certain spiritual paths in creating their relationships with God. Second, when we pray in the merit of our forefathers, we can do so only if we show by our behavior that we value what they valued. If we sever ourselves from our forefathers' values, then we have no right to ask God to see us as their spiritual descendants. We can't ask Him to find favor with us by virtue of the closeness our relatives had with Him.

The concept of merit of the forefathers can then be summarized as follows: Every Jew has certain spiritual potentials and the inherent ability to grow to the same spiritual heights that were reached by our forefathers. Furthermore, we value those potentials. When we pray to God in "the merit of our forefathers," we ask Him to look beyond where we are at the moment, beyond our failings and shortcomings, and to "remember" that we have the same vast spiritual potentials as our ancestors had. We ask Him to grant us things that we may not personally deserve, in the merit of our potentials. When we ask for considerations in the merit of the forefathers, we commit ourselves to developing further in our emulation of them.

The "Deeds of Lovingkindness"

What were these "deeds of our forefathers" that now enable us to pray in their merit? These "deeds" refer to the fact that the forefathers observed the commandments of the Torah even before they were required to do so. They kept the Torah not because it was legally or socially correct to do so, but because they knew that doing so was the will of God, and doing His will was their greatest desire. The forefathers loved God and wanted to be close to Him. The best way to do that was to do what God wanted. Any act that is done outside of obligation, as a demonstration of one's graciousness and desire to give to another, is referred to as "lovingkindness" (chesed).

When we say that the forefathers did acts of chesed, we mean that they had an innate sense of wanting to do the will of God. Whether or not they were obligated to do so did not concern them. The Jews in Moses' times were capable of receiving and accepting the Torah as an extension of the Patriarchs' desire to do what God wanted. The Torah makes God's will obligatory and explicit to the descendants of Abraham, Isaac, and Jacob, so that they can fulfill it.

Every Jew has inherited the forefathers' desire to do God's will simply for the sake of showing love of God, whether or not doing so is an obligation. How much more is this so when God requires something of us. Deep down, every Jew has the desire to do God's will, even if it might be difficult for us to recognize it.

As an example, there are times when Jewish law requires a husband to give his wife a divorce if she requests one. In cases where a husband is recalcitrant and refuses to give his wife a divorce, Jewish law provides for the court of law to use almost any means possible (including physical force) to compel the husband to release his wife from their marriage bonds. On the surface, this presents a difficult situation. Jewish law requires that a divorce be given of the husband's free will. How, then, is it valid for the Jewish court to force him to give it?

Maimonides, a medieval philosopher, says that the deepest desire of any Jew is to do what God really wants him to do,[16] even though the desire might be hidden under a tremendous number of barriers and defense systems. When a man refuses to grant his wife a divorce, he truly wishes to do God's will, even if these feelings are only on an unconscious level. His feelings about his wife may get in the way of his actualizing his truest feelings. He may want to get even with her, he may not want to give up on his marriage—he may have many confusing feelings about what are truly his desires. When the court coerces the man to give a divorce which is mandated by Jewish law, it takes away his confusion and allows him to experience what he truly should be feeling—the desire to do God's will.

Although this scenario may seem comical, it makes a dramatic statement about the inner essence of every Jew. In our deepest inner beings, every Jew wants to do what God wants. When we ask God to remember the lovingkindness of our forefathers, we want Him to remember that they acted above and beyond technical observances of Jewish law and that their greatest desire was to do His will. The fact that we may not yet have reached that level doesn't mean that we don't want to do God's will. We have just been distracted by superficial temptations that thwart our abilities to carry out what we truly believe we should do.

The Talmud says that there are situations in which a person can tear himself away from the merit of his forefathers by despising what they loved. Someone who does this will not be successful in praying for God to remember their merit. This is why, at the end of the *Avot* prayer, we pray for God to bring redemption to the descendants of the forefathers, and we follow this by saying, "for the sake of His Name." We first pray that God will redeem us in the merit of our forefathers, when we still value the spiritual goals our forefathers reached in their lifetimes. However, when we cut ourselves off from those goals, we say that God will still redeem us. In such a situation, redemption will not be in the merit of our ancestors; rather, it will be "for the sake of His Name."

Redemption "for the Sake of His Name"

The idea that God will save us for His Name's sake rather than because we deserve it has a biblical precedent. After God took the Israelites out of Egypt, they received the Torah. Shortly thereafter, they made a Golden Calf, for which God wanted to destroy them. At that point, Moses said to God: "If You destroy Your people, what will the Egyptians and the other nations of the world say? They will say that You were strong enough to conquer the powers responsible for the Egyptian exile, but You were not strong enough to conquer the future kings of the land of Israel. That is why You destroyed Your people in the desert."[17]

Moses' statement meant that the nations of the world would interpret the death of the Jews in the desert as evidence of God's lack of abilities. Even though the Jews might not have deserved to be saved, God could not allow His image in the world to become discredited through their death. Were that to have occurred, the nations of the world would have backtracked from what they already knew about who God was and how He involved Himself in people's lives.

Some time after the sin of the Golden Calf, God wanted to lead the Jews into the land of Israel. They insisted on first spying out the land to see whether or not they wanted to inherit it. The spies came back and reported that the Jews would not be capable of conquering the land and they should not proceed to the land which God had promised them. God was prepared to destroy them for their rejection of the land, but Moses intervened again by saying that if God were to destroy His people, the nations of the world would say that He wasn't capable of bringing the Jews into the land of Israel. The nations would contend that God thought up a scheme to get angry at the Jews so that He could destroy them in the desert.[18]

In both of the above cases, God did not destroy the Jews, even though they deserved it, because something that was fundamental to the purpose of the world would have been lost in the process. In similar fashion, Moses told the Jews at the end of Deuteronomy that there would be a time in the course of history when the Jews would not be worthy of continued existence;[19] nevertheless, God would sustain the Jews, not in their merit, but for the sake of His Name.

Giving Honor to God

There are two types of commandments in the Torah: the *positive* commandments require Jews to do certain acts, and the *negative* commandments require that we refrain from doing certain things. When a person does something he or she is not supposed to do, or omits doing what he or she is supposed to do, there are various things that should be done to rectify such sins.

A person who omits a positive commandment is required to regret the sin and to resolve to do the appropriate act in the future. Once he does this, he is immediately forgiven by God. If he commits a forbidden act and then repents, God does not completely forgive him until he goes through the repentance process of Yom Kippur (the Day of Atonement). If a person violates a commandment for which the punishment is execution or a divine shortening of one's life, forgiveness requires several elements. He needs to repent, go through Yom Kippur, and suffer certain tribulations (*yissurim*) in order to be spiritually cleansed and forgiven. (People can also do certain acts which can obviate the need to suffer afflictions or death as a means of atonement).

The Talmud says that there is a fourth category of sin: the disgracing of God's Name (*chillul HaShem*).[20] Total forgiveness for this cannot be effected until a person goes through the death process, or through a process during life which substitutes for the purification offered by death. For example, one substitute atonement would be a diminished physical enjoyment of the world. He could accomplish this by sleeping less than he ordinarily would and dedicating the extra hours to sanctifying God's Name through learning or teaching Torah.[21] The person still needs to repent, go through Yom Kippur, and undergo tribulations (or a substitute for them). Nevertheless, total purification cannot be effected until the person either dies or goes through a process that substitutes for death.

In the Torah, the commandment not to disgrace God's Name appears to be a simple negative commandment. But if this were true, simple repentance on Yom Kippur should suffice to atone for it. Disgracing God's Name does not carry with it a capital punishment. Why, then, does it require the most drastic of all possible "cures" for true forgiveness?

The reason is as follows: There are two ways in which we show our reverence and love for God: by doing His will, and by showing Him honor. We can evaluate our various behaviors by determining if they reflect God's will or if they show Him honor. When a person sins, he shows that he doesn't care about God's will or honor. When that person repents, his behavior is the same as that of someone who never sinned insofar as they both do God's will, but there is a difference between the two in regard to God's honor. When a penitent person shows that he formerly didn't care about God and now he does, He gives God an honor that the always-righteous person may never be able to give. When a person has to struggle before finally accepting God, he ultimately gives greater honor to God than if he never had difficulties accepting Him at all.

When a person transgresses God's will he cannot undo his act, but when he repents, he can uniquely contribute an acknowledgement that God was right all along. This acknowledgement makes a contribution to God's honor in this world. The victory of God's glory is demonstrated by the penitent's change of heart. A place that was devoid of Godliness is now illuminated, and this illumination contributes to God's glory.

A person who transgresses God's will, then, can still come

back and contribute to God's honor. However, a person who desecrates God's Name is trouncing on God's honor. Insofar as a change in will can be demonstrated by a change in behavior, a transgressor can demonstrate a higher level of honor to God than if he had never sinned at all. The person who desecrates God's Name, in contrast, can never *add* to God's glory in the world. The best he can do is to restore God's honor and glory to their original status. Therefore, the desecration of God's Name receives a greater punishment than other sins because the person who repents for this sin is less able to make restitution.

The strength of the Jewish people as a nation lies in our ability to reveal God's presence to the world. That is our mission, and the act of repentance is therefore part and parcel of that mission. The penitent person stands before God and says, "My repenting makes me part of the Jewish people, because I make a contribution to them through a repentance which shows the honor of God." Showing the honor of God is the contribution that every Jew is supposed to make to the world.

When God tells the Jewish people that He really should have destroyed them, but didn't because of His Name's sake, He is saying that they are necessary to reveal His presence to the world. Were God to destroy the Jews, their mission of revealing Him to the world would be lost. God created the world in order for people to be able to find Him and understand how He relates to the world. He therefore demands that the Jewish people repent and return to Him, instead of destroying them. Through their returning to God, they reveal Him to the world.

When we say that God will redeem the world for the sake of His Name, we mean that we can reach a point where we no longer exemplify, or aspire to, the values of our forefathers. At that point we lose their merit, and we don't have our own merits, but we still have God's merit. However, we have His merit only as long as somewhere within us, we stay committed to revealing His presence and mission in the world. God never gives up on the possibility that every Jew, even a sinner, will eventually reveal something about Him. "The sake of God's Name" is integrally related to the existence and purpose of every Jew, which He will eventually help us recognize and assert.

Redemption with Love

This *Avot* prayer concludes by saying that God will redeem us "with love." One might think that if God has to redeem us for the purpose of manifesting His Name rather than because we are personally worthy, then He would redeem us ungraciously or in a punitive way. This prayer tells us that even if God redeems us for reasons that have nothing to do with our personal merits, He will still do so with love. This is because God will reward our forefathers commensurate with their love for Him.

A Helper, Savior, and Protector

The *Avot* prayer tells us that God is a king who helps, saves, and shields (or protects). The word "help" means that God assists us when we strive to be better, when our very best efforts are not sufficient to make our endeavors successful. The Talmud tells us that God acts as this type of "Helper" in spiritual matters. It says: "The inclination of man tries to overpower him every day. Were it not for the fact that God helps him, he wouldn't be able to conquer his inclination."[22] The inclination to go against God's will is very strong, and we don't have within us sufficient strength to overcome it alone. Nevertheless, God wants us to make our best efforts to fight it. Once God sees that we are doing our best to overcome our inclinations, He helps us by providing the reinforcements that we need to overcome the challenges and to accomplish what we set out to do.

God could have created our negative inclinations equal to, or weaker than, our abilities to overcome them. Why was it necessary for God to create us in a way that requires His intervention for success? The reason is that no matter how much we think we are able to develop ourselves, we must always recognize that we need God and that He plays a role in our spiritual achievements. When we grow spiritually, we need to understand that this is not a solo achievement. Such growth is always done with God's intimate involvement. We were created to be unequal to the task of developing our spirituality alone. We can be successful only if we invite God to be our partner in the venture.

Two ideas are counterproductive to spiritual growth: One is believing that we can develop our spirituality alone. The other is believing that we have to succeed all alone in our spiritual growth, and that until we do so, God will not involve Himself with us. The first situation results in our becoming egocentric and worshiping our own omnipotence. In the second case, we may easily be overwhelmed by a feeling of loneliness, hopelessness, and eventually despair. We need to strive to lead the most moral and ethical life that we can. At that point God says to us, "I'm sensitive to your battle, and I see how hard you're trying. I will come and help you."

We should never think that we deserve no credit for our struggles, even though God is the one who really makes our efforts succeed. When we make a great deal of the effort, God considers it as if we had accomplished the entire task by ourselves. He regards His own involvement as simply a deserved response to us when we try our best.

God is a "Helper" when we try our best and our efforts could come close to achieving our spiritual goals. Sometimes, however, no matter how much we try, our efforts are far from accomplishing what we set out to do. These are times when God acts as a "Savior." He does the task solely by Himself, saving us from situations in which we would succumb to the challenges if we did not have His help. We are in these situations whenever we sin.

Once we do something wrong, we create two problems: First, we need to rectify the deed itself. Second, we create a blemish in our souls when we transgress God's commandments.

Our sin creates an impurity in the spiritual energies that should have been channeled into our souls in a certain way. We do not have within us the ability to remove the impurity created by sin. This situation is similar to someone accidentally spilling food onto a fine garment. Even if the person regrets having done it and tries his best to remove the stains, some residual stain will remain. No amount of regret will make the garment as pristine as it once was.

When we sin, God says that it is up to us to regret what we have done, to verbalize our acknowledgment of the sin, and to make a commitment not to repeat it. We thereby take responsibility for our actions and for obtaining forgiveness from God. God takes responsibility for removing the impurities and renewing our souls to their pristine state. This is how God acts as our "Savior." We merit His purifying us by our wanting Him to do this for us and by asking Him to be our Savior.

When we immerse ourselves in a ritual bath (*mikvah*), we emerge spiritually purified. There is nothing inherently purifying about surrounding ourselves with water; nevertheless, when we immerse ourselves properly, purification occurs. This is so because God tells us that if we do this act, He will bring us a renewed state of purity. It is our yearning for this gift of purity, and our humility in recognizing our need for it, that causes God to grant it. People do not have the ability to create purity and holiness. They are both presents which God gives us once we merit them by desiring them.

God not only acts as a Helper before a crisis, but He also saves us *after* a crisis. When God acts as a protector ("Shield"), He ensures that we don't get into spiritual or physical dangers. We don't realize the extent to which God protects us from dangerous situations. It is easy for us to feel angry at God, to think that if He had not brought us into certain situations, we would not have sinned or we wouldn't have suffered. We don't know how many bad situations we avoid because of God's constant providence over us as a Protector.

When God acts as Helper, He acts in concert with us, as we make our best efforts. When God saves us, He grants purity to us, as a solo action; we can set the stage for Him to grant purity, but ultimately the purity comes from God acting alone. Ordinarily, when He acts as our Protector (Shield), we must have previously repented, but His protection is also something He does alone.

The commentators say that the descriptions of God as "Helper, Savior, and Shield" refer to three Jewish holidays.[23] "Helper" refers to Rosh Hashanah (New Year's), "Savior" refers to Yom Kippur (the Day of Atonement), and "Shield" refers to Succot (Feast of Tabernacles). Rosh Hashanah is the celebration of the birthday of humankind and of the fact that human beings have the ability to make choices. On Rosh Hashanah we focus on the exaltedness of the creation of people, and on our God-given gift of free will. When we exercise our choices in the right direction, God helps us. God's role as "Helper" characterizes the day. Yom Kippur is the day of forgiveness for culpability, at which time God gives us purity. This is a time when God acts as our Savior. On Succot, God gives us the ability to protect the repentance that we have made. This is a time when God acts as our Shield. Thus, on these three Jewish holidays, God acts in His three roles as Helper, Savior, and Shield.

"Shield of Abraham"

There is a rule that the concluding verse and blessing to a prayer encompass within them the most central theme of the prayer that precedes them (Ma'ain hachasimah somech lechasimah). Although the Avot prayer mentions all three forefathers, it concludes by mentioning only one of them: "Blessed are You, God, Shield of Abraham." Why isn't there a reference to all three forefathers here?

God promised Abraham that He would make him into a great nation, bless him, make his name great, and that he would "be a blessing."[24] The promise that Abraham would "be a blessing" meant that his name would be used in a blessing that Jews say. Thus we end the first prayer of the Amidah by saying only, "Shield of Abraham."

There are several reasons for singling out Abraham. First, Abraham was the person who created an indestructible spiritual inheritance of love of God for his descendants. Of all of the things we have inherited, love is the attribute to which we can relate most easily in creating a relationship with God. Therefore, it becomes the most relevant attribute we have when we pray.

A second reason that we mention Abraham's name is that it is possible for Jews to remove themselves from the merit of their forefathers. When we say that God was the "Shield of Abraham," we emphasize that Jews always have the option of repenting and returning to the merit of their forefathers. There is always a part of the Jewish soul that remains untouched and untainted by sin. It is that pure part that contains the seeds of the Jew's return to God and the relinking of that person with his or her spiritual heritage. Through this link, any Jew can regain the merit of the forefathers.

This idea is alluded to in a verse in Malachi: "God will return the hearts of the fathers upon the children."[25] According to one interpretation, this verse means that the love of the forefathers will emerge in the hearts of their descendants.

Implications for Us of the Shield of Abraham Prayer

In this prayer, we seem to praise our pasts more than we praise God. We extol our worthiness to be in a relationship with God by virtue of how great our ancestors were, and by virtue of our possessing their tremendous potentials and qualities. Our praise of God is truly expressed not only for how wonderful He is, but for how He has made us compatible with Himself.

This concept implies that any relationship requires not only an appreciation for one's partner, but also an appreciation for one's own contributions and worthiness. If a person has poor self-esteem, it doesn't matter how wonderful he or she perceives the partner to be. Such an unequal relationship can never result in a true bonding. A parasitic or symbiotic relationship can result, but not a union of two complementary partners.

This prayer also tells us that God is a Helper, Savior, and Shield (Protector). God determines when we need to be protected from dangerous situations, when we need to be helped to get through such situations, and when we need to be rescued from them.

The same applies in human relationships. Sometimes the best way for one person to assist another is by allowing the second person to play an active role in helping himself. When a person is precluded from doing those things that make one feel accomplished, he or she becomes destroyed, not helped. A "helper" needs to have the wisdom to know when to protect

another person, when to assist his or her endeavors, and when
to save the person.

Just as we recognize how detrimental it is to always shield
our loved ones from problems, so we can recognize how
important it is for God not to do that with us. Overprotection
thwarts growth and accomplishment, both of which are necessary for us to develop self-esteem. We can't have healthy
relationships with God unless we recognize that it is not in our
best interests for Him to always be our Protector. Sometimes
He must be our Helper, and at other times, our Savior.

Notes

1. Aruch HaShulchan, *Tefillah*, chapter 91:1, 2.
2. Song of Songs 8:8,9.
3. Song of Songs 8:7.
4. *Otsar HaTefillot*, Introduction to the Amidah.
5. Genesis 14:8–10.
6. *Pirkei D'Rabbi Eliezer*, chapter 27.
7. *Nefesh HaChaim* 2:2, 4.
8. Talmud *Bavli*, Berakhot 7a.
9. Numbers 20:15.
10. Dover Shalom in *Otsar HaTefillot*.
11. Deuteronomy 10:17.
12. Talmud *Bavli*, Yoma 69a.
13. M. Luzzatto, *The Knowing Heart* (Jerusalem: Feldheim, 1982), p. 16.
14. Ibn Pakuda, *Duties of the Heart* (Jerusalem: Feldheim, 1986), Introduction to treatise 3.
15. Nachmanides on Numbers 14:17.
16. Maimonides, *Yad HaChazakah*, Laws of Divorce 2:20.
17. Exodus 32:12; Deuteronomy 9:28.
18. Numbers 14:16.
19. Deuteronomy 32:27.
20. Talmud *Bavli*, Yoma 86a.
21. Gates of Repentance 4:5.
22. Talmud *Bavli*, Sukkah 52a.
23. Shem Mishmuel, *Moadim*.
24. Genesis 12:2.
25. Malachi 3:24.

CHAPTER 5

Resurrection of the Dead

אַתָּה גִבּוֹר לְעוֹלָם אֲדֹנָי, מְחַיֵּה מֵתִים אַתָּה, רַב לְהוֹשִׁיעַ.
(מַשִּׁיב הָרוּחַ וּמוֹרִיד הַגָּשֶׁם)
מְכַלְכֵּל חַיִּים בְּחֶסֶד, מְחַיֵּה מֵתִים בְּרַחֲמִים רַבִּים, סוֹמֵךְ
נוֹפְלִים, וְרוֹפֵא חוֹלִים, וּמַתִּיר אֲסוּרִים, וּמְקַיֵּם אֱמוּנָתוֹ
לִישֵׁנֵי עָפָר. מִי כָמוֹךָ בַּעַל גְּבוּרוֹת, וּמִי דּוֹמֶה לָךְ, מֶלֶךְ
מֵמִית וּמְחַיֵּה וּמַצְמִיחַ יְשׁוּעָה. וְנֶאֱמָן אַתָּה לְהַחֲיוֹת מֵתִים.
בָּרוּךְ אַתָּה יהוה, מְחַיֵּה הַמֵּתִים.

You are mighty, forever, my Lord, You revive the dead, with
great salvation. (You cause the wind to blow and the rain
to fall.) You nourish the living with lovingkindness, You revive
the dead with great compassion, support the falling, and heal
the sick, and release the imprisoned, and fulfill Your faithfulness to those who sleep in the dust. Who is like You, Master of
power, and who can be compared to You? You are a King who
causes death (for the purpose of) bringing the person back to
life, and cause salvation to sprout forth. And You are faithful
to bring the dead back to life. Blessed are You, God, who
resurrects the dead.

Theme of the Prayer

The first paragraph of the Shemoneh Esrai is referred to as the prayer of the *Avot*, because its central theme is how our forefathers found God's presence through His different manifestations in the world and how we use their abilities as models for relating to God's presence in the world.

This second prayer of the Shemoneh Esrai is referred to as *Gevurot*—literally, "Powers." This prayer describes the power of God as He manifests it by nurturing the world through rain. It is a monumental feat that God determines exactly how much rain must fall, and where it must fall (and not fall) in every area of the world. The entire process of rain bespeaks God's mastery of the universe. We say blessings when we see lightning or hear thunder, in recognition of God's power which is manifest through the "pyrotechnics" that accompany rain. These manifestations of God's power make us aware that God, and not man, is truly the master of the world.

Historical Background

The first blessing of the Shemoneh Esrai is related to an event in the life of Abraham. The second blessing is related to an event in the life of Isaac. The seminal event in Isaac's life was the *Akedat Yitzchak*, the "binding of Isaac." When Isaac was 37 years old, God told Abraham to sacrifice Isaac to Him on an altar. Even though this command violated everything that God had taught Abraham about His abhorrence of human sacrifices, Abraham unquestioningly obeyed Him. Abraham and Isaac journeyed together for three days, at which point they reached the place where the Temple was later to stand. God then indicated to Abraham that that was the place where He wanted Isaac to be brought up as a sacrifice. Abraham bound his son on an altar, and was a moment away from slaughtering him, when God sent an angel to stop him. Abraham refrained from hurting his son and sacrificed a ram in Isaac's stead.[1]

The Midrash says that when Abraham lifted up the knife to slaughter Isaac, Isaac's soul left him.[2] This happened either because of Isaac's fear of being killed or because of the emotional intensity of the moment. When the angel told Abraham not to do anything to his son, Isaac's soul was reinstated in him. Isaac was thereby the first person who experienced coming back to life after dying. At the moment that Isaac had been resurrected, the angels said, "Blessed are You, God, who resurrects the dead." This is the blessing that concludes the second prayer of the Shemoneh Esrai.

God's ability to bring the dead back to life is known as *gevurah*—strength. Unlike a mortal king, who prides himself on how many people he can kill, God takes pride, so to speak, in how many dead people He brings back to life.

What is the connection between the beginning of this prayer, which praises God for causing it to rain, and the ending, which praises Him for resurrecting the dead? The answer is that not only does God cause a physical rain and a physical dew to water the earth, but God also brings a spiritual rain and a spiritual dew into the world. This spiritual rain and dew revive those who are dead and need to be brought back to life. If a seed is in the ground, it needs rain in order to grow. It also needs dew to give it moisture on a daily basis, to enable that growth to continue.

Similarly, a human being needs a spiritual dew to enable the soul to come back together with the body after the person has died (resurrection).

The concept of resurrection is one of the cardinal principles of belief for the Jew. It is so fundamental that the Sages instituted this prayer as the second one of the Shemoneh Esrai. This order tells us that once a person recognizes and connects with God (the essence of the first prayer), what necessarily follows is belief in resurrection (the second prayer).

Meaning of the Words

"You Are Mighty Forever . . . You Revive the Dead, With Great Salvation"

The opening phrase means that God's power does not wax and then wane, as people's power does. It is constant over time. In addition, God's bringing life back to those who have perished is seen as an act of "great salvation."

In the Hebrew, we say "You" and God's Name three times in the first verse of this prayer. There were three prophets (Elijah, Elisha, and Ezekiel), as well as some Sages in talmudic times who brought the dead back to life.[3] The Talmud says that God personally holds three "keys" to the world.[4] One of them is the "key" of rain, and one is resurrection of the dead. Those people who have resurrected the dead have been able to do so only because God granted them the power to resurrect. We should not think that anyone has this as an independent ability, alongside God. The ability always comes from the same source—God. That is why we reinforce three times in this verse that this power comes from You, God.

The Vilna Gaon says that the words "You revive the dead with great salvation" mean that when a person dies, he or she may not be worthy of being resurrected by God in the future. However, God has many ways of exercising His lovingkindness and compassion. It is possible that through the cleansing process of *Gehinnom* (where tainted souls are purified), a person might become worthy of being resurrected. Alternatively, God judges the long-term effects of what each person did while alive. These actions might enable the person to merit standing up at the time of resurrection.

This latter idea is that the full ramifications of a person's actions may not be evident at the time of death. For instance, if a person wills money to charity, the good deeds that his estate will ultimately finance would not yet have happened at the time of his death. Similarly, if a person taught others Torah and instilled Torah values in them, the full impact of the teaching might not be realized for many years. All the effects of the students' actions directly resulting from the deceased's efforts might require generations to assess. Therefore, God judges every person when he or she dies, but He also judges them again prior to the time of resurrection of the dead, thus ensuring that the ultimate effects of every person's behavior will be evaluated.[5]

"You Cause the Wind to Blow and the Rain to Fall"

These words are recited or omitted according to the season, because it does not rain during the summer in the land of Israel. Rain is not beneficial there at that time. Therefore, we begin saying these words during the holiday of Shemini Atzeret in the fall, and stop saying them during the holiday of Passover in the spring. If a person forgets to say these words when they are applicable, or erroneously says them when they are not applicable, then the entire Shemoneh Esrai must be repeated once he has completed the second blessing. This idea is consistent with God's power, which is demonstrated by His causing it to rain when rain is proper and causing it not to rain when it would be detrimental.

Once we recognize God's power in this prayer, we then praise Him that He gives it to us. Saying that God causes "the rain to fall" is not truly a request for rain; rather, it is a praise to God in recognition of His power. We make an actual request for rain later in the Shemoneh Esrai, in the ninth prayer.

Technically, we should begin praising God for giving rain at the beginning of the holiday of Succot (Tabernacles) instead of at its conclusion (Shemini Atzeret). However, the Talmud tells us that we postpone praising God for rain until the holiday of Succot is over, so that we can observe the commandment of sitting in the *succah* (temporary outdoor building). Were it to rain at the beginning of Succot, we would be unable to observe this *mitzvah*.

The statement about God's making the wind blow and causing the rain to fall follows the statement about His power and His reviving the dead with great salvation. In addition to the literal definitions of "wind" and "rain," both of these statements also refer to revival of the dead. (This concept will be explained more fully later in this chapter). That God "makes the wind blow" means that He blows back into corpses the souls they once had. That He "makes the rain fall" means that He gives the resurrected people the nurturing that they need to continue to exist.

"You Nourish the Living with Lovingkindness"

In this phrase we acknowledge that God has put into the world whatever is necessary to sustain life. This includes food, water, clothing, and other things. We view His giving us these necessary resources as evidence of His lovingkindness.

"You Revive the Dead with Great Compassion"

Whereas God sustains life with "lovingkindness" (*chesed*), He revives the dead with "tremendous compassion" (*rachamim rabbim*). Resurrection, in and of itself, is an act of compassion. Why do we say here that the compassion is "tremendous"?

The Talmud says that when those who have died come back to life, they arise fully clothed instead of naked.[6] Something similar happens to a wheat plant: A naked kernel of wheat is put into the ground, and it comes out "fully clothed," a fully grown plant with a stalk and a husk. If God deals in this way with a wheat plant, how much more is this the way in which He will deal with the human beings whom He will resurrect! If God makes the human being go through a process of regrowth in resurrection, that process will not be a process of bare growth. Rather, it will include all that is necessary for the human being—that is, clothing. This is evidence of God's "tremendous compassion."

It was once a custom for Jewish men to be buried in their *tallitot* (prayer shawls), so that when they were resurrected, they would awaken properly attired to observe the commandments of the Torah (known as *mitzvot*). When people are not alive, they are not required to observe the *mitzvot*. However, once they come to life, men are obligated to wear fringes on their four-cornered garments. Thus, by being resurrected already properly attired, the new person will not be naked either physically or spiritually. This is also part of God's "tremendous compassion."

After a person dies, there is a tremendous yearning of the person's soul to reunite with the body that served it during life. Another interpretation of "tremendous compassion" is that God is so sensitive to this yearning that He responds to it by allowing the soul to reunite with the body at the time of resurrection.

"(You) Support the Falling, Heal the Sick, and Release the Imprisoned"

There are people who are so weakened by tragedies in life that they are falling. God's granting them the fortitude to go on living is one way in which He supports the falling. This action is considered to be one form of resurrection of the dead. Whereas bringing a dead person back to life is true resurrection, "supporting the falling, healing the sick, and releasing the imprisoned" are mini-forms of resurrection.

Healing the sick refers to God's healing those who are on the brink of death due to illness. Releasing the imprisoned refers to those who are held captive and whose lives are thus no more meaningful than if they were dead. It includes those who at any moment could be killed by their captors, or those who live in fear of being killed.

"And Fulfill Your Faithfulness to Those Who Sleep in the Dust"

This is another reference to resurrection of the dead. The Vilna Gaon says that this verse uses the word "sleep" because although dead people appear as if there is nothing alive about them, their spirituality is always alive. A certain spiritual spark always remains attached to the corpse, and it is from this spark that resurrection will be built at the appropriate time. In this sense, a deceased person is only "sleeping."[7]

"Who Is Like You, Master of Power?"

God is termed "Master" here to emphasize that although there were people in the course of history who resurrected the dead, they were able to do so only because the Master of power granted them some of His ability. They had no capacity to do this without God's granting it to them. That is the first difference between God's resurrective powers and those of humans.

"Who Can Be Compared to You?"

When a human resurrects someone, the effects last for only a few years. When God resurrects people in the future, they will live forever, and there will be no death in the world afterwards. No human being has this capacity. This is the second way in which God's ability to resurrect differs from that of mortals.

"You Are a King Who Causes Death (for the Purpose of) Bringing the Person Back to Life"

This sentence tells us that the sole purpose of God's bringing death into the world is so that He can bring a higher form of life afterwards.

"(You) Cause Salvation to Sprout Forth"

A person cannot see the day-to-day growth of a plant but *can* notice the cumulative growth over a long period of time. This is also the case with the salvation that God creates. It grows slowly. We observe that things in the world die and seem to end. What really happens is that death is a preparation for a higher form of life. There are many times when things seem to be counterproductive to growth, but when the process is over, we can see that the situation really fostered growth. Even though death looks like a final blow, with nothing coming after it, in reality it resembles a plant. Just as a planted seed first disintegrates in the ground and then a sprout emerges, so does a person have to decompose in the ground prior to being reconstructed in a higher way. Part of life is death, which itself is part of the process of salvation.

Another explanation of salvation "sprouting like a plant" is offered by the Vilna Gaon. He says that the actions of one's children can cause the parents (or ancestors) to gain merit in the afterlife. The repercussions of parents' actions grow (like a plant) over time, even after death, and can help the parents merit resurrection.[8]

"And You Are Faithful to Bring the Dead Back to Life"

When we pray these words, we should believe, with complete faith, in God's plan to resurrect the dead. Even though we believe this intellectually, it is important for us to make this idea more real by verbalizing it. In this way, our beliefs do not remain detached abstractions, but rather become heartfelt convictions.

"Blessed Are You, God, Who Resurrects the Dead"

This entire prayer makes five references to God resurrecting the dead. There are two explanations for this number: The first is that there are five different levels to the human soul. (In Hebrew, these levels are known as *nefesh, ruach, neshamah, chayah,* and *yechidah*). The five mentions of resurrection allude to the fact that God will resurrect all five levels of the soul with the body.[9]

The second explanation is that there were three resurrections performed by men in the course of history—one by Elijah, one by Elisha, and one by Ezekiel. The next resurrection that occurs will be during the days of the Messiah. The specific purpose of this fourth resurrection will be to reward those people who cared about the destiny and salvation of the Jewish people throughout history. They will come alive to see this salvation brought to fruition. This will happen when God leads the Jewish people back to the land of Israel. The fifth resurrection will occur when God brings back to eternal life all those who merit the rewards of the world to come. Thus, the five mentions of resurrection in this prayer allude to the five different resurrections that will occur in the course of history.[10]

The Concept of Resurrection

What is the concept of resurrection, and why is it such a fundamental tenet of Jewish belief?

There is a blessing that we make over blossoms in the springtime. It begins: "Blessed are You, God, King of the Universe, who has not left out anything from Your world. . . ." We make a strong theological statement when we say that God did not leave out anything from the world by virtue of the fact that we see blossoms. It would seem more appropriate to make this blessing when we see the fruit of the trees. Nevertheless,

Jewish law says that we make the blessing when we see the blossoms, not the fruit.[11]

The rationale for this idea is very beautiful. There are situations when life appears to end, such as when everything dies in the autumn and goes into a deep freeze for the winter. The moment spring comes, we realize that what seemed to be death was only a figment of our imaginations. Apparent death was only God's way of putting things into a temporary state of dormancy. Subsequently, God invests new energy into trees that allows them to be even stronger than they were the previous year. This is how the physical world operates.

This concept also operates with respect to the human soul. When a person dies, we could easily assume that life is all over and there is nothing to follow. The blossoms teach us that what seems to be a state of death in the lower, physical world is only a stepping stone to a more blessed state later. The same is true of our spiritual state. What seems to be an end is not an end at all. When people die, they are only leaving their physical body in the earth, while God makes a temporary separation between their body and soul. The entire purpose of this process is so God can reunite the body with the soul in the future in a higher state of life. Thus, death is not a final stage but rather a transition point on the way to a higher state of existence.

Our Sages tell us that nobody dies in this world before God reveals Himself to them.[12] If death were an anticlimax to life, it would not be necessary for God to reveal Himself. Obviously, death is the opposite of an anticlimax. For this reason, God personally comes to escort the soul to the next level of its existence, because the body and soul need to be separated from each other in order to accomplish what each needs at the next level of existence. Once they accomplish this, God will reunite them in resurrection. Therefore, the entire process of death is seen as God's personally elevating the person to a higher level.

This is why we thank God that He made the world in such a way that things go into states of dormancy and rebirth rather than just being constant. Otherwise we would think that the world goes on but people have death as their final point. We thank God that He shows us through the world that apparent finality is really a transitional period that allows for a higher stage to follow. We thank God that He allows us to analogize what occurs in nature to our own lives, so that we can see that our lives are not futile. When we see the blossoms, we know that there is a continuity to life, even though there are periods of time during which everything seems to stop.

King David said, "I know that I will never really die, because death occurs only so that one can live on a higher level afterwards."[13] He wasn't afraid to die because he realized that God causes death only in order to allow the soul to separate from the body so that both can attain a higher level of existence later.

Why There Is Death in the World

There is a Jewish principle that every punishment in this world is meant to rectify something. Punishment is designed to be a productive process. We can understand why the process of death and resurrection needs to take place by examining the first instance of death recorded in the Torah.

Death was first decreed upon Adam after he sinned in the Garden of Eden. After Adam ate of the fruit that God forbade him to eat, God told him that he would no longer be able to live forever but would have to die. On the surface, this might appear as God's way of slapping Adam in the face. In reality, this was not the case.

Rabbi Moshe Chaim Luzzatto explains why death became necessary at that time.[14] He says that God's intention in creating man and woman with a body and soul was so that the soul should elevate itself, as well as the body, during their joint sojourn on earth. Through this process, the body would receive soul-like properties. This meant that just as the soul has no physical limitations and cannot die, so would the body become immortal. This would happen only if the person allowed the soul to control the body.

We can create a wall between the body and soul and see them as two different entities, with our soul being for spiritual pursuits and our bodies for physical ones. If we do this, we prevent the soul from totally infusing the body with its spiritual qualities. If the body is deprived of soul-like properties, it succumbs to its physical limitations. When a body is not elevated above its physical limitations, death becomes an eventuality.

The punishment of death that Adam received was not externally imposed by God. Rather, it was a necessary consequence of what Adam did to himself. He legitimized eating as a physical activity separate from what was good for his soul by eating something God commanded him not to eat. In so doing, Adam made a statement that separated his body from his soul, making it subject to mortal limitations.

This is an example of how people bring punishment upon themselves by doing things that subject their bodies to the limits of the physical world.

Luzzatto explains that the wall between body and soul does not make the body incapable of being affected by the soul. The body can still be elevated, but no longer to the point where it won't die. There are still many remaining levels of existence through which the body can be elevated by the soul. Nevertheless, until the Messiah comes, souls will never be able to feed into bodies enough spiritual nourishment for the bodies to remain eternal.

Why Death Is Good for Mankind

Rabbi Luzzatto expands upon this as follows: Death is a consequence of people's inability to fully actualize the soul's potential in elevating the body. Thus, the soul retains this unused potential. The body too suffers, because it is unable to make use of everything the soul has to offer. Thus, as long as the person is alive, both parts of the soul–body partnership suffer. God alleviates this anguish through death.

When a person dies, his or her soul goes to a place known as the World of Souls. There, freed from the body, it grows to the extent that the person developed it during his or her lifetime. It develops according to how much Torah was learned and how many commandments of the Torah (mitzvot) were observed while it was with the body. The body simultaneously goes through a decomposition process which purifies it,[15] allowing the body to rid itself of the negativity put in it through the person's actions. Once the soul has grown to the extent that it can, based on that person's actions, God reunites it with the body at the time He establishes as being best for the world. Once the body and soul are reunited in this way, the soul will be able to give the body what it was unable to give it before. At that point, the reunification is the healthiest partnership possible. The body and soul unite in a true oneness of which they were not previously capable.

Significance of Our Belief in Resurrection

Why is the concept of resurrection such a cardinal belief, and why is it mentioned three times a day in our prayers?

Resurrection speaks to the exact precision of God's reward to people. Nothing in spiritual creation is ever destroyed. Whatever we create spiritually, during our physical sojourn on earth, is brought back to us to the exact extent that we developed it while alive. This occurs when our souls rejoin our bodies during the time of resurrection and afterwards.

This concept invests tremendous, eternal meaning into our every act. Whatever we do remains with us forever because of the everlasting nature of positive spiritual behavior.

Another important principle that we derive, once we know that our souls and bodies will ultimately be unified forever, is that we gain a different appreciation of the importance of our physical being. We see its central role in allowing us truly to develop a unity between our physical and spiritual selves. God is One, and we want to imitate His Oneness. Although God has no body, we want to take our bodies and elevate them with our souls to form a unity. Rather than seeing our body as unholy, the fact that it is resurrected along with our soul teaches us that bodies too have a holy purpose. Resurrection redefines our perspective of the physical, which then helps us appreciate the potential holiness of our physical drives and physical beings.

Physical existence, then, is not to be viewed as independent of spiritual existence. Once we understand that the body is holy, we can appreciate the importance of not using it for unholy purposes.

Implications for Us of the Prayer for Resurrection

The best way for two people to achieve true unity is to understand the importance of bringing out the potentials of the partner rather than making the partner an extension of themselves. The function of a relationship is to help one's partner emerge. The more each individual emerges, the more the couple can merge. Once one accepts this idea, he or she also needs the power and self-discipline to put it into effect.

What sometimes hampers someone from helping a partner emerge is the fear that if the partner grows too much, the other will be left behind.

The prayer for resurrection can suggest to us that people supply their partners not only with their physical needs, but with their psychological needs as well, including whatever is required for people to emerge as individuals in their own right. A person can feel dead to the extent that he or she has unrealized potentials. A partner should attempt to resurrect this person by giving the requisite support and encouragement for realizing his or her abilities and goals. Just as God uses His power to support us physically and spiritually, so should partners do the same for each other.

In this prayer, we extol God's greatness and the uniqueness of His abilities. In human relationships, partners must convey to each other that each cherishes some uniqueness that the other possesses. Each person should frequently let the other know that in some way he or she is special, and is "the best" for the partner. It may take two people a long time to discover what they appreciate and find unique in each other, but the depth of their union depends upon their doing this.

This prayer also refers to God's trustworthiness. In a human relationship, each person needs to know that a partner will be supportive should support become necessary. A positive feeling is conveyed when a person is confident that the spouse will provide support as it is needed. The security that comes from trusting a spouse to provide what is needed, when it is needed, is fundamental to a good relationship.

Notes

1. Genesis 22:13.
2. *Pirkei D'Rabbi Eliezer*, chapter 31.
3. Kings 17:22; II Kings 4:35; Ezekiel 37:10.
4. Talmud *Bavli*, *Taanit* 2a.
5. *Siddur HaGra*.
6. Talmud *Bavli*, *Sanhedrin* 90b.
7. *Siddur HaGra*.
8. *Siddur HaGra*.
9. Iyun Tefillah in *Otsar HaTefillot*.
10. Iyun Tefillah in *Otsar HaTefillot*.
11. *Shulchan Aruch, Or HaChaim* 226.
12. Talmud *Bavli*, *Niddah* 30b; *Pirkei D'Rabbi Eliezer*, chapter 34.
13. Psalms 118.
14. M. Luzzatto, *The Knowing Heart* (Jerusalem: Feldheim, 1982), p. 96.
15. Ibid.

CHAPTER 6

The Holy God

אַתָּה קָדוֹשׁ וְשִׁמְךָ קָדוֹשׁ, וּקְדוֹשִׁים בְּכָל יוֹם יְהַלְלוּךָ סֶּלָה. בָּרוּךְ אַתָּה יהוה, הָאֵל הַקָּדוֹשׁ.

You are holy, and Your Name is holy, and holy ones praise
You every day, forever. Blessed are You, God, the holy
God.

Theme of the Prayer

This third prayer of the Amidah deals with God's holiness. When one prays with a quorum (a *minyan*), the Shemoneh Esrai is repeated aloud for the benefit of the congregation. During the repetition, the following Kedushah prayer is inserted in lieu of this prayer:

> We will sanctify Your Name in the world, in the same way that they (angels) sanctify it in the highest heavens, as it is written by the hand of Your prophet, "And one called to another and said, 'Holy, holy, holy is the Lord of Hosts, the whole world is filled with His glory.'" Those facing them say, "Blessed"—"Blessed is the glory of God from His place." And in Your holy Writings the following is written: "God will reign forever—Your God, Zion—from generation to generation, praise God.
>
> We will tell of Your greatness and for all Eternity we shall sanctify Your holiness, and Your praise, our God, shall never be removed from our mouths, forever and ever, because You, God, are a great and holy King. Blessed are You, God, the Holy God.

Historical Background

The Midrash tells us that this prayer's concluding blessing was first uttered by the angels when Jacob had his first prophetic vision.[1] He had come to the place on which the Temple was later to be built, and he saw a ladder with angels ascending and descending on it. At the top of the ladder he saw the Gates of Compassion open. This vision inspired him to sanctify God's Name, at which time the angels declared, "Blessed are You, God, the holy God."

The Concept of Holiness

This prayer is the only place in the entire Shemoneh Esrai in which we say that God's attribute of holiness prompts the holy to praise Him. What is the significance of identifying holy people with praising God's holiness?

God is described by two similar expressions. One says that God is *Sovev kol Almin*—"He encompasses all worlds." The other says that He is *Memaleh kol Almin*—"He fills all worlds."[2] The description of God as "encompassing all worlds" defines God before He created the world, existing as an entity independent of anything else. We define God in relation to His world, even though God exists independently of His relationship to the world. We do so because, as human beings, we can't fathom something that exists outside of time and space. The description of God as "filling all worlds" defines God as a Being who expresses Himself through the world that He created. We *can* comprehend a Being described in these terms.

The perspective of angels causes them to define God as a Being that "encompasses all worlds." Since angels, in their inherent essence, have no relationship to space and time, their perceptions of God can be independent of space, time, and how God relates to the world. Therefore, on a certain level, angels can define God in a purer way than mortals can; they can relate to God in a vacuum, so to speak. Human beings, then, relate to God in the physical world and define God in terms of that world. Angels, on the other hand, can understand God as an independent entity but cannot understand His manifestation in the material world.

It is our function to see God through the camouflage of the material world. There are no physical camouflages in the celestial realms where the angels dwell. Angels never see anything that clouds God's Oneness. When we perceive God in the material world, we integrate His presence with the physical world and bring to fruition the purpose of the physical world. In other words, when we understand the physical world as a manifestation and extension of God's will, we unify the spiritual and material realms. In this respect, we are superior to the angels.

When we describe God as being "holy" (*kadosh*), we really mean that He is aloof from, or is above, the material world. When angels refer to God as being holy, they see His exaltation above the world.

The praise of God's holiness by Jews and by angels are connected. The Midrash says that the angels are not allowed to praise God until the Jewish people do so first.[3] What is the significance of this statement?

God has a commitment to making His will manifest in the physical world. Angels are the messengers who take His manifestation into our world. This fact is reflected by the angels' first referring to God as being holy; that is, they see Him as being exalted above the material world. Next, the angels refer to God as *HaShem tzevakot*, the God who is the "Master over the constellations." They recognize that God is involved in the affairs of the universe. They conclude by acknowledging, *meloh kol ha'aretz kevodo*, "the earth is filled with His glory." This is a recognition by the angels that God involves himself in our material world. The angels understand that they have a role to play in bringing God's commitment to the physical world. They recognize that God not only is exalted above the world but interacts with it as well.

The Uniqueness of Jacob

Of the three forefathers, Jacob had the best ability to recognize the spiritual mission behind everything material. He best understood that everything in the physical world is a manifestation of God's will and that material things were created only to serve a spiritual purpose. This unity of physical existence with spiritual purpose is known as *Emet*, or "truth."

When Jacob saw a ladder in his spiritual vision, the bottom of it was on the earth and the top was in heaven. From this, Jacob understood the meaning of true holiness. God is not only in heaven, but He manifests His presence through the spiritual purpose which underlies every physical thing. True holiness personifies the idea of an exalted God who gives of His exaltation into this world.

The angels going down to earth in Jacob's dream symbolized God's giving into the world. The angels ascending the ladder symbolized people's recognition that God has invested the physical world with a spiritual purpose and elevated the world to that purpose. These symbols teach us a powerful lesson. They teach that the extent to which we recognize the spiritual essence of God's giving into the world and our giving it back to God is the extent to which God increases the spiritual essence that He lets flow into the world.

Blessing God's Holiness

The third prayer of the Shemoneh Esrai ends with the words, "Blessed are You, God, the holy God." The Midrash says that God's pleasure with the world reaches its peak when He sees the Jewish people speaking about His holiness. When they say the blessing that God is the Holy God, God holds onto His throne and hugs a picture of Jacob and promises to remember the plight of the Jews in their exile.[4] This means that when the Jews ratify God's existence in the world, God, so to speak, hugs Jacob for recognizing that the world is here for a spiritual reason and for trying to bring it to fruition in his life. When we look at the physical world and see the Godly purpose behind it, we are acknowledging that God is a holy God. The angels can't say Kedushah until we first indicate that God's purpose fills all of the earth. Once we acknowledge God's holiness on earth, then angels become messengers of God's purpose in their heavenly realms.

The significance of our praising God with holiness is that we thereby show that everything physical has a spiritual function. The recitation of *Kedushah* by a Jew is the means by which we ratify God's purpose in having created the world as well as our purpose in being Jewish.

Implications of Holiness for Human Relationships

A holy relationship between people does not imply that people avoid connecting with the material world. It does imply that whatever involvements people have with the physical world should not become dominant themes in their lives. Holy people balance the physical with the spiritual, such that they control their physical drives and enjoy them only in ways that will spiritually elevate them. In this way their physical pursuits serve spiritual goals.

Human relationships have a physical and a spiritual component to them as well. A holy marital relationship is one in which the physical enjoyment of the couple is a celebration and expression of the spiritual unity that already exists between them. This attitude instills into the relationship a sense of self-dignity and dignity for one's partner. It is this qualitative appreciation for ourselves and others that allows us to connect with them on higher levels. Each of these higher levels preserves the other person's sense of dignity and allows it to emerge. The enhancement of this dignity as an outgrowth of the relationship creates a great spiritual love between the two individuals.

Notes

1. *Pirkei D'Rabbi Eliezer*, chapter 35.
2. Zohar, *Raya Mehemna, Pinchas; Tikkunim* 57.
3. *Tanna Dvei Eliyahu Zuta* 25.
4. *Tanna Dvei Eliyaha Zuta* 25, and *Tanya Rabati*.

CHAPTER 7

The One Who
Grants Knowledge

אַתָּה חוֹנֵן לְאָדָם דַּעַת, וּמְלַמֵּד לֶאֱנוֹשׁ בִּינָה. חָנֵּנוּ מֵאִתְּךָ
דֵּעָה בִּינָה וְהַשְׂכֵּל. בָּרוּךְ אַתָּה יהוה, חוֹנֵן הַדָּעַת.

You graciously give man discerning knowledge, and teach
people understanding. Graciously grant us from Yourself
discerning knowledge, understanding and intellect. Blessed
are You, God, who graciously grants discerning knowledge.

Theme of the Prayer

In this prayer we ask God to grant us the wisdom to discriminate between issues, values, and pursuits that appear to be similar. We often conceptualize wisdom as a faculty that allows us to extrapolate from our experience or accumulated knowledge to novel situations. Judaism tells us that by virtue of our connection with God, we can possess forms of wisdom that are outgrowths of our relationship with Him. This divinely granted understanding allows us to discern between values and activities that appear superficially identical, but which have critically different effects on our lives and our souls. These are the types of wisdom for which we petition God in this prayer.

Historical Background

The biblical origin of the blessing for knowledge is based in an incident in the book of Genesis. The Midrash says that this blessing was recited by the angels when they saw that God taught Joseph the 70 languages of the nations of the world, via the angel Gabriel.[1] Joseph needed to know all 70 languages as a prerequisite for assuming the post of second-in-command to the Pharaoh of Egypt.

A second opinion says that God taught Moses the secret powers of all of God's Names. When the angels saw this, they exclaimed, "Blessed are You, God, who grants knowledge."[2]

This prayer acknowledges that wisdom is a gift from God. This is why it must begin with the words, "You graciously grant. . . ." Otherwise, we might think that we developed our intelligence ourselves. We view Joseph and Moses as role models of individuals who were worthy of divine gifts of wisdom. The significance of Joseph learning 70 languages is that God gave Joseph whatever he needed in order to be a ruler over Egypt. He did this because Joseph had already become a ruler over his own passions. Joseph rose to power only after he had passed the test of not succumbing to the seduction by the wife of Potiphar. Once someone demonstrates internal leadership, as Joseph did, he or she can be ready for external leadership.

Spiritual wisdom is the product of one's spiritual receptivity. Moses was privy to knowledge of God's Names because his ego did not block his "spiritual antenna." He was therefore completely receptive to divine "wave lengths" of knowledge.

Order of This Prayer in the Shemoneh Esrai

Although all of the Amidah prayers have independent importance, there is also a rationale for the order in which they appear in the Shemoneh Esrai.

We began the Amidah with three prayers of praise to God. In this fourth prayer, we make the first of thirteen requests, the request for discriminating knowledge. It is first because such knowledge allows us to see differences between things, an ability that we always need. Also, without first having this type of knowledge, we would not know what to ask for in the twelve requests that follow, or in our private prayers. Only by understanding the essential differences between things can we know what we can make holy.

Why We Say God Has Granted Us Knowledge

This first personal request is the only Amidah prayer that prefaces a request with the statement that God graciously gives us something. We say that God graciously gives us knowledge, before requesting that He continue to grant it to us. We do this because spiritual growth, as expressed in the remaining Amidah prayers, requires a transition period. By saying "You grant man knowledge" and then making a request for knowledge, we provide a transition between the prayers of praise that precede this prayer and the prayers of request that follow it.

A second reason we say, "You graciously grant knowledge"

is to reinforce to us that intelligence and wisdom are not innate assets that we have independent of God's participation. Although we are genetically endowed with various aptitudes, there is a deeper level of knowledge that depends upon the depth of our relationship with God. The parts of our potential that become actualized through brainstorms and insights are special gifts from Him.

There is another reason for mentioning God's graciousness, and that is related to the structure of the prayers on the Sabbath and Jewish holidays. On those days, the thirteen requests of the weekday Amidah are replaced by a prayer that discusses the essence of the particular day. This change is made because people are not concerned about their daily affairs on these holy days and therefore don't make the usual petitions, and also because the Sabbath and holidays are themselves sources of blessing.

At the conclusion of these days, we make Havdalah ("Division"). This is a prayer that denotes the termination of the holiness of the day and marks our return to the nonsanctified nature of the weekday. We add the following after the first verse of this prayer: "You have graciously given us the ability to study Your Torah, and You have taught us to do the statutes of Your will. And You have made a distinction, Lord our God, between that which is holy and that which is secular, between light and darkness, between Israel and the (other) nations, between the seventh day and the six days of Creation. Our Father, our King, begin for us, in peace, the days that come to greet us, devoid of all unintentional sin, and cleansed of all iniquity, and cleaving to You in awe."

Havdalah may be said only if we can discern the difference between the secular and the holy, and between the holiday and the weekday. Therefore, the capacity to discriminate is a prerequisite for Havdalah.

Technically, it is still the Sabbath or holiday when we begin the evening prayers in which Havdalah is recited. Since we don't make requests on these days, how do we request the knowledge we need in order to discriminate between that holy day and the weekday? We can't presume that we possess this knowledge unless we ask God for it. The compromise solution is to begin saying the weekday prayer, acknowledging God as the grantor of knowledge, and hope that He will follow by actually granting us knowledge. Then we can recite the Havdalah prayer and follow it with the weekday portion of the prayer, asking for knowledge.

Why are specific differences between the holy and secular, between light and darkness, between Jews and non-Jews, and between the Sabbath and weekdays enumerated in the Havdalah of the prayer for wisdom? The reason is that the two contrasted categories have elements of holiness, or lack of holiness, that make them different from each other. We can discern these differences only if we purify ourselves spiritually. Thus, in the Havdalah of this prayer, we ask God to "Give us a week cleansed of sin and iniquity, and cleaving to You in awe."

Meaning of the Words

"Knowledge and . . . Understanding"

"Knowledge" (*daat*) in this prayer does not mean factual knowledge, but rather the capacity for evaluation, qualitative discernment, and so on. Mere book-learning can be attained without God's intervention. "Understanding" (*binah*) refers to having a relationship with that which we come to understand. Accomplishing this involves discernment, deduction, and intuition.

"Unintentional Sins and Iniquity"

The Havdalah prayer refers to "unintentional sins" and "iniquity." Unintentional sins are those that we commit accidentally. Even though they are done unintentionally, they still have a negative effect on us. "Iniquity" refers to sins that we commit intentionally. Once we do so, it becomes easier for us to repeat that sin. We therefore ask God to cleanse us of previous sins so that we will not be predisposed to repeat them.

Implications of Knowledge for Human Relationships

A person who doesn't discriminate between people, who more or less relates to everybody in the same way, will tend to have only superficial relationships. If one does not choose to discern the true differences between individuals, then all relationships are interchangeable. When no discrimination is used, the implication is that no note was made of another's unique abilities. If those go unnoticed, they will not be utilized to create a cohesive bond in any resulting relationship.

When we use our discriminating knowledge to select a person with whom we wish to relate, the resulting relationship has the capacity for depth and significance. Our discriminating and choosing selectively implies that we have grasped the uniqueness of the other and that we value it. When we find something for which we've searched, we appreciate the person who possesses it all the more. True appreciation, therefore, depends upon discriminating how a person's qualities set him or her apart from all others.

It is for this reason that the word *daat*—discriminating knowledge—implies the capacity to separate similar things from one another. It also means to form a close bond. When the Bible refers to people being intimate with one another, it uses the term *daat*. One truly bonds to a spouse when there is deep knowledge of the spouse's uniqueness.

Notes

1. *Shebolei Leket*, *Tefillah*, chapter 18.
2. *Pirkei D'Rabbi Eliezer*, chapter 40.

CHAPTER 8

The One Who Desires Repentance

הֲשִׁיבֵֽנוּ אָבִֽינוּ לְתוֹרָתֶֽךָ, וְקָרְבֵֽנוּ מַלְכֵּֽנוּ לַעֲבוֹדָתֶֽךָ, וְהַחֲזִירֵֽנוּ בִּתְשׁוּבָה שְׁלֵמָה לְפָנֶֽיךָ. בָּרוּךְ אַתָּה יהוה, הָרוֹצֶה בִּתְשׁוּבָה.

Return us, our Father, to Your Torah, and bring us close, our King, to Your service, and return us with complete repentance before You. Blessed are You, God, who desires repentance.

Theme and Historical Background of This Prayer

This prayer for repentance is based on what happened to Reuven, the firstborn son of our forefather Jacob. After the death of his stepmother, Reuven stressed to Jacob in an inappropriate manner that Jacob should be more involved with Reuven's mother. Due to his impulsiveness, he lost certain spiritual benefits that should have been his due by virtue of being the firstborn of Jacob's twelve sons. He regretted this tremendously, and after realizing his error, Reuven repented for the rest of his life.

When Moses blessed the tribes of Israel with words from God, he told the tribe of Reuven, "Reuven will live in this world and not die in the world to come" (*Yechi Reuven v'al yamot*).[1] This was an announcement that Reuven's repentance was finally accepted by God. When the angels heard these words, they said, "Blessed are You, God, who desires repentance."

Structure of the Prayer

There are fifteen Hebrew words in this prayer, just as there are fifteen Hebrew words in a verse in the Prophets which speaks about repentance. That verse says, "The wicked man shall leave his path, and the man of iniquity his thoughts, and he should return to God. And God will have mercy on him, (and he will return) to our God, for He forgives abundantly."[2] As the Day of Atonement comes to a close, we recite the Neilah prayer, in which, as our final petition to God we say that His ultimate desire is not to put to death those people who have misused life. God's ultimate desire is for us to return to Him after we sin, so that He can embrace us again. The fifteen words in the repentance prayer allude to the verse in the

Prophets that speaks so eloquently about God's desire for
people to repent. God wants nothing more than for us to
return to Him.

The number 15 also has mystical connotations. The Kabbalistic commentaries tell us that there are seven heavens and that
these have seven spaces between them. From the highest
heaven to the Throne of Glory is an additional "distance," for
a total of fifteen levels. The fifteen words of this prayer allude
to the fifteen levels of space between ourselves and God. When
we repent, we can transcend these fifteen levels and reach the
Throne of God.[3]

Each letter in the Hebrew alphabet has a numerical value.
This prayer begins and ends with the Hebrew letter *heh*, which
has a value of 5. The numerical value of the first and last *heh*
added together is 10, and the number 10 alludes to the Ten
Days of Repentance, from Rosh Hashanah until Yom Kippur.
Although God always wants us to repent, He is especially
eager for us to do so during the ten days between the Jewish
New Year and the Day of Atonement.

All of the above refers to the extent to which repentance can
bring us close to God. The words of the prayer, as we shall see,
explain the process by which this is brought about.

Relationship to the Previous Prayer

Why is this prayer the second request we make, and how is
it connected to the previous prayer for knowledge? How do we
make the transition from knowledge to repentance?

Since returning to God depends upon Torah study, we first
ask God for discriminating knowledge and insight. Once we
have these faculties, we can apply them to the learning of
Torah. Through Torah study, we have a vehicle of connection
through which we can return fully to God.

Men and women both have an obligation to learn Torah,
although what they are required to learn, and the framework
in which they are supposed to learn, is different for men and
women. In times when women learned Torah from their moth-
ers in the home, women did not have to learn Torah from

formalized study; today, women have a requirement to learn Torah formally.[4]

Another reason for this order of Amidah prayers has to do with our perspective about life. We have a level of awareness, or knowledge, which is essentially the same on a day-to-day basis. Each of us tries to use our knowledge, based on trial and error, experience, and so on, to make each day better than the one before. There is a second type of knowledge as well, which results in our making more than simple, mechanical improvements from day to day. It consists of our acquiring a different perspective about life. With a new perspective, things that weren't important yesterday are important today, and vice versa. This form of knowledge, known as *"daat,"* "discriminating knowledge," involves qualitative and not just quantitative changes. This qualitative shift to a different mind-set is what is required for repentance.

Meaning of the Words

"Return Us, Our Father, to Your Torah"

We ask God, "as a father," to "return us to Your Torah." This means that God, acting as a father, will always take His children back, even if they have abandoned the learning of Torah or the performance of its commandments.

Jewish law says that it is the responsibility of a father to learn Torah with his children. If the father is unable to teach his child Torah, either because he's not a good teacher or because he himself hasn't had the opportunity to learn Torah, then the child can learn Torah in school. However, the ideal method of transmitting Torah is directly from the father. This method creates a connection of generations, providing a rich relationship which enhances the child's learning.

In addition, a father teaching Torah to his child enhances the relationship between the parent and child. The father is a better father, and the Torah becomes a richer Torah for the child, because of the love and the chain of generations that are transmitted. Thus, when we ask God to give us the desire to learn Torah, the time to learn, and the wisdom to understand it, we ask Him to do so as the ultimate Father.

There is a second reason why we ask God to act as a father in returning us to Torah. There are things in life from which we shy away. When we're not psychologically ready for something, we tell others who try to encourage us that we're not interested. Often, we subsequently realize that what we were offered was really something with which we should have become involved.

Normally, we feel embarrassed if we reject the overtures of strangers and later want to use what they offered. Most people don't want to face the humiliation of confronting someone whom they have rejected for incorrect or inappropriate reasons. When the person who offered us something was a loving mother or father, however, it is easier for us to face our mistakes. No matter what children do, they know that their parents love them. Because of their abiding love for their children, good parents won't throw something back in their children's faces if the children change their minds and want what they previously rejected. Parents give their children an abiding sense of security which enables children always to return to their parents.

And so, we ask God to return us to Torah as a child returns to his father. We might have been offered Torah at some point in our lives and rejected it. We might even have studied it and decided that we had better things to do. At a certain point, however, we decide that we want to come back to Torah, but we feel embarrassed. We need never feel embarrassed when we return to Torah. Just as a child is always welcome to come home, we can always return.

People who commit themselves to behavior that is inconsistent with Torah values should never feel too embarrassed to change. For example, there was a Jewish woman who dated a non-Jewish man for five years but in the end she just couldn't marry him. There was something inside her that simply didn't allow it. When she was a teenager, she had rebelled against Judaism. When she became older and wiser, she wished to return. Wasn't she embarrassed? Not at all. She realized that she was coming home, and no one rejects a person who wants to come home.

"Bring Us Close, Our King, to Your Service"

"Service" (*avodah*) has several interpretations. According to some commentaries, it means the totality of mitzvot (commandments).[5] We serve God by doing all the things we are required to do, as well as by avoiding all the things we are not supposed to do. This verse refers to our fulfilling our obligations to God. Therefore, we call Him a "King" and ask Him to bring us closer to serving Him.

According to other commentaries, "service" specifically refers to prayer.[6] *Avodah* means "work" and is the word used to denote physical labor. Even though prayer is something spiritual, it is termed "work" because prayer requires us to work out a lot of internal conflicts, goals, and our sense of direction. We must be honest with God and with ourselves when we use prayer to communicate with Him, and doing this requires work.

When we speak to God, we can't say one thing and mean something else. What we say must be true, but it also needs to be presentable to God. For instance, we can't ask God to let us win a lottery because everyone in our community has more money than we do and we want the same luxuries that they have. It may be true that we have fewer luxuries than our neighbors, but why should God relate to that?

Prayer is supposed to be an opportunity for us to evaluate and reevaluate our needs, in the company of God. We should keep asking ourselves why we want something, why something is important, and how having it will enable us to grow spiritually. Every Jew, together with God, evaluates his or her individual needs. This process of review is the "work" of prayer.

"Return Us with Complete Repentance"

In this prayer, we seem to make redundant requests of God. First we ask God to help us return to Torah. Next we ask Him to help us pray. Then we ask Him to bring us back to Him with full repentance. One would think that the return to Torah and prayer would encompass any possible type of repentance. If so, why is it necessary to add, "and return us with complete repentance before You?"

This repetition teaches us that there are two particular mitzvot, more than any others, that help us come close to God. These are the learning of Torah, and prayer. All mitzvot are important, but Torah study and prayer intensify the bond between people and God in the strongest way.

The Talmud discusses the reason why Torah study brings us so close to God. The Talmud says, "A transgression can extinguish a mitzvah, but a transgression can never extinguish Torah."[7] This statement requires some explanation. Jews do not believe that each transgression cancels out a mitzvah, or vice versa. There is no accounting sheet where, if a person does twenty negative things and ten positive things, he comes out as a "minus 10." Rather, God sees the negative things that we do as barriers to our ability to receive from Him. Therefore, when we sin, God causes us to go through certain purifying processes in order to remove these barriers. Once the barriers are removed, God rewards us fully for all of the positive things we have done.

In this way, our positive and negative actions are seen as two separate accounts. Our negative behaviors prevent us from absorbing and appreciating spiritual reward. God takes away these barriers in many different ways. Once they are out of the way, we can fully appreciate the reward which he gives us for our positive actions.

When the Talmud says that "a transgression extinguishes a mitzvah," it doesn't mean that a sin eradicates what is accomplished by a mitzvah. The good that is accomplished by even one mitzvah is too great to be diminished by something negative that a person does. The act of doing any mitzvah creates a certain eternal spiritual energy. In addition, it creates a sense of a closer connection with and deeper commitment to God. Doing anything that is God's will brings us one step closer to Him. It creates a sense of commitment, responsibility, and obligation to God by virtue of having done what He desires.

When we sin, we create negativity and we also take one step away from God. It is in this sense that a transgression takes away from what we accomplish when we do a mitzvah. A transgression can't negate the essential quality of a mitzvah, but it takes away from the exhilaration of closeness and connection to God which we would otherwise feel.

This is not the case with the effects of transgressions on the consequences of Torah study. A person who observes the special mitzvah of learning Torah creates such an intense bond with God that the connection is always retained. Transgressing cannot entirely remove this special closeness. There is some kind of "super-resistance" that is created by learning Torah. Therefore, if someone wants to rebuild his closeness to God, he should ask God to help him learn Torah.

Repentance, or returning to God, accomplishes two things: First, it makes us recognize what we should, or should not, do in the future. Second, it reinstates a connection with God that had been lost. The mitzvah that can best reconnect us to God is the one that can remain unaffected by our transgressions. In order to return to God, we need to start by reinstating a connection with Him, especially if we are still mired in transgressions. Repentance, in its fullest sense, is a long process which could take many years. The exhilaration and nurturing that comes from a connection with God gives us the energy to improve our behavior. The connection with Torah gives us the strength to begin a complete return to Him.

This is why God said during the First Temple era, "I don't care that the Jewish people worshiped idols, and I don't care that they were steeped in immorality. I don't even care that they did things that were tantamount to murder. If they had not abandoned Torah study, I would not have destroyed the Temple."[8] By this, God meant that had there only been a connection with Torah learning, the light that would have been created by it would have brought the Jews back to Torah observance. Even though the Jews' behavior was not acceptable, had they only allowed themselves to be nurtured by a sense of connection to God, He would not have had to resort to destroying the Temple. Slowly, through Torah study, they would eventually have realized how negative were the things they were doing, and they would have stopped doing them.

The Mitzvah of Prayer

Once we ask God in this prayer to return us to Torah, we then ask Him to bring us close to prayer (*avodah*). Prayer is a mitzvah which, like Torah study, also brings us close to God. People who decide to change their lifestyle to become more observant must slowly but surely adopt a total change in viewpoint about the world. Such people change their goals, their values, and their behavior in becoming observant, and they begin to look at the world in a totally different way. For example, the focus of nonobservant Jews may be to ask themselves how they can become more successful financially, or how they can gain more status and prestige. Observant Jews will try to see God's presence in the secular and material world and notice His connection with the world. Whereas secular people may ask what they can get from the world, observant people ask what they can give back to God through living in the world. When we have more of a Jewish perspective about the world, we see more of God in the world around us.

Prayer, more than anything else, creates consciousness of God. When we stand in front of a Being who is invisible, and we talk to Him, we make a statement that there is a God and that He listens to us. We also show that we are obliged to pray to Him and to create a relationship with Him through the communication of prayer. Prayer is thereby a monumental connection with God, making a statement about the reality of God for us. Torah study is the vehicle for a connection with God, and prayer is the statement through which that connection is deepened. It is for this reason that we ask God in this prayer to help us with these two mitzvot. Once we have these two aids, we can ask God to return us with perfect repentance. Even if it takes us years to return fully, we will be on the right track with Torah and prayer. The resulting repentance will be "before You" (lifanecha). It will be so sincere that even God will testify as to its authenticity.

It is difficult to learn Torah. One might struggle for hours to understand a certain concept. Therefore, it seems reasonable that we ask God to help us understand Torah ("Return us to Your Torah"). However, it is less understandable why we ask God to help us do mitzvot. ("And bring us close to Your service"). Either we do mitzvot or we don't. Why do we need to ask God for assistance in doing them?

The Ethics of the Fathers says that one who throws off the

responsibility of doing mitzvot is burdened by another set of obligations. Conversely, one who accepts the yoke of heaven upon himself by doing what he or she is supposed to do is relieved of other responsibilities.[9] The process by which this happens is that we say to God that we really want to do what He wants us to do, and we make our best efforts to do so. God responds by removing barriers that get in the way of our observing the mitzvot.

We need God's help to make a shift from involving ourselves in secular pursuits to a new set of religious involvements. Making this happen requires prayer. For example, let's say that a person wants to attend a Torah class on Wednesday nights. Every time he or she is ready to go, something comes up, perhaps a late-night meeting at work, or a last-minute phone call, or a social obligation. The person must ask for God's help both in removing the actual impediments and in helping the person make the class a priority. Once God helps remove the barriers, the person can then implement the appropriate changes so that he or she can return to God.

Returning Anew

Repentance is not simply a matter of doing something a little differently by altering details of how it is done. Repentance is predicated on having a different perspective about life, which causes different behavior. This is the connection between the previous prayer (discriminating knowledge) and the present one (repentance). We ask God for an appropriate perspective so that through our life we can see things in their reality, not in their illusions. Without *daat*, repentance is meaningless; it simply alters details of our existence without making any real changes.

This new mind-set is really a whole new life. If we retain our old perspectives and make only mechanical changes, nothing is really new in our lives. But when we adopt a new perspective, we have the sense that life is completely different and that every day is a new beginning.

This explains why there are two different biblical sources for prayer. One source tells us to pray for things that we need, and a different source tells us to pray for repentance (*teshuvah*). In the first case, we pray for financial success, health, and everything else that we need, on the basis of the Torah verse, "And you should serve God with all of your heart and with all of your soul."[10] We pray for material and physical things because we require them in order for our lives to continue. Since God brought us into the world, it is reasonable for us to request of Him the fulfillment of these needs.

In Hebrew, the word for *repentance* is the same as the word for *return*. The commandment to pray for *teshuvah* comes from the verse, "Bring words with you, and return to God."[11] Rabbenu Yonah says this means that there is a commandment for us to pray to God to ask Him to help us do *teshuvah*.[12] We ask God to help us do *teshuvah* when we have blocked God from giving to us. When we do *teshuvah*, we don't simply ask God to continue giving to us. We ask God to give us a whole new life.

Who says that we can ask God to give us entirely new lives? It is one thing to ask God to provide for us within the lives that we already have, but it is another to ask God to give us entirely new lives. For this, we need a source separate from the general mitzvah of prayer. This is what the present prayer in the Shemoneh Esrai addresses. It is not enough for us to want to make mechanical revisions in our behavior. True repentance requires God's help in allowing us to start life anew by seeing the world from a different perspective. We have to want to change, but God has to grant us a new perspective so that our resolve is successful, and so we may have the opportunity for a new life.

The Totality of Teshuvah

The human faculty essentially consists of thought, speech, and action. We operate in all three of these realms. Therefore, when we return to God, we must return in all three of these areas. Some people think that *teshuvah* is behavioral change and doesn't involve the ways we think or speak. This is not true, because when we create a relationship with God, every faculty is a gift from Him and a bridge to Him.

One might think: "Isn't it enough for me to change my behavior and my speech? Can't I at least have the freedom to think any way that I choose?" The truth is, that isn't possible. Whereas action is related to our physical existence, and speech is related to a higher level of existence, thought is directly related to our souls. If our minds have not really returned to God and we still fantasize about things that are prohibited, then our souls are not yet "standing before" God. Physically we may act robotically in doing the right things, but when we compartmentalize ourselves in this way, we have not made a complete connection with God.

In this prayer, then, we ask God to help us return to Torah. Torah study is principally done with speech. Our mouths should be involved with understanding God's will. Next we ask God to help us serve Him with actions. Once these two are accomplished, we ask God to make us really return to Him. This request refers to our thoughts, to what goes on in our hearts and in our desires. Our speech can change in obvious, observable ways. Our actions can also change in measurable ways. Our thoughts, however, are not observable to anyone else; only God can know what we truly think. We ask that these thoughts also come before Him with sincerity: "And return us with complete repentance before You."

Implications of Repentance for Human Relationships

In this prayer we don't ask God to accept us as we are, with no strings attached. This prayer underscores the fact that people make mistakes in their relationships with each other, just as they make mistakes in their relationship with God. In both situations, rectifications need to be made, and people sometimes find these difficult. It can be hard for them to admit that they made mistakes, even if they know that they did. Change is also difficult for most people to make, even when they know that it is necessary.

In this prayer we ask God to give us the tools to effect changes in ourselves. This idea teaches us that whenever a person needs to change him or herself in order to improve a relationship, the person should never feel that it is a solo undertaking. Partners should always feel comfortable turning to each other and asking for the time, encouragement, and concrete help needed to effect changes. A spouse should also be available to help the partner change.

Nevertheless, the one who needs to change must accept responsibility for modifying his or her behavior. Meanwhile, the spouse should be patient in helping, often by providing the tools that will enable the needy partner to grow and thereby to enhance his or her self-esteem and self-confidence.

Notes

1. Deuteronomy 33:6.
2. Isaiah 55:7.
3. Commentary on *Machzor Kol Bo*.
4. Shulchan Aruch, *Or HaChaim* 47:4. See Taz and Magen Avraham.
5. Etz Yosef in *Siddur Otsar HaTefillot*.
6. Sfat Emet, *Shabbat Shuvah* 5645.
7. Talmud *Bavli*, Sotah 21a.
8. Midrash on Lamentations, *Pesichta* 2.
9. Ethics of the Fathers 3:6.
10. Deuteronomy 11:13.
11. Hosea 14:3.
12. Gates of Repentance 1:41.

CHAPTER 9

The Gracious One Who Forgives Abundantly

סְלַח לָנוּ אָבִינוּ כִּי חָטָאנוּ, מְחַל לָנוּ מַלְכֵּנוּ כִּי פָשָׁעְנוּ, כִּי
מוֹחֵל וְסוֹלֵחַ אָתָּה. בָּרוּךְ אַתָּה יהוה, חַנּוּן הַמַּרְבֶּה
לִסְלוֹחַ.

Forgive us, our Father, for we have sinned unintentionally.
Pardon us, our King, for we have purposely sinned,
for You pardon and forgive. Blessed are You, God, the gracious
one who forgives abundantly.

Theme and Historical Background of This Prayer

The biblical background for the above blessing is an event in the life of Judah, the fourth of Jacob's sons.[1] Judah was married to a woman named Shua, with whom he had three sons—Er, Onan, and Shelah. Er married Tamar, but he sinned and was taken from the world. Onan then married Tamar, with whom he was supposed to have children in order to perpetuate Er's name. Onan was punished for not wanting to have children that would be "credited" to his brother's name, and he also died. The obligation of levirate marriage then fell on Shelah. (Levirate marriages occurred in biblical times. When a man died without leaving children, his brother married the widow in order to perpetuate the man's lineage. Such marriages are no longer performed.)

Since Judah saw two of his sons die after marrying Tamar, he was afraid that there was something about being married to her that resulted in the deaths. Therefore he had no intention of allowing Shelah to marry her. He used a delaying tactic, telling Tamar that Shelah was still young and that she should wait until he matured before marrying him.

With the passing of years, Tamar realized that Judah had no intention of giving Shelah to her as a husband. In the meantime, Judah's wife died. After mourning her, Judah journeyed to a crossroads. Tamar disguised herself as a prostitute, seduced him there, and became pregnant by him.

It is difficult to understand how someone of Judah's stature could have succumbed to a prostitute. This difficulty is addressed by our Sages. The incident between Judah and Tamar occurred years after Judah and his brothers had sold Joseph into slavery. At that point, our Sages say, Judah had fallen spiritually. He could have prevented the sale of Joseph by opposing his brothers, but he didn't. When the ten brothers brought Joseph's blood-soaked garment back to their father and deceived him into believing that Joseph had been killed by a wild animal, Jacob felt tremendous anguish. The brothers became angry with Judah for not having anticipated their father's reaction and using his qualities of leadership to stop them from selling Joseph. Immediately after this episode, Judah went off on his own and married Shua, and had children with her.[2]

Our Sages say that Judah became involved with Tamar only because he had fallen spiritually. When he met her at the crossroads, he did not recognize her, and God brought a tremendous inclination upon him to want to have relations with her. Judah fought very hard not to succumb to this desire, but God, as part of His providence in the world, ensured that the desire would be too strong to overcome. It was necessary for Judah and Tamar to unite, because this union would produce the progenitors of the Davidic dynasty and the Messiah himself. For this reason, there was a special angel who was assigned the task of pushing Judah back to Tamar every time he attempted to go away from her and return to the road.[3]

This is not meant to whitewash Judah's actions, since had he not fallen spiritually, he would not have been put into this position with Tamar. Nevertheless, God wanted Judah's and Tamar's seeds to unite, in order to start the Davidic dynasty. There are many Kabbalistic reasons as to why the Davidic dynasty had to be established through such a complicated and seemingly distasteful course. In any event, Judah's actions are viewed as a spiritual fall combined with divine providence.

Tamar was a spiritual woman. She wanted to have relations with Judah because she knew that great children were destined to come from her union with him. She made sure to ask him for some type of identification, in order to have proof later that her children were Judah's. Since Judah had no ready identification, Tamar asked him for some type of security, and he gave her his emblem and one of his distinctive garments. Some days later, he tried to send Tamar a goat in lieu of his emblem and cloak, but Judah's messenger was unable to find her, so Tamar retained his security.

It is interesting to note that the goat was the same type of animal with which Judah had sinned in the sale of Joseph.

Judah had slaughtered a kid and dipped Joseph's coat of many colors in it, to make it look as if Joseph had been killed. His sending a goat to Tamar, then, had a symbolic meaning: it suggested that because Judah was involved in selling Joseph and then lied to his father about it, he again got into a situation involving a goat. His initial spiritual failure with Joseph allowed him subsequently to become entangled with Tamar.

Tamar became pregnant with twins. Three months later, when her pregnancy became evident, Judah, as the governor of the province, was told that Tamar had become pregnant through prostitution. Since Tamar had not remarried, it was assumed that her pregnancy was a result of prostitution, although no one knew with whom. It is prohibited for an unmarried woman to have sexual relations, although if she does so, it is not normally a capital crime.[4] For reasons discussed in our commentaries, however, Judah decided that Tamar was to be put to death for her act of prostitution.

As Tamar went to her death, she made a tremendously moral decision. She was pregnant by the very same man who had judged and sentenced her. She could have felt that Judah also had no right to go unpunished. But she knew that Judah was a very important person, and she did not want to embarrass him. So she decided: "If Judah admits his involvement with me when I show him his emblem and cloak, fine. He will then be making the decision to allow himself to be embarrassed. If he doesn't admit that it was he who lived with me, however, then I am prepared to say nothing and go to my death." (From this incident, the Talmud derives that it is better for a man to throw himself into a fiery furnace than to embarrass his neighbor publicly.[5])

Tamar held up Judah's emblem and cloak and asked, "Whose emblem and garment are these?" Judah then admitted responsibility and further acknowledged that her pregnancy was his fault because he deceptively led her to believe that one day she would marry Shelah. It was clear to Judah that her actions were for the sake of heaven and that she had seduced him because she wanted to bring spiritually great children into the world.

In this story, Judah ignored his personal honor and admitted his deed, despite personal embarrassment. He acknowledged that Tamar was righteous and that he was to blame. The Talmud says that when Judah proclaimed, "She is right. I am responsible for her pregnancy," God forgave Judah. At that moment, the angels in heaven said, "Blessed are You, God, the Gracious One, who shows so much compassion and brings so much forgiveness into the world."[6]

As we saw at the beginning of Chapter 8, Reuven repented for the rest of his life after inappropriately involving himself in his father's personal affairs. Therefore, the fifth prayer in the Shemoneh Esrai, the blessing of "God desires repentance," is associated with Reuven. Judah also repented, but he didn't do so for the rest of his life, changing his entire lifestyle. He had engaged in an act that required forgiveness (even though the actual act with Tamar is viewed as providential), but his action was not viewed as stemming from a basic character flaw. Reuven required a lifelong examination of his personality and lifestyle, because what caused him to err was his haste, which was considered such an ingrained trait that it required a lifelong process of rectification. Therefore, the prayer for repentance is associated with Reuven, and that of forgiveness is associated with Judah.

Relationship to the Previous Prayer

The prayer for forgiveness is the sixth one in the Amidah. Our Sages separated the issues of returning to God (*teshuvah*) and receiving forgiveness from God by making them two separate prayers. In the fifth prayer of the Amidah we asked God to assist us in our going through the changes necessary for repentance. This sixth prayer asks for forgiveness for those things we have done wrong.

The separation of these two prayers conveys a message: We might otherwise think that we do *teshuvah* so that we won't be held culpable for inappropriate things we have done. Splitting them makes the statement that we want to change, even if we can't be forgiven and even if we still have to suffer negative consequences. Our desire to make a change for the future warrants a request all its own. This separation of the two negates the idea that we might want to return to God for egocentric reasons, or that repentance is nothing more than a technique to undo our responsibility for past actions.

For this reason, the prayers are ordered so that we first have to want to change and become better, something valuable in its own right. Even if we didn't live the way we should have yesterday, we ask God for the strength to make today better. Whether or not we will be forgiven for what we did yesterday is not really an issue. Once we do *teshuvah*, we then ask God to forgive our past sins. Thus we see that changing ourselves is the central issue, and not being held responsible for our past is a secondary issue that follows.

Our best petition when we ask God to forgive us is to have already changed our deeds as well as our perspectives on life. Once we have done this, we may ask God not to punish us for our past misdeeds, since we no longer represent the same people we were when we sinned.

In Jewish thinking, one way that God provides correctives (*tikkunim*) for our pasts is by having us go through difficult circumstances. When we ask God to forgive us, we simultaneously petition Him to consider the changes we have already made of our own free will. As penitents, we ask that these changes take the place of external correctives which God would otherwise have to create as therapy for us. It is only when changes do not come about through our self-judgment that they need to come about through God's intervention through punishment.

Judaism recognizes the need for specific therapies to undo certain impurities and lack of sensitivity. When we recognize the correctives that we need, and we undergo some form of lenient therapy, we ask God that this substitute for having to undergo difficult therapies. Sometimes our self-imposed corrective involves doing more mitzvot, or doing them with more dedication, or being more selfless.

As an example, the Talmud speaks about someone who violates a certain commandment in a rebellious way. The usual punishment for that sin is a certain type of spiritual death (*karet*).[7] Such a person might rectify this by increasing his learning of Talmud from one to two pages a day; another person, who normally sleeps eight hours a night, might decrease the sleep to six and use the additional two hours to work on his devotion to God. In these situations, people diminish their physical life in some way and substitute something spiritual. Doing this can substitute for *karet*, the punishment to which they would otherwise need to be subjected.

Meaning of the Words

God as "Our Father" and God as "Our King"

We ask for two things in this prayer: To be forgiven and to be pardoned. We ask for forgiveness from a Father for things we did in error. We ask to be pardoned by a King for things we did on purpose—a more severe level of sinning. These two ideas reflect two relationships with God: as children to a father, and as servants to a king.

We experience the relationship of a child to a father in our sense of closeness to God. God has literally tied himself to us, in the same way that a father gives over his seed to create his children. God similarly gives of His essence when he endows each of us with a soul at birth. The Jewish soul, then, consists of the "chromosomes" of God. In this sense, we are inextricably bound up with God, similar to a father–child connection.

By virtue of our having some part of God within us, God sees us as His children, no matter what we do. Our sins are viewed only as mistakes, no matter how grievous they are, because sinning is not consistent with the nature of the soul that we have within us. Our sins express, not our essence, but only a temporary straying away from who we really are. As God's children, we ask God to forgive us for these errors. "Forgiveness" (*selichah*) means that God completely wipes away a sin. As long as we have a relationship with our Father, all that needs to be removed is the sin itself. The second relationship between God and the Jewish people is that of a king to his servants. When God created the world, He had a goal for it. He wanted people to realize His presence in and dominion over the world. God knew that people would find happiness and fulfillment through this realization. God wanted the world to develop in a certain direction, and He "hired a work force" to bring to fruition His greatest hopes and plans for the world. God gave people the mission to fulfill this realization, and He blessed them with the potential to carry out the task, but He also expected them to dedicate their lives to this mission. This was God's way of saying that human beings have the capability of realizing the true purpose of the world's existence. God's appointment of people to do His will was the way in which He asked us to form the "government" to make this happen.

Every Jew is a minister in God's Cabinet, charged with the responsibility of making God's goals come to fruition. He made us take the oath of office, made us dedicate ourselves to total allegiance, and made us totally accept our mission. This is what is meant by a person accepting the "yoke of Heaven" upon himself. The person accepts that he will be a loyal Cabinet minister in the government of the world and pledges allegiance to the President of the world.

There are two types of acts for which we ask forgiveness in this prayer: Acts of error, and purposeful acts. As was just mentioned, insofar as we are children of God, every transgression is viewed as an act of error. However, when we aren't careful enough in discharging our duties of office when acting as God's Cabinet members, our falling short brings disgrace to the government. This is why we ask God to pardon us as a king pardons a servant who has purposely acted inappropriately.

Our Sages say that when a person does *teshuvah*, he must correct his own mistake as well as help others correct the same mistake. He must do this because there are two elements to every sin we commit. First is the mistake itself, and second is the disdain that we show for the government of God by not taking enough care to discharge our duties of office properly. Therefore, in order to rectify the error itself, we must act correctly. Then, to rectify our lack of loyalty in serving God, we must bring others to serve God in the way that we are supposed to serve Him. The greatest expression of loyalty is showing that we not only do correct things ourselves, but we also care about others serving their required missions, issued to them by God.

There are two ways in which we ask God to react to us—

with forgiveness and with pardon. When we relate to God as our Father, He can completely take away a sin. This is the forgiveness for which we ask in this prayer. When we relate to God as our King, He can only pardon us. This is analogous to a president pardoning a criminal. The act itself is not reversed, but the lack of loyalty that the criminal demonstrated is erased. Thus we ask God to pardon us as a King for that part of our sin which demonstrates disloyalty.

"Blessed Are You, God, the Gracious One Who Forgives Abundantly"

We end this prayer with a blessing that God is tremendously gracious (chanun) and also forgives abundantly. The Torah tells us, "He will cry to me and I will hear, for I am gracious."[8] The prophet Isaiah also tells us to return to God because "He forgives abundantly."[9] We shouldn't think that God has forgiven us so many times that He has run out of forgiveness. God never gets tired of forgiving us.

The idea of "who forgives abundantly" exists on two levels. When we say that God is marbeh lisloach, we mean that God has a multitude of forgiveness available in a quantitative sense as well as in a qualitative one.

Rabbenu Yonah, who wrote one of the most famous works on repentance, says that as soon as anyone has the slightest thought of wanting to change, he or she is already granted forgiveness.[10] This is not to say that at that point the person undergoes a purification process and is bonded back to God. That purification involves a very intricate, soul-searching process. But God makes it easy for us to be forgiven and to move on, even when we have felt only one intense moment of wanting to repent.

A second example of God's "abundant forgiveness" occurs when a person decides that he wants to return to God because terrible things are happening in his life. He has tried everything else to make things better, so he may as well try teshuvah. He's being very pragmatic, without having any philosophical commitments or regrets about the past. Even though he has ulterior motives in changing his actions, the Torah tells us that this level of repentance is still accepted by God. Clearly, it's not the most sophisticated way of returning to God, and it is hoped that the person will build a more meaningful type of return. Nevertheless, God still accepts it.

A third example is a situation in which a 97-year-old man repents on his death bed, as he is breathing his last. He vows that he will never go astray again, he will never again involve himself in illicit relationships. God still says that his *teshuvah* is acceptable, even though he is no longer physically capable of transgressing as he did previously. God accepts our *teshuvah* at any point in life when we have a change of mind and see the difference between what is right and wrong, what is proper and improper.

King David said in the Psalms that God asks a person to repent until his last moments here on earth (*Tashuv nefesh ad dakah*).[11] When is a person's last moment? *Ad dikduka shel nefesh*—when the person has no more energy left in him.[12] If he repents even at that point, God accepts his *teshuvah*.

All three of the above examples are facets of God's "abundant forgiveness" (*ribui selichah*). They all demonstrate how easy God makes it for us to return to Him. We can have deep thoughts of repenting in a single moment. We can repent because of hardships that befall us, or we can repent during our last moments of life. These examples constitute the first level, the quantitative aspect, of "abundant forgiveness."

A second form of *ribui selichah* is demonstrated when God gives such credence to the *teshuvah* that it makes the person great. For instance, if a person does many sins and then appreciates how far those actions were from what they should have been, it is possible for all of the sins to become mitzvot. God can take all of the transgressions of a penitent (*baal teshuvah*) and transform them into mitzvot, provided the person uses these transgressions to foster a stronger commitment to God. God says that the *baal teshuvah* is greater than a totally righteous person (*tzaddik*) in His eyes. He also says that He considers a penitent as if he were just starting life anew, and He overlooks the penitent's past life. All of these things give a qualitative depth to the *teshuvah*. God wants so much to forgive that He invests our repentance with greater meaning than it might otherwise have.

Two of God's attributes are *rachum* and *chanun*. *Rachum* refers to God's doing things that are necessities for us. He does them out of compassion. *Chanun* refers to those things God does for us that are beyond necessities. He gives us these things as gifts, out of His tremendous lovingkindness. The fact that God makes it easy for us to do *teshuvah*, at whatever level we are willing, is a reflection of His giving us what is necessary. We have so many weaknesses and shortcomings that if God didn't open up every potential avenue for us to repent, we wouldn't do it. We would just pile up so many mistakes that we would have no way of existing.

At the end of Yom Kippur we say: "God, we're made of flesh and blood, and we're destined to return to the earth. If You don't forgive us, we can't even live."[13] Thus a certain aspect of forgiveness is a necessity, and the *Rachum* attribute of God grants this. But we conclude the repentance prayer of the Shemoneh Esrai by saying that God is *Chanun*: He gives us opportunities to repent that are not necessities. It is not a necessity for God to allow our sins to become mitzvot, nor to consider a penitent to be greater than a totally righteous person, nor to allow a penitent to start life anew. These things are beyond necessities.

We conclude the prayer for repentance by thanking God both for the necessary forgiveness that He grants us and for the aspects of forgiveness He gives that are beyond necessities. We thank Him that He gives out of His overwhelming love for us.

Implications of Forgiveness for Human Relationships

A critical component of our relationship with God is that He forgives us when we make mistakes. The same is required within human relationships. If a spouse won't forgive, and doesn't let go of the partner's past shortcomings and errors, disappointments will accumulate. These hurts will eventually be unloaded in a destructive manner. A cumulative history of mistakes and disappointments can never be undone without forgiveness.

Forgiving and forgetting is the only way to keep such mistakes from ruining a relationship. The fact that God has "an abundance of forgiveness" suggests that this must also be part of any human relationship. The ability to apologize, and to accept apologies, is critical to maintaining any relationship between people.

Notes

1. Genesis 38:1.
2. Genesis 38:1; Rashi 38:1.
3. *Bereishit Rabbah* 85:8.
4. Talmud *Bavli, Avodah Zarah* 36b; Nachmanides on Genesis 38:24.
5. Talmud *Bavli, Sotah* 10b.
6. *Shebolei Leket*, chapter 18.
7. *Vayikrah Rabbah* 25:1; Gates of Repentance 4:11.
8. Exodus 22:26.
9. Isaiah 55:7.
10. Gates of Repentance 1:9.
11. Psalms 90:3.
12. Talmud *Yerushalmi, Hagigah* 2:1.
13. See *Atah noten yad laposhim* in the Neilah service.

CHAPTER 10

Redeemer of Israel

רְאֵה נָא בְעָנְיֵנוּ, וְרִיבָה רִיבֵנוּ, וּגְאָלֵנוּ מְהֵרָה לְמַעַן שְׁמֶךָ,
כִּי גוֹאֵל חָזָק אֶתָּה. בָּרוּךְ אַתָּה יהוה, גוֹאֵל יִשְׂרָאֵל.

Please look at our affliction, and fight our battles, and redeem
us quickly for Your Name's sake because You are a
mighty Redeemer. Blessed are You, God, Redeemer of Israel.

Theme and Historical Background of This Prayer

When an angel discovers something about God that it didn't previously know, it becomes exhilarated and excited. This insight inspires the angel to sing praises to God. The same occurs with people. For example, when the Jews who left Egypt during the time of the Exodus crossed the Red Sea, they sang a praise to God, not simply because they were saved but also because their experience allowed them to know God in a way that they hadn't known Him before.

When someone is confused about a relationship, he or she isn't happy about it. For instance, a woman might socialize with a man but not be sure if he is a warm or caring person. If, on a particular occasion, it becomes clear that he is both, that knowledge makes the woman very happy. There is a tremendous excitement that comes with being able to appreciate another person and to see him or her as being positive and good.

The situation that resulted in the blessing of redemption occurred when the Jews were still in Egypt, in the midst of the most difficult oppression. God made four promises of redemption to the Jews, via Moses. He said that He would take them out of Egypt, save them from the Egyptians' hands, redeem them, and take them to Himself as a nation. (There was a fifth promise as well—that God would bring the Jews into the Holy Land—but the first four promises are seen as the critical steps of redemption).[1]

The first three promises refer to God saving the Jews from the clutches of negativity. First, God said that He would physically remove the Jews from danger. Next, He promised to protect them from the Egyptians catching up with them once they had left Egypt. Then He promised to redeem them; this meant that even though there would no longer be an external danger, God would redeem them from the internal captivity that was created by their being in Egypt. Once He redeemed the Jews, God promised to take them to Himself as His nation.

After God expressed these four promises of redemption to the Jewish people, the angels exclaimed, "Blessed are You, God, who redeems Israel."

Order of This Prayer in the Shemoneh Esrai

This prayer of redemption (*geulah*) is the seventh prayer in the Shemoneh Esrai. In the fourth prayer we asked for discriminating knowledge. With that insight we can make changes in our lives that show that we want to go on a new path (repentance, the fifth prayer). Then, in the sixth prayer, we asked for forgiveness, to remove impediments from our pasts.

This prayer seems to be out of order because it will be followed by requests for health and wealth and then by the prayer for God to take us back to Jerusalem. It would seem that this prayer would more appropriately be paired with the later prayer whose theme is returning to Jerusalem.

All of the prayers in the Shemoneh Esrai are sourced in verses from the Prophets or Scriptures. There is a verse in Psalms that says, "The God who forgives all of your sins, the God who heals you from all of your ills, and the God who redeems you from all of your destruction."[2] The sequence of events is forgiveness, health, and redemption from internal destruction. The psalmist stated that once God forgives us for our pasts, He no longer holds us responsible for them, and as a result it is unnecessary for us to continue undergoing difficult circumstances that normally cleanse us of our sins. It would seem from this verse that the order of prayers in the Shemoneh Esrai should be for forgiveness, then for healing, and only then for redemption. In actuality, we pray in the Amidah for redemption before health.

When a Jew is afflicted with an illness, there is a spiritual purpose behind it, even though we may not always know exactly what it is. If we truly repent for our past, it is possible to obviate the need to undergo sickness whose purpose might be to purify us. In King David's reasoning, God forgives us, bypasses the need for us to be ill, and therefore heals us spiritually and physically.

This isn't the sequence in the Shemoneh Esrai. One reason is that if the prayer for healing were to come immediately after the prayer for forgiveness, the seventh prayer would be for health and the eighth would be for redemption. We know that no matter what, the Messiah must come within 6,000 years of the Creation of the world (we are now in the year 5751 from the Creation). God is committed to making sure that His ultimate goal in creating the world comes to fruition by the end of 6,000 years of human existence. This will be realized by the coming of the Messiah.

When the 120 men of the Great Assembly wrote the prayer for redemption, they felt that it should be seventh in the Amidah, paralleling the seventh thousand-year period from the creation of the world. This tells Jews that no matter what, God is committed to bringing the Messiah to the world by the Jewish year 6000.

When we pray for the Messiah to come, we are reassured that the context of the prayer guarantees that he will come. An analogous situation occurs when someone buys something; he or she feels more secure about the purchase if it comes with a guarantee. Similarly, the prayer for redemption is specifically taken out of its order in a scriptural verse to teach us the lesson that God is behind the plan for the Messiah to come, and it's a guaranteed plan. It must happen. Knowing this gives us an inner confidence and dispels any doubts when we pray for the Messiah's coming. The men of the Great Assembly tell us in this prayer that we should never stop praying for the Messiah to come, since it is guaranteed to happen.

There is a second reason why this prayer is taken out of the position it would have according to scriptural verse. God frequently causes things to happen to us that are intended to remedy the past. A certain therapy may work without our making any spiritual changes. Simply by virtue of our having gone through certain difficulties, our spiritual chemistries can be changed. Our souls can be spiritually transformed by virtue of crises we undergo without our being aware of the meaning of these crises. Thus we might go through healing processes without knowing it, because they occur in the inner resources of our souls.

God often provides us with certain therapies. If we don't pick up the message of a given therapy, God alters the plan. Thus God may cause us to become ill or may give us difficult circumstances. Sometimes we may not pick up the communication, or may reject the message. When that happens, God may try to communicate the message in another way.

An ill state of health can come and go without any visible changes in us. Perhaps, though, the change has been subtle, occurring in the inner resources of our souls. Or it could occur because we did not utilize the first opportunity and God altered His approach. Ill health followed by good health is not necessarily a result of our having changed. Therefore, praying for health directly after forgiveness in the Amidah is not necessarily the order in which these two events occur in the real world. Health may come even without forgiveness.

We are endowed with certain spiritual potentials which we can use to grow and become everything we were intended to be. If we follow a lifestyle that doesn't allow us access to our potentials, these potentials go into "captivity" and we can't use them. This situation is described as our being in a state of spiritual bondage. When we are "redeemed," we give something, and we get something in return.

For a Jew, redemption means that we gain access to a part of ourselves that was not accessible before. It doesn't mean that we are born anew, or that we are given some external spiritual revelation. It means that we can get to the "prizes" within us that we weren't previously able to use. Redemption is a direct result of our making changes and obtaining forgiveness for our pasts. We go through *teshuvah* and acquire forgiveness from God, and then we are able to pursue our mission. When God forgives us, He says to us: "I see that you are working on yourselves for the future. I will no longer hold you responsible for your past, nor will you be held back because of it." Once our past no longer bogs us down, we can get on with our unique mission in life.

Therefore, we pray for personal redemption *after* praying for repentance and forgiveness. Once we decide to change the future and God no longer holds us responsible for the past, we can devote all of our energies toward realizing our true purposes in the world.

It is now understandable why we pray for redemption, rather than for physical health, after forgiveness. Health may come with or without forgiveness; true redemption can come only after forgiveness.

Meaning of the Words

"Look at Our Affliction"

When we say "look" in this prayer we mean that we want God to become intimately involved with us. We also want Him to be aware of how oppressed we are by the nations of the world.

"Fight (Rivah) Our Battles"

The Hebrew word *riv* refers to a dispute outside of a courtroom. (Once a case goes to court, it is known as *din*). We ask God to give us the strength to resist the influences of exile, to which we might otherwise wish to succumb. While in exile, we may have no desire to resist the temptations of the secular world and the immoral influences around us. We ask God to help us want to resist this spiritual corruption. Once we start to battle this urge, we ask God to fully and quickly redeem us. There is an urgency to our request lest delaying the redemption result in numerous spiritual casualties.

"For Your Name's Sake" and "You Are a Mighty Redeemer"

The first phrase refers to the fact that even if we are unworthy of redemption, God will redeem us so that His ultimate purpose for the world will come to fruition. Our calling God a Mighty Redeemer means that even if we don't deserve to be totally redeemed, God will counter accusing arguments that contend that we don't deserve to come out of exile.

"Redeemer of Israel"

When we conclude this prayer with "Blessed are You, God, Redeemer of Israel," we acknowledge that we recognize God's constant involvement in our process of redemption.

Significance of Redemption While We Are in Exile

In this prayer we ask God to redeem us while we are still in exile. One type of exile is created when we use our spiritual potentials in ways that they were never intended to be used. When we mischannel these energies, they are referred to as "being in exile." When we pray for spiritual redemption, we ask God to help us rechannel the energies into their proper places.

In the blessing at the end of the prayer, the verb "redeems" is in the present tense. This is because God redeems us on a daily basis from our negative inclinations (*yetzer hara*). Our negative inclinations get us to do things that mischannel our spirituality and thereby cause internal exile. Were it not for God's assistance in fighting these negative inclinations, we would give in to them. God's helping us to overcome our negative inclinations is what redeems us from self-imposed exile.

The Meaning of Exile

A story in the Talmud[3] relates that Rabbi Yosi went into a ruin to pray. While he was praying, Elijah the Prophet waited for him in the doorway. When Rabbi Yosi finished his prayers, Elijah greeted him and asked, "Why did you enter a ruin of Jerusalem?" (It was forbidden to enter a ruin.).

Rabbi Yosi replied, "I was traveling and I needed a place to pray."

Elijah responded, "You should have prayed along the road."

Rabbi Yosi defended himself. "I was afraid that had I prayed by the road, I would have been interrupted by passersby."

Elijah admonished him, "You should have prayed an abridged version of the Shemoneh Esrai."

Rabbi Yosi later proclaimed to the Sages: "On that day I learned three things from Elijah the Prophet: One shouldn't enter a ruin; one is permitted to pray along the road; and when one prays along the road, he should pray an abridged version of the Shemoneh Esrai."

This story teaches us something profound about how we

should relate to exile. Rabbi Yosi lived two generations after the destruction of the Second Temple. His "praying in a ruin" meant that he had engaged God in a philosophical debate about the lack of usefulness of exile for the Jews. Through his arguments, he hoped to persuade God to end their exile. Elijah taught Rabbi Yosi that rather than trying to persuade God to end the exile, one's prayers should be directed toward asking God to help us journey through the hazards of being in exile. This is what is meant by the statement that "one should pray along the road."

The Talmud says that Rabbi Yosi didn't want to "pray along the road," meaning that he didn't know if he could withstand the challenges of living in exile, because he was afraid that they would make him lose his connection with God. The necessity of "praying an abridged version of the Shemoneh Esrai" signifies that we needn't fear that we won't be able to bond with God in exile. In this story Elijah tells us that we are equipped to maintain a closeness with God even in the worst of times during our exile.

It is especially significant that it was Elijah the Prophet who taught Rabbi Yosi this lesson. Elijah is the person who will herald in the end of the exile and begin the ultimate redemption, accompanied by the Messiah.

The prayer for redemption in the Shemoneh Esrai emphasizes our need to ask God to help us make use of our exile rather than praying for Him to end it prematurely. The redemptive process lies in our accepting the challenges of exile. The journey of exile was designed to push us to ask for God's greater help in our lives. Our asking God to give us the courage, insight, and spiritual strength to overcome the challenges of exile brings redemption.

Implications of Redemption for Human Relationships

One level of redemption occurs when people learn to actualize whatever potentials exist in a given situation. This means that when people learn how to cope in a bad situation, their freedom from it begins. Such coping requires honesty in identifying what the situation is, followed by an appraisal of how they can best grow from it.

People should be honest about what problems they need to face in their relationships. They need to ask themselves what they can learn from the difficulties, how they can grow from them, and how they can best confront them. Challenges are aspects of people's relationships that should enable partners to grow from them, rather than to be destroyed by them. If difficulties are properly confronted, the process of working them through can ultimately deepen a relationship. There is benefit to be derived from "redeeming" a problem rather than denying it or allowing oneself to be victimized by it.

Notes

1. Exodus 6:6–8.
2. Psalms 103:3, 4.
3. Talmud *Bavli*, *Berakhot* 4a.

CHAPTER 11

The One Who Heals the Sick of His People Israel

רְפָאֵנוּ יהוה וְנֵרָפֵא, הוֹשִׁיעֵנוּ וְנִוָּשֵׁעָה, כִּי תְהִלָּתֵנוּ אֶתָּה,
וְהַעֲלֵה רְפוּאָה שְׁלֵמָה לְכָל מַכּוֹתֵינוּ, כִּי אֵל מֶלֶךְ
רוֹפֵא נֶאֱמָן וְרַחֲמָן אֶתָּה. בָּרוּךְ אַתָּה יהוה, רוֹפֵא חוֹלֵי
עַמּוֹ יִשְׂרָאֵל.

Heal us, Lord, and we will be healed, save us and we will be
saved, since our praise is to You. And bring about a
complete remedy for all of our afflictions, for You are God, a
King who is a faithful and compassionate healer. Blessed are
You, God, who heals the sick of His people, Israel.

Theme of the Prayer

This is the eighth prayer in the Shemoneh Esrai. The Levush (a commentator on the prayerbook) tells us that the number 8 is symbolically related to healing. Baby boys are circumcised on the eighth day of life, and then they require healing. The prayer for healing is eighth in the order of the Amidah prayers to symbolize the circumcision. It alludes to the idea that one should not be afraid to perform the mitzvah of circumcision, for God heals the circumcised baby.

Historical Background

The historical background to this prayer comes from a biblical event which allowed the angels to discover yet another facet of God's greatness—that He is a healer. God commanded Abraham to circumcise himself at the age of 99, and he did so. God visited Abraham on the third day after his circumcision and sent the angel Raphael to heal him.[1] After Abraham recuperated, the angels, seeing that God had the ability to heal, said, "Blessed are You, God, who heals the sick among your people, Israel." Thus the prayer's being eighth in the Amidah symbolizes the circumcision day.

The Meaning of Healing

The opening words of this prayer are based on a verse from Jeremiah: "Heal me, God, and I will be healed, save me and I will be saved."[2] Jeremiah said these words when he was totally heartbroken over the destruction of Jerusalem that was to take place. He became sick because he was spiritually distraught, and so he turned to God and asked to be strengthened. He needed to know that God would "hold his hand" while the

137

devastation occurred. He asked God to help him have the spiritual strength to deal with the crisis.

Jeremiah served as his own doctor. He recognized that his sickness came from his heart, from his spiritual distress over the tremendous loss to come. In diagnosing the real source of his problem, he turned to God, saying: "In my spiritual distress, I can turn nowhere, except to You. I need to be healed by You, and only then will I be healed." A doctor could only give him palliatives. Jeremiah understood the true source of his pain. Only with spiritual comfort could he truly be healed. That is why he reiterated the words, "Heal me, and I will be healed." True comfort and healing could come only from God.

When we are ill, only our symptoms are usually treated. Yet the physical manifestations of poor health are frequently outgrowths of something going on within us. In addition to this, when we undergo tremendous stress or pain, it is very hard for us to access our souls. We can see this problem from the life of King Saul; when he was depressed, he lost contact with divine inspiration (*ruach hakodesh*).[3] Anyone who is depressed loses touch with his soul, especially if he feels angry or resentful. These emotional states are not conducive to happiness, and happiness is a prerequisite for receiving divine inspiration.

Relationship to the Previous Prayer

Jeremiah knew that his physical pain stemmed from his spiritual agony, and he was not willing to go anywhere else but to God in order to feel better. The prayer for health comes after the prayer for redemption because we experience a great deal of inner frustration as long as we are not spiritually free and spiritually redeemed, and this frustration itself can lead to ill health.

When we have potentials that are not exercised, we can become ill. Therefore, we must ask to get in contact with our potentials when we ask for redemption. Actualizing our fullest abilities puts us in a healthier state of mind and creates a healthier state for our soul. Once we have emotional and spiritual strength, we can deal with the physical ailments that are the products of our spiritual frustrations.

Jeremiah said his prayer as an individual ("Heal me . . . save me . . .") because he felt the anguish of his circumstances more strongly than did anyone else. In contrast, we ask for collective spiritual healing when we say, "Heal us, God, and we will be healed, save us, and we will be saved."

Next we add, "and bring a full healing to all of our afflictions." This is a request for God to heal us physically. Maimonides says that everything in the physical world reflects that which exists in the spiritual world,[4] including the entire realm of medicine and communicable diseases. This is why we first ask for spiritual healing and then healing for the physical manifestations of spiritual disease.

A Context for Viewing Illness

Another facet of this concept relates to how we view illness. Illness presents a tremendous religious challenge. Most of us want to be healthy, and sickness is hard for us to deal with, especially when it lasts for more than a few days. It keeps us from doing what we want to do and being what we want to be. It's a limiting and humiliating experience.

Jews believe that health comes from God. In contrast, many people think that if they go to the right doctor they will be fine. How do we reconcile the reality—that when the doctor treats us, we often do get better—with the religious perspective that God heals us?

Ibn Pakuda, a Jewish philosopher, says that God could heal people without medicine or other treatments. God is capable of doing anything. However, He didn't want healing to occur as a unilateral act on His part, without our involvement. God wants us to be challenged by illness. We can grow through the challenges of being sick, by realizing that there is a God behind the illness who directs our lives.[5]

One person who gets pneumonia could be treated with antibiotics; another person might die from it. Science can't explain why one person responds to a certain therapy and another doesn't. When we confront the variables of the "laws of nature" without ultimate certainty about how they will operate on an individual basis, we are pushed to see that there is a hidden factor behind creation. This is exactly what God wants us to realize.

God wants us to see Him where His presence is not obvious and to be able to discern Him in concealed places. It is no feat to see things in a place that is well lit, but becoming acquainted with a dark room and then discerning figures in the darkness requires attention and scrutiny. Part of our self-development is to refine ourselves so that we can discern God, even in the most concealed places, and see how He is everywhere and involved in everything. As we discover God through the concealment, the world around us becomes a more significant one, and we ourselves become more fulfilled.

We each live with both our apparent selves and our deeper selves, in both the apparent world and the deeper world. This duality gives us a whole arena in which we're challenged to find God in the concealed places. Some people think that God isn't here. He is here. We often don't see Him, but the more we develop ourselves spiritually, the more we can discern God behind the scenes. Illness challenges us to do this.

The idea of developing spiritually through discerning God in hidden places not only is a challenge, but also is the definition of our relationship with Him. Ibn Pakuda stated, "If a person completely attributes to the natural world the importance of that which affects him"—that is, if someone thinks that "Mother Nature" and natural law are responsible for everything that happens to him—"then that person develops a relationship with nature. If that occurs, the person will be provided for according to what natural circumstances can give him."[6]

Developing a relationship with nature means that sometimes nature will provide very good things and sometimes it will provide things that are not acceptable. The laws of nature say that illnesses are not curable beyond a certain point, that certain things degenerate past a point where they can come back to life again. Nature has the ability to cause rebirth, but it also has limitations, as do all physical things. If we relate ourselves to the physical world and decide to harness only the laws of nature, then what we get will be subject to those same limitations. They will also define the extent of the relationship that we have with the world.

On the other hand, if we recognize that there is a God who directs nature from moment to moment, we will hook ourselves up with the Creator and Director of nature. We will develop a relationship with the Master of nature, rather than merely with nature. If we relate only to nature, then we can't expect the supernatural. If we address our attention to God because we realize that nature can't hurt or benefit us unless God wants it to do so, we thereby open up the possibility of going beyond the bounds of nature. We can be provided for directly by God.

This concept is vividly portrayed in the book of Joshua, when the Jews of the desert entered the land of Israel and began to conquer it.[7] The first city they needed to conquer was Jericho, which was surrounded by seven virtually impenetrable walls. God told the Jews to go around the walls once a day for six days and seven times on the seventh day. Then they were to blow the shofar and celebrate victory. They did so. After they celebrated their victory, the walls crumbled and they entered the city, where they caught the inhabitants by surprise.

This episode occurred because God wanted the Jews to know with certainty that they were limited within the laws of nature. By circling the walls they realized that according to the laws of nature, it was impossible for them to enter the city of Jericho. The blowing of the shofar was their call to God to help them, and the celebration of victory came from their certainty about God's abilities. Once they realized that God is the Master over Nature, they finally got into the city.

When the Israelites entered their own land, they would tend their own crops, animals, and the like. The first thing that God wanted the Jews to know was that their ultimate relationship should be with Him, not with the forces that outwardly looked responsible for agricultural success. The Jews could enter Jericho only after demonstrating trust in God. This is why they entered the city on Shabbat, which is the day that symbolizes trust in God. It is the day of trust in God because on this one day we refrain from work, and it is possible not to work only if we trust God. Otherwise people would be afraid that their farms, crops, and animals would not be maintained if they refrained from working one day a week.

The Israelites' trust in God was so strong that they celebrated victory even before the walls of Jericho fell. Once they had leapt over the symbolic walls of nature and completely connected themselves to God, they were capable of doing anything. On the other hand, Jericho's inhabitants trusted nature. They felt secure in their belief that the walls would shield them from all harm. So, when their walls crumbled, they experienced the limitations of their belief in nature.

In order to accentuate the concept of trust in God, we emphasize God's Name when we say, "Heal us, *God*, and we will be healed." We view doctors and healers as messengers of God, capable of bringing the healing which is ultimately provided by God Himself. One of the commentaries says that there are many avenues where we may go in order to be healed, but in such cases, the sickness will return; only if one turns to God can there be an ultimate healing in which the sickness will not come back.[8]

This is very enigmatic. We know that we go to doctors who heal us, and our illnesses don't come back. However, as long as we live only within the parameters of nature, we are always vulnerable to the laws of nature. Only if we link ourselves to God and allow ourselves His protection can we become invulnerable to the laws of nature.

For this reason, when many people take medicine, they precede it with a prayer: "God, who is the Master healer, should will that I become well, and this medicine should do what it can do (to bring about healing)."

Once we view God as the ultimate Master of our lives, we change the way we look at sickness. Once we stop trying to conquer nature, we can deal with what God tries to communicate to us by causing us to get sick. We can still view sickness as a limitation, and we can still try to be healed through medicine and the like. However, if God doesn't want us to be well, no amount of running to health professionals will cure us. We may not know why God wants us to be sick at a certain time, but we do know that there is a purpose to the sickness. It is accomplishing something.

The fact that a baby boy requires circumcision teaches us that our actions are required in order for the world to become perfected. Furthermore, it teaches us that being sick, and going through the process of being healed, is an integral part of our development and growth. When God brings us into the world, He makes the statement: "I brought you into this world imperfect, and it is up to you to perfect yourselves. Sometimes this process of perfection is painful. Nevertheless, it promotes personal growth and healing." God waits in the shadows as He helps us heal and grow, while we deal with our imperfections. This is why the eighth prayer of the Shemoneh Esrai, which alludes to the circumcision, is that of healing.

One of the worst parts of being sick is the feeling of being alone and betrayed, beaten down and conquered. We need to remember that being sick means that God is by our side, using sickness as a means for spiritual healing. This is why we end the prayer for healing, "Blessed are You, God, who heals the sick of His people Israel."

Jews have the unique perspective that healing is part of the format of growth and development rather than an inconvenience that comes into our lives. The greater our potentials are, the greater is our frustration when those potentials are not reached. Insofar as Jews have a unique mission and challenge, God will communicate with us in unique ways. The Torah teaches that God knows us in a love relationship different than any other in the world. Therefore, He will bring to bear on us many different situations that will allow our souls to become pure.[9]

Spiritual frustration breeds illness, and such frustration is most heightened in the Jewish soul. Because we are endowed with a special mission, we have a deeper need for fulfillment than do others. When our lack of perfection results in the delaying of our fulfillment, we feel frustrated. The greater our mission, the more frustrated we feel. Our heightened frustration breeds greater illness for us than for others, and so the Jews particularly need God to heal us.

Meaning of the Words

"Our Praise Is to You"

As long as someone views healing as coming from the doctor, and feels that it is the doctor who deserves his thanks, he has further concealed God's role in the world. In seeing the doctor as the cause of his healing, he has further concretized the role of nature in causing sickness. Therefore, we say to God, "We're not going to make that mistake. If You heal us, we will use the process of healing to reveal Your role in the world." This is what is meant by, "because our praise is to You." If You heal us, we won't extol the virtues of the doctors, the techniques and the medicines. We will turn to You in gratitude for having sent us these people as Your agents of healing.

"A King Who Is a Faithful and Compassionate Healer"

We refer to God as a king in the context of each Jew having a mission, which can be thwarted during illness. The director of those missions is God, in His role as a king. Since God causes us to get sick in order for something to happen to our spirituality, we must trust that He is a "compassionate healer."

We must also know that God is "compassionate" and would bring sickness upon us only if it were to our benefit to undergo it. Once He does this, and then heals us, we can recognize His role in the healing. That recognition in itself is a step toward spiritual growth. We are then ready to move on to the next stage, which is the delight that we have in recognizing that God is a healer as well.

Once we recognize the need for spiritual healing, we can then ask for healing for all of our physical afflictions. "And bring about a complete remedy for all of our afflictions." This is the theme of this entire prayer.

"Who Heals the Sick of His People, Israel"

We pray for someone to be healed among "His people, Israel," because each Jew has a unique role and mission and needs to make a unique contribution to the world. We ask God to heal the sick person in that merit, and to give him or her strength out of the process of healing. We do not simply say, "Master of the Universe, so-and-so would like to be healthy, so please heal him." We ask God to heal him because as long as that person is sick, he cannot make his unique contribution to the Jewish nation at large.

Implications of Healing for Human Relationships

Scientists and doctors have publicized the fact that depression, anxiety, anger, and other negative emotions affect people's biochemistry. Poor emotional health may contribute to heart problems, stomach or intestinal ailments, suppression of the immune system which fights disease and infection, and hormonal disturbances. Similarly, when people suffer physical ailments, they often develop emotional problems as a reaction to the limitations and discomforts imposed on them. Thus there is a well-established reciprocal connection between the mind and the body.

Physical health is also juxtaposed with spiritual health. When people do not adequately nourish their spiritual health by doing the commandments in the Torah, their souls suffer. Since a soul energizes the body, just as one's emotions do, a malnourished soul will not be capable of sustaining the optimal physical health of the body. Similarly, when people are physically ill, they will be limited in how well they can perform the commandments. Since the performance of mitzvot nourishes the soul, the soul will also suffer when the body has poor health.

Even though people can only be agents of healing, they can endeavor as much as possible to help their spouses be physically, emotionally, and spiritually healthy. They can provide support systems to prevent poor health from occurring in the first place. When one spouse is physically sick, the other should do whatever he or she can to ensure that the person does not become emotionally sick as well. In addition, a supportive spouse can help keep the partner's physical or emotional sickness from affecting the latter's spiritual well-being.

Notes

1. Talmud *Bavli, Baba Metzia* 86b.
2. Jeremiah 17:14.
3. I Samuel 16:14, 16.
4. Maimonides, *Yad HaChazakah, Hilchot Daat*, chapter 2.
5. Ibn Pakuda, *Duties of the Heart* (Jerusalem: Feldheim, 1982).
6. Ibn Pakuda, *Duties of the Heart, Shaar HaBitachon*.
7. Joshua 6.
8. *Zohar Chadash, Balak*.
9. Amos 3:2.

CHAPTER 12

Satisfy Us from Your Bounty

בָּרֵךְ עָלֵינוּ יהוה אֱלֹהֵינוּ אֶת הַשָּׁנָה הַזֹּאת וְאֶת כָּל מִינֵי תְבוּאָתָהּ לְטוֹבָה, (וְתֵן בְּרָכָה,) (וְתֵן טַל וּמָטָר לִבְרָכָה) עַל פְּנֵי הָאֲדָמָה, וְשַׂבְּעֵנוּ מִטּוּבֶךְ, וּבָרֵךְ שְׁנָתֵנוּ כַּשָּׁנִים הַטּוֹבוֹת. בָּרוּךְ אַתָּה יהוה, מְבָרֵךְ הַשָּׁנִים.

Bless upon us, Lord our God, this year, and all of its types of produce for good. And give a blessing (in the winter we substitute the words, ''bring dew and rain for a blessing'') on the surface of the earth. And satisfy us from Your bounty, and bless this year like the good years. Blessed are You, God, who blesses the years.

Theme of the Prayer

We begin this prayer by saying, "Bless upon us, Lord, our God." We pursue making a livelihood only after first acknowledging that we do so only in the context of a relationship with God. Before we go to work, we recognize that God is the ultimate provider and our success is up to Him. If we believe that God provides for us, then we won't try to bring down God's blessing by engaging in illegitimate behaviors. If people have no relationship with God when they make a livelihood, they may do anything that works. Values can quickly disappear when money is at stake.

On the other hand, if we start our day by saying that our success depends upon God's providing it, then it is inconceivable that He wants us to use dishonest channels in order to obtain His blessing. We therefore begin this prayer for sustenance by saying that God is our provider. This is a major step toward our acting correctly in our business dealings, and it reinforces for us that we shouldn't haughtily think that our success is due solely to our efforts.

This idea is eloquently portrayed in the biblical background of this prayer, described below. From an economic perspective, Isaac was correct in thinking that he should leave the place he lived in and take his business elsewhere. This is why God had to tell him that, since he had reached a level of total dedication to God, it was not appropriate for him to move from a holy land to an unholy place. To do so would have been a denial of who he was. His actions teach us that we should never pursue our livelihoods in a way that would make us deny who we are. If we have bread on our tables but are not the people we're supposed to be, then what will we have accomplished?

Isaac needed to pursue a livelihood, but God directed him not to do it in a way that would compromise his existence. Similarly, our first obligation is to our spiritual stature. The

One who provides the livelihood will provide it even if we don't follow the rules of better economics, as long as we maintain our spirituality. Our first responsibility is to ask ourselves, "Who am I, and will this livelihood compromise my spiritual stature?"

Overall, this prayer stresses the fact that we are challenged with making a livelihood. That challenge should be a positive one from which we can grow. We should follow Isaac's example in being aware of the spiritual growth that we can attain by viewing livelihood in its proper perspective.

Someone may say, "Spiritual stature is very nice, but it won't mean much if I starve to death." This biblical story teaches us that God has the wherewithal to provide livelihood under any adverse circumstances. If we preserve our spiritual stature, not only will we get what it is natural to get, but God can also provide over and above what nature decrees.

This idea is communicated very beautifully in a commentary on the prayerbook known as the *Kolbo*. It notes that the prayer for sustenance begins with the letter *bet* and ends with the letter *mem*. The Written Torah (Five Books of Moses) begins with the letter *bet* (*Beraishit*), and the Oral Torah (Talmud) begins with the letter *mem* (*Mai'aimatai*). A person who learns the Written Torah, which begins with a *bet*, and the Oral Law, which begins with *mem*, will be blessed with a livelihood.[1] This means that the spiritual pursuit of learning Torah will not impede our ability to procure a livelihood. To the contrary, God will provide for us if we study Torah.

It's not a coincidence that there are hints about both the Written Torah and the Oral Torah in this prayer for livelihood. A man may have the attitude that only the Written Torah is important. He might feel that he doesn't have time to study the "sophisticated" content of the Talmud. Thus, he may be willing to sacrifice a minimum of time studying the basics of Judaism, as presented in the Five Books of Moses, but he may not be willing to take time away from making money to study Talmud. This prayer reinforces to us that the blessing of livelihood begins with our study of the Five Books of Moses, but it doesn't come to fruition until we study the Talmud as well.

It is for this reason that the Jews had a course of study that lasted for 40 years, when they were in the desert after their exodus from Egypt. Although they learned many different things from the Torah during this time, the one thing they learned consistently and without interruption was that God would always provide for them. During these 40 years God provided them with everything they needed—food, drink, clothes, shelter—so that they would know intimately that God was their provider and would continue to be so in the land of Israel. Once settled in Israel, they would have to spend time and energy following the natural methods of providing for themselves through agriculture and business. It was God's intention that by giving them a 40-year program in His ability to provide for them, they would not later turn the pursuit of a livelihood into an end unto itself.

What is the whole purpose of the land of Israel? It was given to us to heighten our spiritual development. The land of Israel has an inherent holiness which can be productively reaped by those who live on its soil. But, when pursuit of livelihood and belief in one's own control of nature obscure one's spiritual mission, the potential holiness that can be gleaned is wasted. Therefore, God gave the Jews a preparatory course so that they would always recognize that if they pursued spiritual goals, He would provide for them.

Historical Background

The historical roots of this prayer for financial sustenance and livelihood come from the book of Genesis. There was a famine in Isaac's lifetime, and he thought that he should do what his father had done when famine struck. Abraham had relocated to Egypt, temporarily leaving the land of Israel. When Isaac contemplated doing the same, God told him that even though his father had done this, Isaac was forbidden to leave the land of Israel, because Isaac was considered to be a "perfect sacrifice." Isaac's having been bound on an altar to God with perfect dedication sanctified him in a unique way. He was thereby disqualified from ever leaving the land of Israel. Egypt was the symbol of total impurity, so God enjoined Isaac to remain in Israel despite the famine and reassured him that he would prosper.

Isaac remained in Israel and tended a poor plot of farmland. The year was a bad year for everyone else, but Isaac's land produced 100 times its expected productivity for a nonfamine year.[2] When the angels saw this, they said, "Blessed are You, God, that You are ultimately the source of the blessing of livelihood that comes to this world." Despite all the natural circumstances that confront us, God is the ultimate provider. His ways do not necessarily conform to statistics or predictability. Therefore, when we seek a livelihood, we follow Isaac's approach in petitioning God rather than relying solely on natural phenomena.

Man's need to make a living has been both his blessing and his curse. When Adam and Eve were expelled from the Garden of Eden, their need to earn a livelihood resulted from their having transgressed God's command.[3] Prior to this sin, human beings were to be provided for directly by God, without having to exert any effort. Our Sages say that when Adam and Eve were in the Garden of Eden, angels "brought them meat and filtered wines for them."[4] (Obviously, "meat" and "wine" are meant in more than their usual literal senses). Thus, Adam and Eve did not have to concern themselves with providing a livelihood for themselves.

After they sinned, God brought certain curses into the world. One of these was, "by the sweat of your brow you shall eat bread."[5] This meant that people would subsequently have to work to make a living. At first blush, this seems to imply that by virtue of the sin of Adam and Eve, we are all saddled with the terrible burden of having to make a living. This seems to be a slap in the face by God to all of their descendants, and a punishment for billions of people in subsequent generations. This hardly seems fair.

Actually, any punishment by God acts toward a purposeful end and is not seen as a vengeful act. One might think punishment is something akin to God's saying, "You double-crossed me so now I'm going to set you straight." God's statement to Adam, "By the sweat of your brow, you shall eat bread," seems to be a curse, when one considers Adam's previous state in Paradise. Nevertheless, it was most purposeful. Before Adam sinned, the distraction of making a livelihood would have been detrimental to his spiritual stature. Adam's and Eve's spiritual states were so exalted that for them to have to push buttons, wait for trains and buses, or drive to work would have been a total waste of time and a degradation of their spiritual stature. Once Adam had plummeted spiritually by bringing negativity into his life, God felt that the most appropriate thing for him to do would be to work. Working would challenge him in the marketplace and would make him constantly depend on God. This was a curse in comparison with his initial exalted state, but was the most appropriate thing for his spiritually lowered condition.

Ibn Pakuda says that the job market produces all kinds of unique spiritual challenges, accentuated by the pressure of having to make money. These challenges do not occur through any other avenues.[6] Once Adam had sinned, he needed the pressure of not knowing if he would have food to eat. He needed to be confronted with tests of his integrity, and he needed to relate to others. Also, because of Adam's spiritual plummet, he would not have used large amounts of free time wisely.

This situation is what is referred to in the *Ethics of the Fathers* when it says, "Beautiful is Torah study that is accompanied by the labor of making a livelihood."[7] Someone who has plummeted spiritually can use time in derogatory ways that only take the person away from who he or she is supposed to be.

Our having to go out and make a living was intended by God to be another rung on the spiritual ladder. Needing to make a living was meant to encourage us to develop. On the other hand, there is nothing today that can deny our spirituality as much as the excuse to pursue a livelihood.

Many people never become a fraction of what they could be. They excuse themselves by saying: "What could I do? I had to make a living, so I couldn't use my talents and energies to develop my spirituality." The need to make a livelihood can stimulate a tremendous degree of productivity and growth in people. God's saying that we have a responsibility to provide for ourselves opens up tremendous spiritual potentials—in terms of philosophy, behavior, and character. At the same time, it presents many potential deviations, such as greed, selfishness, and thinking that we make things happen all by ourselves.

Order of This Prayer in the Shemoneh Esrai

Why is this prayer for livelihood the ninth one in the Shemoneh Esrai? The ninth chapter of Psalms (which is currently numbered as the tenth chapter) states, "The rich person lies in ambush trying to pounce upon a poor person, like a lion in its den."[8] The greedy rich man devises all kinds of schemes to grab the poor person. Once he lures the poor person into his trap, he closes the net on him and captures him.

The commentators ask, "What kind of rich person robs poor people?" If someone wants to stage a holdup, he does it to a person who has something to steal rather than to an indigent person. Nevertheless, King David says that the rich person lies in ambush preparing to rob the poor person.

The Talmud says that this verse refers to rich people who control the markets with unfair practices.[9] Their practices don't hurt the rich, who have enough resources to deal with such market manipulation. However, it slowly pushes the middle and lower classes out from the markets and destroys them. In King David's time the rich were left with greater and greater shares of the market after exercising their unethical practices. Thus Psalm 9 speaks about the greedy rich person trying to destroy the poor.

The prayer for livelihood was placed ninth in the Shemoneh Esrai in order to connect it to the idea that is conveyed in the ninth Psalm. Although at first glance this connection may seem far-fetched, a closer look shows how well related these ideas are. This prayer attempts to convey the attitude that procuring a livelihood should never compromise our essential natures. When God directed man to go out and make a living, His intention was not for man to make a living by destroying everything and everybody in his path. The connection of the "nines" reminds us that if we don't see livelihood in its proper context, we could become greedy monsters. In our greed, we could even be willing to destroy poor people. This kind of greed is a denial of the humanity that we are always supposed to maintain.

The prayer for livelihood follows the prayer for health because someone who is sick is not concerned about livelihood. Health comes before livelihood in the concerns of most sick people. Only when we are healthy do we worry about our livelihoods.

Meaning of the Words

"Bless This Year"

Even though this prayer refers to livelihood, it also stresses time. When we ask for health, we don't ask God to "bless this year with health." Similarly, we don't ask Him to "bless this year with knowledge" or to "bless this year with personal redemption." Yet, when it comes to livelihood, we ask God to "bless this year."

In the financial world, one speaks in terms of a fiscal or a budgetary year. In this prayer we acknowledge the fact that God makes decisions about our livelihoods on a yearly basis. Every Rosh Hashanah (New Year) we ask God to give us everything that we require during the coming year so that we may actualize our potentials. This is why we call Rosh Hashanah a "Day of Judgment." It doesn't mean that we say to God on that day, "Listen, I need a $100,000 job so I'm asking You to give me that job." Rather, we turn to God and ask Him to help us be everything that we should be. One thing we need in order to realize our spiritual potentials is a livelihood. Therefore, we ask God to "bless this year" so that we can live up to these potentials.

Many of our commentators say that when we ask God for a livelihood, we should ask Him to give it to us with pleasantness and not with pain, in permissible ways and not in forbidden ones.[10] If we get our livelihood through forbidden channels, we've lost sight of the whole purpose of wanting a livelihood.

Most people are open to the idea of introspecting and to forming a relationship with God on Rosh Hashanah. On that day, God judges us according to how we present ourselves. If we present ourselves as righteous people, God judges us as righteous people. He judges us *baasher hu sham*—as we are at that time and place.

The concept of *baasher hu sham* is taken from the story about Ishmael, Abraham's son by his concubine Hagar.[11] When Ishmael and Hagar were in the desert, Ishmael took sick and would soon die of thirst if no water could be obtained. Hagar called out to God, who sent an angel to show her a source of water, thus saving Ishmael's life.

When the ministering angels saw that Ishmael's life was about to be saved, they complained to God: "How can you save the life of this man? He is destined to harass the Jews and to be a murderer." The Torah tells us that God saw Ishmael *baasher hu sham*—in his state of righteousness at that moment, without regard to the fact that in the future he would be wicked.

On Rosh Hashanah we read the Torah portion that contains the episode of *baasher hu sham*. This portion reinforces to us that we are all judged on that day according to our spiritual situations at that time.

On Rosh Hashanah, then, God decides what each person's livelihood will be for the following year. For example, He might decide that for a certain farmer's crops to grow, thirty inches of rain will be needed. He might thus decree that there will be thirty inches of rain over the following year.

The Hebrew word for year, *shanah*, has the numerical value of 355. This corresponds to the number of days in the lunar year, and that is why it is called *shanah*. However, *shanah* also means "to change." Even though a decision is made on Rosh Hashanah as to how much money a person will earn in the coming year, or how many inches of rain will fall, the benefit to the recipient is subject to change. Thus, even if the amount of rainfall is determined by God on Rosh Hashanah, where and when it will fall changes from day to day. If the recipient of the rain actualizes the commitments he made on Rosh Hashanah, the rain will come in the right season. The Gemara says that if the person is deserving, the rain will fall in the fields, but if he is not deserving, it will fall in the hills, where it has little use.[12] The rain can come in a way that reflects God's lovingkindness, or in a way that makes it a punishment.

Thus, God's blessing is always available, but our actions can change the blessing. Therefore, in this prayer we ask God to let His blessing "fall upon us"—*barech alenu*. There is nothing deficient in God's blessing, but we ask Him to make sure that His blessing comes upon us. We are the ones who can prevent the blessing from coming into its rightful place.

"Bless . . . Its Produce for Good"

In this prayer, we ask God to bless our year and our crops. We want our general economic situation to be good, and we also want our specific agricultural situation to be good. If our general economic situation is good but the agricultural one is not, then things are really not good for us. People can't eat money.

The reason we ask God to bless the year and the crops *letovah*, "for good," is that there is a spiritual danger in God's providing abundantly for us. When a person has a lot of material things or money, he can forget about God. The Torah teaches us that "Yeshurun got fat and kicked."[13] When we become too satiated with materialism, we may rebel against the One who provided for us. The whole purpose of having a livelihood is so that we can be close to God. There is no point in gaining a livelihood while losing the perspective about why we are living.

We ask to grow spiritually every day, thereby allowing the blessing that was apportioned to us on Rosh Hashanah to come in its proper place and time. We also ask for it to feel satisfying.

"Satisfy Us from Your Bounty"

The Talmud says that when a person dies, not even half of his desires will have been fulfilled in his lifetime. The nature of our attachment to the physical world is such that it creates greater and greater appetite. "Someone who makes his first hundred wants 200; when he makes 200 he wants immeasurably more."[14] The fact that a person has been blessed doesn't mean that he feels as though he is. When someone who has something always wants more and more, he never truly has anything. Therefore, we first ask God to give to us, and then we ask to be happy with what we have.

This is why it says in *Ethics of the Fathers*: "Who is rich? The person who is happy with what he has."[15] In this prayer of the Shemoneh Esrai we ask God for the ability to be happy with our portion.

We ask to be satisfied with a good livelihood in order not to be hungry. This state will allow us to devote our minds and feelings to our spiritual growth. Someone who constantly pursues what he feels he lacks cannot spend much time or energy on spiritual development. When a person says that he will make time to study Torah after making his first million dollars, it is rare that he follows through on the promise. Once he's made the first million and is confronted with his promise, he is likely to say, "I'll study Torah after I've made my second million."

One version of this prayer reads, "from Your bounty" and the other version reads, "from *its* bounty." "Its bounty" refers either to the bounty of the land of Israel, or to the bounty of the year. This prayer was originally constructed for the inhabitants of the land of Israel. They asked God to satisfy them with the bounty that was allotted to that land. Alternatively, it refers to the bounty that was allotted to them for the year. The two versions of the text differ according to whether the prayer is said in the land of Israel or in the Diaspora. Someone who is in Israel says, "Satisfy us from its bounty." Outside the land of Israel, one says, "Satisfy us from Your bounty."[16] According to other opinions, it doesn't matter where one is; one should always say, "from its bounty," because there is a primary blessing that goes to the land of Israel, from which there is a spillover to the rest of the world.[17]

Rabbi Yonasan Eibeshutz, a great ethical figure, said that "Satisfy us from Your bounty (goodness)" means that we ask God to satisfy us from that which He considers good. This is a specific reference to food that is kosher.[18] It is possible inadvertently to eat foods that we are not supposed to eat. What saves us from the mistake of unwittingly eating something non-kosher? One thing is our caring enough to ask God to keep such mistakes from happening.

Technically, we are not culpable for mistakes that occur without our knowledge. Nevertheless, truly committed Jews care whether or not mistakes are made. We ask God to help us make sure that everything that we eat is kosher. Foods that are not kosher create spiritual havoc within us. We are what we eat, and we produce what we've eaten. For this reason, Rabbi Eibeshutz said that eating nonkosher food is frequently responsible for people having difficulty raising their children.

According to this interpretation, "Satisfy us with Your bounty" means that we want to be nurtured by God. We want to be provided for by Him with positive things, including what we eat.

Implications of Livelihood for Human Relationships

This prayer implies that marriages depend upon one or both partners assuming responsibility for making an honest livelihood. If a person who should be assuming that responsibility is not doing so, one should not seriously consider marrying that individual. Our Sages express the idea that wherever food is not available, peace becomes a challenge. Someone may be unable to control the fact that although he makes appropriate efforts his endeavors simply don't pan out. Nevertheless, serious attempts at earning a living must be made.

This prayer also tells us that we should feel satisfied with the livelihoods that we make. In general, people should learn to be satisfied with what they have; this applies not only to one's livelihood but also to one's spouse. Even when a spouse is essentially a good person, a partner can undermine the marriage by always feeling he or she deserves better. A person who never feels satisfied with what he or she has will always be insecure, and this feeling will unsettle the spouse as well. People should strive to find happiness in the financial and marital portions that they have.

Notes

1. Commentary, *Machzor Kol Bo*.
2. Genesis 26:12; Rashi on Genesis 26:12.

3. Genesis 3:19.
4. Talmud *Bavli*, *Sanhedrin* 59b.
5. Genesis 3:19.
6. Ibn Pekuda, *Duties of the Heart, Shaar HaBitachon,* chapter 3.
7. *Ethics of the Fathers* 2:2.
8. Psalms 10:9.
9. Talmud *Bavli*, *Megillah* 17b.
10. Talmud *Bavli*, *Megillah* 17b.
11. Genesis 21:17.
12. Talmud *Bavli*, *Taanit* 22b; Baraita Etz Yosef in *Otsar HaTefillot.*
13. Deuteronomy 32:15.
14. Ecclesiastes 5:9.
15. *Ethics of the Fathers* 4:1.
16. Iyun Tefillah in *Otsar HaTefillot.*
17. Iyun Tefillah in *Otsar HaTefillot.*
18. Yaarot Devash on Shemoneh Esrai.

CHAPTER 13

The Ingathering of the Exiles

תְּקַע בְּשׁוֹפָר גָּדוֹל לְחֵרוּתֵנוּ, וְשָׂא נֵס לְקַבֵּץ גָּלֻיּוֹתֵינוּ,
וְקַבְּצֵנוּ יַחַד מֵאַרְבַּע כַּנְפוֹת הָאָרֶץ. בָּרוּךְ אַתָּה יהוה,
מְקַבֵּץ נִדְחֵי עַמּוֹ יִשְׂרָאֵל.

Sound the great ram's horn (shofar) for our freedom, and
        raise a banner to gather in our exiles, and gather us
together from the four corners of the earth. Blessed are You,
God, who gathers in the scattered ones (the exiled) of His
people Israel.

Theme of the Prayer

This prayer asks God to gather us together and bring us back to the land of Israel during the time of the Messiah. The seventh prayer of the Shemoneh Esrai requested redemption within exile. We ask God there to help us overcome the challenges of exile while we remain in exile. This prayer, in contrast, is a request for redemption that will end our exile and return all of the Jews to our land.

Historical Background

Jacob had twelve sons; his favorite was Joseph, a son of his wife Rachel. When Joseph was a teenager he had a prophetic dream from which he understood that he must bring his entire family down to Egypt at some point in the future.[1]

When Joseph was 17 years old, his brothers sold him into slavery. Jacob was led to believe that Joseph had died; he was not told that Joseph was alive and well in Egypt. Some years later Joseph became the viceroy to the king of Egypt, unbeknownst to his father and brothers who were still living in Canaan.

God caused there to be a famine in Egypt and its surrounding countries. The famine forced ten of Joseph's eleven brothers to come to Egypt to buy food. Joseph recognized his siblings, but they did not realize who he was. Joseph then devised a ploy to force the youngest of his brothers, Benjamin, to come down to Egypt and thereby fulfill his prophetic dream. He imprisoned one of his half-brothers, Shimon, on the pretext that he was a spy, and threatened to kill Shimon. Shimon could prove his innocence only if the other brothers brought Benjamin to Egypt.

When the brothers returned to Jacob and told him the viceroy's plan, Jacob at first adamantly refused to let Benjamin leave. Jacob had already lost his favorite son, and a second son, Shimon, was imprisoned in Egypt. Jacob could not bear the thought of something bad happening to Benjamin, the only other son of his beloved Rachel.

Jacob finally allowed all of his sons to leave when all of their food ran out. They had to go to Egypt to replenish their supplies. When they left, Jacob felt as if his life's work of building a Jewish nation had been destroyed. He felt that he had already lost three of the requisite twelve tribes, and these lost tribes were irreplaceable.

When all the brothers were in Egypt, Joseph concocted another ploy. This time he attempted to imprison Benjamin. His brother Judah then forced a confrontation with Joseph, at which point Joseph revealed his true identity to his brothers. Eventually, Jacob too was brought down to Egypt to join his family.

Jacob became revitalized after seeing Joseph alive after so many years of believing him to be dead.[2] When Jacob lived to see all twelve sons safely together with him in the land of Egypt, the angels sang out in praise to God, "Blessed are You, God, who gathers in those who have been dispersed of His nation Israel."[3]

When Jacob's sons had sold Joseph, they had then taken his coat of many colors and dipped it in blood; then they showed it to Jacob and told him that Joseph had been killed by a wild animal. Jacob was so distraught that he refused to be comforted for what he believed was the death of his son. The Or HaChaim (a commentator on the Torah) says that when the sons tried to comfort Jacob during his week of mourning, they came with all of their children. Their rationale was to show Jacob that although he had indeed lost Joseph, he also had many other children and grandchildren. They tried to shift his focus away from what he had lost onto what he still retained.

Jacob refused to be comforted because he knew that each of his sons had a unique contribution to make in the creation of the Jewish nation. If one of the twelve tribes was missing, then the foundation of the Jewish people was incomplete. The whole function of the Jewish people could not come to fruition as long as any one component was missing.[4]

The apparent loss of Joseph meant to Jacob that, as talented as the Jewish people might be, a unifying component was missing: without the critical element of the tribe of Joseph, and without his unique leadership talents, there would be no Jewish people. They could not form a cohesive whole, they could not teach a message to the world, and they would not be able to survive in the future.

When Jacob went to Egypt and saw that Joseph was still alive, he realized that God had ensured the cohesiveness, integrity, and survival of the nation that Jacob had spent his life building. He realized that God watches over the foundations of the Jewish people and will not allow the Jewish nation to perish. It had seemed to him that according to the laws of natural history, the tremendous talents of the Jews were dispersed. When Jacob realized that this was not so, and that God was mindful of the destiny of the Jewish people, the angels exclaimed: "Blessed is God who gathers in the exiled of His people Israel." God ultimately unifies the Jewish people and ensures their spiritual and physical survival. This is part of God's promise for the survival of the world and for the coming to fruition of its goals.

There is a midrash that says that while Jacob mourned the loss of Joseph, God said to Himself, "You're mourning your son and asking questions about Me, and I'm busy making your son a king in Egypt."[5] This illustrates the drama of the idea encapsulated by "who gathers in the exiled of His people Israel." Throughout history, there have been times when the energies of the Jewish people seemed to be dispersed forever. In reality, the nation's purpose and ultimate cohesiveness has been ensured since its inception. God guarantees an ultimate unification of the Jewish people, which will bring us back to our national peoplehood and goals.

In this prayer we ask God to unify the critical components of the Jewish people in the future, just as He has always done in the past. Just as He collected Jacob's children from their disparate places, so should He collect all of us from the four corners of the earth. In contemporary times, Jews not only are dispersed to the physical ends of the earth, but also have hidden themselves in the spiritual ends of the earth. We need God's help in reunifying us into one people.

One of the commentators expresses this sentiment very beautifully: "The soul of our father, Jacob, should be happy again. He should be happy with us, and we should be happy with him."6 There is a cognizance on Jacob's part that his children are not together physically, emotionally, nor ideologically. This hurts him. Therefore, we pray that God will help us in the same way that He soothed Jacob's pain—by unifying his children. We ask God to help Jacob be happy once again that his family is back together. We also ask to be happy that we are part of Jacob's family.

It is tremendously poignant that our forefathers felt a deep longing for their children to come back together again. They saw us as a family. We sometimes don't see ourselves as a family, and we don't function as one. That hurts our forefathers and foremothers. In this prayer we ask that, in the same way that God made Jacob happy by bringing his entire family together, so should He do it again.

The prayer says that "we should be happy with him," that is, with Jacob. If we cannot unify and actualize ourselves as a cohesive unit, then we will each be missing something that is needed for our personal happiness. If the group does not function as an integrated whole, then each member loses some of his or her optimum productivity and the group as a whole loses its total productivity. Unless all Jews are united, we cannot appreciate our own identities within the family, but can function only as individuals. If Jacob is happy with us—meaning we are all united—then we can be happy with him.

Order of This Prayer in the Shemoneh Esrai

This prayer for redemption follows the prayer for livelihood, for two reasons. One reason is that the land of Israel was created to be the most beneficial place for the Jews to grow in their relationship with God. It was God's plan that in Israel, Jews would have a home environment that would provide for their unique agricultural, political, and sociological needs. With all of their needs taken care of, Jews would be able to access the special spirituality of the land and grow to ever greater heights.

This idea is conveyed beautifully in a description of the land of Israel that appears in Deuteronomy. It says that the land of Israel "has neither too little, nor too much."[7] The function of the land was to enable Jews to create and maintain a relationship with God. Were the land to have too little, the Jews would be overly worried about their livelihood. Were the land to have too much, people would be worried about how much they might lose. Therefore, the land was described as a place properly measured to have exactly what was needed. In Israel, Jews would be free to dedicate their time to that which was most important—developing a relationship with God.

When we pray to return to the land of Israel, we ask God to enable us to live where our economic situation is in balance with our spirituality. Once we put our economic situation in perspective, we prepare ourselves to return to the spiritual state of redemption in the land of Israel. Redemption and livelihood are always tied to each other. In fact, a verse in Ezekiel says that "the fruits will be bountiful, and the economy will be healthy, because your day of the ingathering of the exiles has come."[8]

The second reason for connecting the prayers of livelihood and ingathering of the exiles is in the relationship between physical bounty and spiritual bounty. The first ten generations of the world enjoyed tremendous physical bounty. This paralleled the tremendous spiritual potentials that people had at that time. There was a balance between the spiritual strength that people could have and the physical gifts that could be utilized. After ten generations, God saw that people were obsessed with physical bounty and used it to detract from their spiritual pursuits. God then brought the Great Flood, after which the world became completely different: the physical bounty of the world was tremendously diminished.

The Malbim (a commentator) explains that when people lowered their spiritual stature, the physical blessing that was offered them also declined.[9] Were the physical blessing to have remained the same as before, they would have preoccupied themselves with material pursuits to a point of self-destruction. God understood that people didn't have enough spirituality to elevate themselves commensurate with the amount of physical bounty provided. Thus He diminished the physical bounty to keep it in balance with people's spiritual capabilities.

The balance between physical bounty and our spiritual potentials is an ever-changing one. Once we are ready for an ingathering of our exiles, returning to the land of Israel and greeting the Messiah, we will be on a higher spiritual plane. Once we reach that higher spiritual stage, God will bless us with greater physical bounty. The Prophets tell us that in the time of the Messiah the fruits will grow bigger, they will be tastier, livelihood will be easier to come by, and so on.[10] There is a direct relationship between our spiritual growth and our ability to integrate the physical into our spiritual lives. For this reason, the prayers for livelihood and the ingathering of the exiles are connected.

The earlier prayer for redemption concludes by saying that God "redeems Israel." This tenth prayer concludes by saying, "who gathers in the scattered ones of *His people* Israel." The former blessing refers to Jews who don't merit going back to the land of Israel. When God redeems us under circumstances in which we're not meritorious, it is only because we belong to the nation of Israel. God has accepted upon Himself the responsibility to redeem us as a group. God loves us and will never forsake us, even if we are not individually deserving of true redemption. On the other hand, when we ask God to take us back to the land of Israel, as we do in this prayer, we say that we are prepared to live on a higher level of holiness, that we want to live as we should in the land of Israel. In such a case, we are referred to as "His people Israel." (In the Torah, we find that when the Jewish people sinned God referred to them as "Moses' nation." This occurred when they made a golden calf shortly after God gave them the Torah.[11] When they acted in accordance with His will, He referred to them as "My nation."[12])

Meaning of the Words

Three Expressions of Ingathering

There are three expressions of ingathering in this prayer: "Sound the great ram's horn for our freedom," "raise a banner to gather in our exiles," and "gather us together from the four corners of the earth."

There were ten tribes that went into exile prior to the exile of the tribes of Judah and Benjamin. These tribes (colloquially referred to as the "ten lost tribes") were exiled somewhere in "the dark mountains." We don't know exactly where they went. Some part of them went even further away and were lost to the Jewish people. (The word "Jew" is derived from the word "Judah," since most Jews today are descendants of the tribe of Judah.)

The Vilna Gaon says that the first two expressions of redemption in this prayer refer to the ten tribes, one part of whom disappeared into the dark mountains, and one part of whom disappeared "beyond the Sambatyon river."[13] We ask God to reunite these ten tribes with the two other tribes. We also ask that, once this is done, He gather together the remnants of the two remaining tribes, who are currently dispersed among the four corners of the earth.[14] This prayer asks God to bring these three groups back together again.

This prayer reinforces the idea that Jews are lost until we find every one of our brethren. God directs the historical process that first disperses the Jewish people and then brings us back together again. As individuals, we can't actualize our ideal functions until all Jews come back together again. Jews do not believe that what really matters is for each person to act individually and do what is best solely for himself or herself.

The commentators say that the three expressions of redemption in this prayer parallel the sequence of redemption in the time of the Messiah.[15] The first stage will be the gaining of our freedom in the countries of exile. The second stage will be a gathering together of all the Jewish people to one central location, in exile. In the third stage, we will go back to the land of Israel as a unified force. These stages reflect what happened to us during our exodus from Egypt 3,300 years ago. First we gained freedom while we were still in Egypt. Then we were gathered together in one principal region of Egypt. Finally, from that region, we all left Egypt and eventually were given the Torah.

"A Great Shofar"

What do we mean when we ask God to sound a great shofar? When Abraham brought his son Isaac for an offering, God told him not to kill his son. God had only wanted to test Abraham, to see if Abraham was *willing* to sacrifice Isaac. Nevertheless, Abraham had a deep desire to demonstrate, in reality, his dedication to God. He yearned to bring his act of sacrifice to fruition, so God provided him with a ram whose horns were caught in a nearby thicket. Abraham took this ram and did with it what he had planned to do with Isaac. In this way, Abraham concretized his desire to serve God in the ultimate possible way. God responded to Abraham's action by saying, "I will consider everything that you had wanted to do to Isaac as if you had actually done it to him."

A midrash says that no part of the ram that Abraham sacrificed was wasted, because he sacrificed it with total dedication and devotion. "The left horn of the ram was the shofar that was blown when the Torah was given. The sinews were made into strings for the harp which was used by King David. . . ." Similarly, all of the other parts of the ram were incorporated into objects that had lofty spiritual uses. The right horn of the ram, which was much larger than the left one, is the shofar that will be blown by Elijah the Prophet during the ingathering of the exiles. This is what is referred to as the "great (huge) shofar."[16]

This midrash suggests a number of historical impossibilities. Could sinews last hundreds of years and become part of King David's harp? Could one of the ram's horns last over 3,000 years and be blown in the time of the Messiah? The Maharal of Prague explains that this midrash does not mean that the different parts of the ram literally became incorporated into various holy instruments. It means that all of the emotions that Abraham invested in the ram were not wasted.[17] Even though he expressed his devotion to God with a certain ram, his act made an everlasting mark, which enabled his descendants to do what they did.

Abraham's dedication to doing the will of God enabled God to give the Torah to his descendants. Abraham's act enabled his descendants to say, "*Naaseh venishma*," "We will do what God asks us to do in the Torah, and then we will understand the 'whys' and 'wherefores' of the commandments." Abraham's dedication to God resulted in King David's descending from him. King David poured out his love for God in the book of Psalms. Abraham created the spiritual potentials which later grew into the acceptance of the Torah, the writing of the book of Psalms, and all of the spiritual developments throughout Jewish history until and including the time of the Messiah. All of these were products of Abraham's spiritual roots. He planted them in such a way that they would blossom forever, revealing all of the different manifestations of God until the time of the Messiah.

What does "leaving a lasting mark" in Judaism mean? It means that once the Jewish people experience a tremendous spiritual height, an indelible mark is made on our souls. Even if we later fall from that height, and even if most of its impact disappears, the fact of having once experienced it makes a lasting impression.

As an example, imagine that a person wrote something on a piece of paper and later erased it. Normally, no matter how well it is erased, some impression will always remain on the paper where the words were once written. If someone subsequently doesn't remember what was previously written, he can still fill up the impression and rewrite the page. When something written is erased, it is not totally destroyed; the impression that remains allows the original story to be reconstructed.

The concept of "impression" is also true in spiritual matters. When something spiritual ceases to exist, an indelible mark is left by the fact that there was once an expression of it in an intense moment. For example, before a soul comes into this world, God makes it take an oath that it will be righteous.[18] The commentators ask, "Why is it necessary for a soul to take an oath before it comes into this world?"[19] All Jewish souls were present when God gave the Torah at Mount Sinai and were bound by the oath they made then: "*Naaseh venishma*," "we will obey the Torah, and then we will listen to the reasons for doing the commandments." Why does God make souls take an additional oath?

The reason is that the original oath of *Naaseh venishma* left an impression on each soul, and the second oath "reminds" the soul of the intensity of the experience at the giving of the

Torah. A second oath is necessary because the soul may have been exposed to situations that were insensitive to the first oath. The depth of the first oath can never be totally erased, and the second oath "reminds" the soul of its original commitment.

The shofar is a vehicle by which we bring impressions to reality. In Abraham's case, he had a mission to accomplish by offering Isaac as a sacrifice to God. In reality, he wasn't able to accomplish the totality of the act, but nevertheless he tried to bring all his devotion and desire to do God's will to fruition by sacrificing the ram. Thus Abraham took a will, a desire, a feeling, an impression, and brought it to a reality. The shofar will forever remain that which awakens within us the levels of impression and brings them closer and closer to reality.

Maimonides says that the shofar symbolizes the verse, "Wake up, you people, from your slumber."[20] When we hear the shofar, the sounds reawaken an impression that is already there. The reality of Jewish history is that the further we are from the time of the giving of the Torah, the more removed we are from our spiritual heights. Therefore, the shofar must become bigger and bigger. That is why we speak about a "great shofar."

At the giving of the Torah some 3,300 years ago, the Jews were at their spiritual height and they saw the world in its truest sense. As we go ever further away from that spiriual height, the reality of Revelation becomes more and more diminished, while the impression becomes greater and greater. This is why we say to God, "Blow on a *great* (huge) shofar." As history marches on, most of our spiritual greatness becomes an impression. We need a huge shofar to awaken what is always there but is dormant inside us, as an impression.

"The Scattered Ones"—The Exiled Sparks of Holiness

In this prayer we say that God "gathers in the scattered ones of His people Israel." This means that God brings together our personal, dispersed sparks of holiness, which have been displaced from their proper places and functions because of our being in exile.[21]

"Ingathering of the exiles" doesn't refer only to bringing together people who have been dispersed. It also refers to the parts of an individual's soul coming together. An individual's spiritual vitality and energy can become mischanneled in many directions. The Talmud says that "the Messiah will not come until we bring all the spiritual energies back to their proper point of correct channeling."[22] To the extent that our energies are mischanneled, they are not where they are supposed to be. If this is so, we cannot have a full experience of life. We each have a limited supply of energy, and if we waste it, then it can't be used in the way that it's supposed to help us actualize our spiritual potentials.

Unifying as One People

Abraham publicized the belief in one God, contrary to what the rest of the world believed at that time. The world is made up of a diverse group of people, with no two people being alike. Abraham was able to proselytize his belief in God and to rally people from totally different backgrounds under his banner. Abraham didn't say: "Everybody's different, their beliefs are different, and they have the right to believe in whatever they choose. I might as well give up trying to influence them and keep my beliefs to myself. Let them do their thing, and I'll do mine."

There are twenty Hebrew words in this prayer. They symbolize the twenty generations that existed in the world prior to Abraham. This is as if to say that in the merit of Abraham, we will again be collected together as one people.

Abraham knew that the truth could ultimately unify diverse groups of people. In this prayer, we recognize that people might think that it is impossible for God to unite the Jewish people, because they have such diverse opinions, backgrounds, and places of residence. From the allusion to Abraham, however, we see that everybody can be united under the banner of God. In the time of the ingathering of the exiles, all Jews will again be united in the service of God.

Implications of the Ingathering of Exiles
for Human Relationships

Two marriage partners generally come from different backgrounds, and their perspectives, needs, and ways of thinking are not the same. Making marriages transcend these differences is no easy task.

This prayer implies that people from diverse backgrounds need to establish some spiritual goal in order to forge healthy relationships. Such goals can transcend all of the differences that otherwise exist between any two people. Apart from this central, unifying spiritual goal, all other components of a relationship might be considered negotiable.

True freedom is not obtained by people standing their ground about every minute detail of their lives. Sometimes the greatest freedom depends upon being able to establish a primary spiritual goal. When both spouses have many nonnegotiable positions that are at odds with each other, a satisfying compromise becomes impossible. For such people, the inability to compromise results in a lack of freedom. Setting spiritual goals sometimes frees people from having immovable positions about many other areas of their lives.

Notes

1. Nachmanides on Genesis 42:9.
2. Genesis 45:27.
3. *Shebolei Leket*, chapter 18.
4. Or HaChaim on Genesis 37:35.
5. *Pesikta D'Rav Kahana* 17.
6. Tanya Rabati.
7. Deuteronomy 8:7–10. See *Akedat Yitzchak Shelach*.
8. Ezekiel 36:8.
9. Malbim on Genesis 8:21.
10. Talmud *Bavli, Shabbat* 30a.
11. Exodus 32:7.
12. Exodus 32:4. See *Midrash Rabbah*.
13. *Siddur HaGra*.
14. *Siddur HaGra*.
15. Dover Shalom in *Otsar HaTefillot*.

16. *Pirkei D'Rabbi Eliezer*, chapter 31.
17. Maharal, *Beer HaGolah*.
18. Talmud *Bavli*, *Niddah* 30b.
19. Talmud *Bavli*, *Niddah* 30b, Maharsha's commentary.
20. Maimonides, *Yad HaChazakah*, *Teshuvah* 3:4.
21. Yaarot Devash on Shemoneh Esrai.
22. Talmud *Bavli*, *Abodah Zarah* 5a.

CHAPTER 14

Restoration of Justice

הָשִׁיבָה שׁוֹפְטֵינוּ כְּבָרִאשׁוֹנָה, וְיוֹעֲצֵינוּ כְּבַתְּחִלָּה, וְהָסֵר מִמֶּנּוּ יָגוֹן וַאֲנָחָה, וּמְלוֹךְ עָלֵינוּ אַתָּה יהוה לְבַדְּךָ בְּחֶסֶד וּבְרַחֲמִים, וְצַדְּקֵנוּ בַּמִּשְׁפָּט. בָּרוּךְ אַתָּה יהוה, מֶלֶךְ אֹהֵב צְדָקָה וּמִשְׁפָּט.

※ ※ ※ ※ ※ ※ ※ ※ ※ ※ ※ ※

Return our judges to us, as they were in the earliest times, and the ones who gave us counsel, as at first. And remove sorrow and groaning from us. And rule over us, You, God, all by Yourself, with lovingkindness and compassion. And we should come out righteous in judgment. Blessed are You, God, a King who loves righteousness and justice.

Theme of the Prayer

This is the eleventh prayer of the Shemoneh Esrai. In it, we ask for the restoration of the judges and counselors whom we used to have.

The Sanhedrin

The highest court of Jewish law was known as the Sanhedrin. We ask for its restoration in this prayer. Rabbi Yonasan Eibeshutz wrote, "As long as we had the true Jewish court in its appropriate place next to the holy Temple, the presence and dignity of God rested upon the Jewish people."[1] The Sanhedrin was not a place where two people slugged out their differences. Rather, it was viewed as a place that personified the presence of God (Shechinah) among the Jewish people.

Maimonides wrote, "The son of David (the Messiah) will not come until the Sanhedrin is back in its place."[2] When the Messiah comes, there will be a renaissance of spiritual revelation, and the manifestation of God. Thus both of the commentators quoted here indicate that the Sanhedrin represents holiness and the presence of God among the Jewish people.

In secular society, a court of law is a place where people legally wash their dirty laundry. When two people are unable to resolve their conflicts by themselves, they must come before a judge who makes them do what is right. In secular terms, courts of law represent the failure of people to live up to what they are supposed to be.

When the Jews went into exile, one of the things they lost was their Sanhedrin, with everything that it represented. One of the modern tragedies that results from the absence of this centralized power is that some women have difficulty obtaining religious divorces. When the Sanhedrin existed, its Sages had it within their power to force unwilling husbands to give their wives divorces. Nowadays, a woman can be left without redress if she wants to get out of a marriage and her husband is unwilling to give her divorce papers. This unfair control by the husband of the wife's right to remarry is not because of a flaw in Judaism per se; rather, it is something that we have lost because we did not appreciate Judaism for what it was.

In this prayer there is a connection between the Sanhedrin and the state of being under the reign of God. Rabbi Yonasan Eibeshutz says that the establishment of the Sanhedrin was not simply God's way of creating law and order. It was also God's way of manifesting His presence to the world.

Historical Background

The book of Exodus says, after the giving of the Torah, "And these are the ordinances (laws of justice) that should be placed before them. . . ."[3] Following this preface is a series of intricate laws that form the basis of the talmudic tractates of *Baba Kamma*, *Baba Metzia*, and *Baba Batra*. These tractates deal with issues of monetary damages and monetary problems. When God told Moses that those were the ordinances he should place before the people, the angels blessed God and called Him a King who loves righteousness and justice. What was so significant about this event that it prompted the angels to bless God?

Samuel judged the Jewish people. He lived prior to, and during, the reign of King Saul. The judges who followed Samuel were not quite as committed to their roles as Samuel had been. He used to travel from city to city in order to bring justice into the lives of the Jewish people.

At the end of Samuel's life, the Jews came to him and told him that he was too old to continue judging them. They wanted him to anoint a king in his stead. Prior to that time there had never been a king over the Jewish people. Samuel was initially terribly disturbed by their request, and he turned to God to ask for His guidance. God told Samuel that if the Jewish people asked for a king, he should arrange for them to have one.[4]

Appointment of a Jewish king over the Jewish people is one of the 613 commandments of the Torah.[5] Once the Jews had settled in the land of Israel, they were supposed to appoint a king, destroy Amalek, and then build the holy Temple. Nevertheless, Samuel felt rejected by the Jewish people. When he then turned to God for guidance, God's response was that Samuel should not feel hurt—that the people had rejected not Samuel but God Himself.[6]

Relationship to the Previous Prayer

The previous prayer asked for God to gather together all the exiled Jews, and to bring us back to the land of Israel once we are ready to go back to His home. When we are ready to live in God's home, we will also be ready for the restoration of His justice.

The Functions of a Legal System

The Ran, a medieval Jewish commentator, says that there are two ways of viewing the concept of justice. One view is that a legal system is "for the betterment of society." Without a socio-legal system, everyone's individual needs, desires, and goals would result in a chaotic society.[7] It says in the *Ethics of the Fathers*, "Were it not for the fact that people are afraid of the government, one person would swallow up the next."[8] From this perspective, a legal system is necessary in order to preserve the social peace. In fact, one of the seven commandments that were given to Noah's descendants was that they should set up courts of law.[9]

The other view of the laws of justice is as a format that creates an atmosphere in which God can live in this world with us. According to this perspective, there could conceivably be a law that creates a spiritual state in the world, but does not preserve the social order. For example, Jewish law says that a person may not be executed by a human court unless certain conditions have been met. The criminal would have had to be warned by two witnesses, prior to his capital crime, that the act he planned to carry out would subject him to the death penalty. Unless he were to acknowledge that he understood the punishment that awaited him, and that he planned to do the deed anyway, the court could not execute him.

This teaches us that no one is truly evil unless he deliberately does something which he knows is evil, and whose consequences don't concern him. Unless someone reaches that level, we don't have the right to rule out his life. On the other hand, if the courts must go to such lengths in order to execute criminals, such people might proliferate. Were this to occur, the social order would not benefit from the legal restrictions on punishment.

The Ran says that the opposite is also possible. A law could be good for the social order, but not be conducive to bringing God's holy presence into the world. Therefore, Jewish laws of justice can be distinguished according to which function they best serve.

The Ran underscores that the function of the Jewish judge was primarily to help create an atmosphere in this world in which God's holy presence could rest. This is why there were so many exacting laws about the kind of person that a judge needed to be. He had to be someone of exemplary character. His personal character had to be a vehicle that brought God's spirituality into the world.

This concept extends to such a degree that the Talmud says that when a proper judge judged, God Himself came into the courtroom. The judge perceived God's spiritual inspiration, and was then able to appropriately counsel the litigants as to what they should do. Proper judgment included a very intense contact with God, which then facilitated the judge's ability to say what was right and what was wrong. His legal decision would be rendered according to which consequences would allow God to live in this world.[10]

According to the Ran, one purpose of having a king was to maintain the social order when it was threatened. The king had the right to institute certain laws to preserve the social atmosphere, which might be adversely affected were there judges without kings. To this end, a king had the right to punish someone without any warning. He could also confiscate property and do other things whose purpose was to maintain the social order.[11]

After proposing the above, the Ran says that by and large, the social order is served by the judge rendering proper judgment. If a legal system is good enough to bring God's presence into this world, then it normally creates a social order as well. As an example of this, the town of Bnai Brak in Israel has no police department. The people there live with the discipline of Torah, which obviates the need to have police.

The Ran then suggests a second reason as to why there was a king. He says that the king instituted and enforced that which the judge found to be important. Thus, in theory, a king's role is to maintain social order; in practice, his role is to institute the behavior that the judge believes will allow God to dwell in this world.

The Ran adds that the Jews also needed a king in order to maintain a certain stature vis-à-vis the nations of the world. The Jews' mistake with Samuel was that they wanted a king *instead* of Samuel, not in addition to him. They wanted social order without the divine inspiration that should have preceded it, and which should have been the basis on which the social order rested. They only wanted a government that would run like all other governments. That is why God said to Samuel, It is not you whom they have rejected. They have rejected Me.

There was an entire era when the Jewish people were judged by judges. Jewish law says that the king was the only person who was required to write a Torah scroll for himself, and carry it around with him. Since the king's focus and his concerns had to do with the social order, it was always possible that social issues would distract him from the spiritual ones that should have been his ultimate concern. Therefore, the king was liable to depart from the laws of the Torah. This is why he required his own personal Torah scroll. It was intended to remind him of who he was supposed to be, and what ultimate role he was supposed to play for the Jewish people.

Judges as Vehicles of God's Judgment in This World

Imagine the following scenario: A man named Abe kills a man named Barry. Abe is apprehended and brought to trial. In court, two witnesses named Charlie and David testify that Abe indeed murdered Barry. The court finds Abe guilty, and sentences him to be executed.

After Abe is sentenced, but before he is executed, two more witnesses come to court to testify. Edgar and Frank testify that they don't know if Abe murdered Barry or not. However, they do know that Charlie and David could not have witnessed the murder in question, since Charlie and David were with Edgar and Frank at the time the murder took place. Moreover, Edgar and Frank testify that they were all nowhere near the scene of the crime at the time it occurred.

The Torah says that in this type of scenario, witnesses such as Charlie and David are known as "plotting witnesses." The Torah mandates that Charlie and David are to be executed, and Abe is to be released. This is because "plotting witnesses" (*eidim zomemim*) are to be subjected to the same punishment that would have been meted out to the defendant, had their testimony not been invalidated.

Paradoxically, if Abe had already been executed prior to Edgar and Frank's invalidation of Charlie and David's testimony, Charlie and David are not killed.[12]

This sequence seems totally illogical. It would seem that if Abe were executed erroneously, the plotting witnesses should also be executed. Similarly, if Abe were not executed, then the plotting witnesses should also not be harmed.

Nachmanides, another medieval Jewish commentator, says that the logic behind this sequence is as follows: The caliber of judges was so high that when they judged, "God was standing in the courtroom." In other words, the judges' efforts to bring about justice was important enough to merit the presence of God. Since God was there and was connected to the judges, if He had not wanted a defendant to die, the judges would have sensed that something was awry. At that point they would not have condemned the defendant to death.

If Abe had not killed Barry, but the court had Abe executed, then—according to this logic—God must have had some reason (known only to Himself) for wanting Abe to leave this world. If God had wanted Abe to die, the punishment given to the plotting witnesses would no longer be a punishment of death.[13]

Leaving aside the complexity of this particular scenario, it illustrates how a proper court of law was viewed. The type of people who created the system of justice were those who were expected to be able to bring God into a courtroom.

Judaism does not believe in the concept of a jury, although it does believe in the importance of testimony by eyewitnesses. A legal system based upon a secular jury composed of everyday people has nothing in common with how a Jewish court of law was designed to function. The Jewish system is based on the deep philosophical concept that man cannot judge man; only God can judge man. Jewish judges were vehicles of God's judgment in this world.

God as Our Judge

The beauty of the Sanhedrin can now be better appreciated. It represented an environment within which God was invited to manifest His divine presence. In the "Justice" prayer of the Shemoneh Esrai, we ask God to rule over us. We don't want a secular king to rule us. We want God, Himself, to "feel comfortable" dwelling among us and directing our lives. Every action of ours should be molded by our feeling the presence of God, and by deciding whether or not He would want us to do a given act. We should want to make God more comfortable with our actions, rather than chase Him away by what we do.

This clarifies why the angels exclaimed that God is "a King who loves righteousness and justice," after the Torah and its social laws were given to the Jews. The angels were impressed that God miraculously revealed His Torah to the Jews. Nevertheless, the angels were concerned that the Jewish people would not be able to carry the concepts of the Torah into their mundane daily lives. How would the Jews deal with their fellow Jews? How would they conduct their business affairs? How would they adjudicate legal matters? After the supernatural revelation by God on Mount Sinai, the Jews had to plummet back into the mundane realities of daily life, without His manifest presence.

This is why God immediately followed the giving of the Torah with the words, "These are the laws of justice (*mishpatim*)" that will preserve the Sinai experience and the divine presence. These "social laws" were not merely for the purpose of preserving a social ethic. They were designed to continue the entire revelation of Sinai within the confines of a mundane life.

It is easy for us to be inspired when we sit in a classroom, or in a synagogue, and hear a religious figure give a moving talk. However, when we make the transition back to our homes or to our places of business, it is difficult to maintain God's presence in front of us as a reality. The *mishpatim* are means through which we can integrate the greatest manifestations of God into our daily lives. That is how we make the laws of justice transcend the simple function of rules that facilitate an ordered society. When the angels saw that God had endowed the Jewish people with a vehicle by which they could permanently recreate the Sinai experience on a daily basis, they blessed Him.

The Talmud says that when a Jewish judge judges correctly, he becomes a partner with God in the creation of the world.[14] The Jewish legal system was not constructed to be merely a social convention, with God's sole interest being to establish law and order. The Jewish social laws were designed to continue the Sinai experience, and to bring the reality of God into our daily lives. A person who tries to implement these laws becomes a partner with God as he preserves God's revelation of Himself to the world.

Redemption with Justice

There is a verse that says, "Zion will be redeemed with justice."[15] It emphasizes that the Jews will be redeemed from exile only through their asking for a type of justice that will allow God to dwell in this world with them. Thus we need to discipline ourselves in a way that can make the return of God a realistic possibility.

It is tragic that we lost the Sanhedrin when we were exiled. In exile, we have lost so many spiritual gifts that it seems we will never be able to return to God. We lost the gift of prophecy forty years before the destruction of the Second Temple, and we lost the centralized courts of law (Sanhedrin) when that Temple was destroyed. If we needed a Sanhedrin when we lived in the land of Israel, then we certainly need one now that we are not all living in Israel under a centralized governing power.

Even though we need a Sanhedrin more than ever now, we cannot have one without being the kind of people who originally gave us our power. The power of the Sanhedrin came out of the Jews' desire to live with the type of discipline that allows God to dwell with us in this world. We can't have the power of the Sanhedrin unless we want God to be a part of our daily lives. We can't have this gift back unless we sincerely ask for all that it entails.

There are many spiritual gifts that we could use, but we have to make places for them in our lives, and in ourselves. If we are not willing to make space for God's dwelling among us, then the Sanhedrin, prophecy, and God's ruling us cannot have their desired effects. The exalted function of the Sanhedrin was reflected in its being located in the courtyard of the Temple. The importance of the Sanhedrin was that through it God dwelled in our midst. When we demonstrated to God that we no longer wanted Him to dwell with us in the land of Israel, He exiled us from that land, allowing the Temple to be destroyed and the Sanhedrin to be dismantled.

Meaning of the Words

"Return Our Judges . . . and the Ones Who Gave Us Counsel"

The Vilna Gaon explains this prayer as follows:

A "judge" was a person who determined what the law was, and/or had the ability to enforce a judge's decisions. This could include not only judges, but kings as well.

"In the earliest times" refers to the years when the Jewish people had their first government—that is, the time of Kings David and Solomon.

"Counselors" were advisors. "Who gave us counsel, as at first" is a reference to the time and the wisdom of Moses and Aaron. Technically they were not kings, but they gave excellent advice about how people should observe the law.

We pray here for God to give us people who can enforce the

law when Jews are not at a spiritual level where they will accept the law of their own accord. At the same time, we need the spiritual enlightenment of their judgments to be equal to that invested in the law by Moses and Aaron.[16]

"Remove Sorrow and Groaning from Us"

This can be interpreted to mean that when we decide we do not want God in our lives, many people suffer from the resulting lack of justice. When there is no justice, advantage is taken of righteous and good people.[17] When there aren't proper courts of law, and justice is not properly meted out, people suffer and groan. But when God will bring back appropriate justice, the suffering of our people will be alleviated.

In the secular world, people do their best to stay out of court. From a Jewish perspective, however, the greatest blessing for the world is when God sits on His Throne of Justice and metes out true justice. That is the best way to right the injustices of the world. The idea of letting every person be free to do what he or she feels is right is the most cursed situation imaginable. This is why we say in the blessing, "God loves righteousness and justice." He loves justice because it brings everything to where it is supposed to be. When things are the way they are supposed to be, that is truly a state of blessing.

"Remove sorrow and groaning" has a second interpretation. It is eloquently expressed in a prayer that we say Friday night, after welcoming the angels to our Sabbath table with the "Shalom Aleichem" prayer. In it we say that the conditions of exile have created such turmoil in our lives that we can't pray properly. We've lost our proper values, we've lost our proper perspectives, and we're confused. On Friday night we escape from the nonsense of the week, and we begin to feel the pleasure of true values. In that state of mind, we ask God to help us communicate with Him in the way that we really should be able to do.

In the midst of our "sorrow and groaning," we can't even think straight. Without the clarity of what our true values should be, we are always in a state of sorrow and groaning. We didn't want God, so He left. Now that He's gone, we have to make decisions about our lives, devoid of His presence. When left totally to our own devices we are likely to make many poor decisions. The sorrow and groaning come from a lack of clarity about what decisions we should make. We ask God to take away our sorrow by dwelling among us, thereby enabling us to make the correct decisions about how to lead our lives.

Removing the Sorrows of Exile

The Vilna Gaon said that three factors have been responsible for many of the Jews' problems during their exile over the previous 1,900 years. The first factor is corrupt leaders and judges. The second factor is living in environments that weaken our spiritual health. Problems are created when we are influenced and harassed by people around us who make it difficult to live in appropriate ways. The third factor is our internal *yetzer hara* (drive to do what is wrong), which encourages us to do the wrong things.[18]

This prayer addresses all three reasons for our having problems. When we ask God to restore our judges, we are asking for people who will interpret the law correctly and give us heightened spiritual advice. This is necessary to remove the problems created by corrupt leaders. Unfortunately, some of our worst suffering throughout history was caused by Jewish leaders who were misguided.

The Torah predicted that various punishments would befall the Jews if they didn't keep the commandments. God said that one of the severest punishments would come from within the Jewish people themselves.[19] Therefore, our first request is for a restoration of exemplary leaders. We don't want to suffer because our leaders have their own prejudices and their own axes to grind. We want leaders who will preserve the spiritual standards that make us who we are supposed to be.

We next ask God to take away "sorrow and groaning." The word "sorrow" (*yagon*) refers to being saddened and depressed by nothing in particular, and "groaning" (*anachah*) refers to suffering that comes from a particular problem. We ask God to take away the sadness and suffering that come from our surroundings. Some commentators say that if we had good leaders, sorrow and suffering would automatically stop, and we would then have spirit and pride in ourselves, which are incompatible with sadness and suffering.[20]

The third thing we ask is for God to "rule over us by Yourself." Our negative inclinations should not rule over us. We want the only governor of our lives to be God, not our internal drives that wish to do things against His will. No government can effectively rule if it has two kings. We ask God to reign over us by Himself, not in conjunction with other forces.

This prayer asks for the restoration of justice and a judicial system that are comparable to what we had in biblical times and in the time of the First Temple. Our ability to have the most glorified type of judicial system really depends on what we want for ourselves. There is a concept that God rewards or punishes us in accordance with our actions, measure for measure (*middah keneged middah*). If we institute an internal system of justice and try to discipline ourselves according to it, then we merit being blessed with an external judicial system that will ensure the caliber of our spiritual potentials as a nation. If we trounce upon the internal discipline that we should demand of ourselves, and don't judge ourselves or introspect about how to improve from within, we cannot expect to get the Sanhedrin back. What we value and emulate internally becomes the merit for our deserving true justice in the outside world.

The Talmud says, "When there is justice in the world below, there is no justice that needs to be decided in Heaven. When there is no justice in this lower world, then God must mete out justice from above."[21] If we judge ourselves, then God will not have to do so for us. If we shirk our responsibilities, then God must enforce justice from His world. When that becomes necessary, God sends us many different agents of judgment. Sometimes, the nations of the world are His agents of judgment.

Thus, there is a direct connection between how the world executes justice and our own internal spiritual condition. If we work on improving ourselves, God will not bring us to greater spiritual awareness through trials and tribulations administered by the nations of the world. If we improve internally,

God will grant us leaders who will allow Him to dwell in our midst, so we will not need to be punished by the nations around us.

This idea is eloquently expressed in Deuteronomy: "Judges and law enforcers you should put in front of you in all of your gateways (in all of your cities)."[22] The Chassidic commentators interpret "gateways" in this verse to mean, not entrances to cities, but rather "gateways" that allow access to each person.[23] All individuals should set up their own judges to make sure that whatever enters their eyes, ears, mouth and so on does not defile their soul or body within. That is, before we read something, we should decide if it is worthwhile reading. Before we eat, we should decide if the food will enhance or detract from our spirituality. Before we speak, we should decide if our speech is inappropriate or allowed. Every Jew should judge, prior to acting, whether the results will be spiritually beneficial or detrimental. We should then enforce these decisions accordingly. Every gateway into the human being is a gift from God that needs to be protected, judged, and disciplined.

This prayer concludes that God, rather than our negative inclinations, should rule over us, with "righteousness and justice" (*tzedakah u'mishpat*). We can be judged by God Himself or by courts of law that God establishes. Jewish liturgy often refers to "courts of Heaven" (*bet din shel maalah*); these courts operate primarily with justice. The heavenly agents that God establishes are set up to judge within the framework of the law. God, however, may elect to judge a person by Himself, without the process of law. Ideally, we should all want to be judged directly by God rather than by His appointees, because God's relationship with us is not only that of a judge to a subject, but also that of a father to a child. When the judge who decides your fate is also your father, you have a much better chance of receiving a compassionate sentence!

God's direct judgment is referred to as "righteousness" (*tzedakah*), whereas the judgment of the courts of Heaven is referred to as "justice" (*mishpat*). In this prayer we ask God to influence the courts of Heaven such that our innocence will be manifest to them, whether we stand before our Father or before His agents. This is why we conclude the prayer by asking God to find us "righteous in judgment" (*vetzadkenu bamishpat*). We should be judged favorably in the courts of law as if we were being judged directly by our father.

As much as God loves us and would like us to be judged favorably, He also wants to see that justice is done. Therefore, this prayer ends with the blessing that God is a "King who loves righteousness and justice." If we stand before God, He will give us a more lenient judgment than if we stand before His agents. But God doesn't want us to rely on His mercy. He wants us to live up to a standard that will allow us to emerge meritoriously from a court of law. We shouldn't have to bank on the privileges of our unique relationship with God. Even though God loves to grant us mercy, He also loves justice. We should demand a standard of behavior from ourselves that will allow us to be found righteous even within a court system.

Implications of Restoring Justice for Human Relationships

There must be justice and fairness in human relationships. People must take responsibility for their misdeeds, and respect others, in order for human interactions to work. Unfortunately, spouses too commonly feel at liberty to act callously toward each other. People should monitor their actions according to how an impartial judge would view them. No one should take a spouse for granted, or be above judging his or her own personal behavior and trying to make sure that it is exemplary.

Good relationships depend upon the willingness of both partners to judge themselves objectively and strive to act with fairness and mutual respect. People who avoid reviewing their relationships, who "shove things under the carpet" so as to avoid discomfort, damage their relationships. People in healthy relationships measure their behavior by the yardsticks of truth and fairness. People can't feel good about themselves as long as they whitewash their actions. They also can't feel good about their relationships if they treat their partners in ways that violate their inner sense of what is right and wrong.

On the other hand, we can't be punitive with others and rationalize our behavior by saying that God loves justice. We must act with others the way we would like them to act with us. Justice must be tempered with compassion and common sense. Pure justice, meted out by someone who sets him or herself up to judge others, destroys relationships. Criticism, even when it is warranted, must be delivered in a kind and compassionate manner; it must be designed to encourage and spur others on to greater growth, not to hurt or destroy them.

Notes

1. Yaarot Devash on Shemoneh Esrai.
2. Levush, quoting Maimonides.
3. Exodus 21.
4. I Samuel 8:22.
5. Deuteronomy 17:15.
6. I Samuel 8:7.
7. Derashot HaRan—*Shoftim VeShotrim*.
8. Ethics of the Fathers 3:2.
9. Talmud *Bavli, Sanhedrin* 56b.
10. Nachmanides on Deuteronomy 17:11.
11. Maimonides, *Yad HaChazakah*, Kings, chapter 4.
12. Talmud *Bavli, Makkot* 5b.
13. Nachmanides on Deuteronomy 19:18.
14. Talmud *Bavli, Shabbat* 10a.
15. Isaiah 1:27.
16. *Siddur HaGra.*
17. Ezekiel 9:4.
18. Ezekiel 9:4; see Metzudat David.
19. Leviticus 26:17.
20. Etz Yosef in *Otsar HaTefillot.*
21. *Devarim Rabbah* 5:5.
22. Deuteronomy 16:18.
23. Sfat Emet, quoting R. Chaim Vital.

CHAPTER 15

He Who Breaks Enemies and Humbles Rebellious Sinners

וְלַמַּלְשִׁינִים אַל תְּהִי תִקְוָה, וְכָל הָרִשְׁעָה כְּרֶגַע תֹּאבֵד, וְכָל אֹיְבֶיךָ מְהֵרָה יִכָּרֵתוּ, וְהַזֵּדִים מְהֵרָה תְעַקֵּר וּתְשַׁבֵּר וּתְמַגֵּר וְתַכְנִיעַ בִּמְהֵרָה בְיָמֵינוּ. בָּרוּךְ אַתָּה יהוה, שֹׁבֵר אֹיְבִים וּמַכְנִיעַ זֵדִים.

And for the slanderers let there be no hope, and may all evil be instantly destroyed. And all of Your enemies should be quickly cut off, and the rebellious sinners You should quickly uproot, and smash, and break, and humble quickly in our day. Blessed are You, God, who breaks enemies and humbles rebellious sinners.

Theme of the Prayer

Jews do not believe in indiscriminately "turning the other cheek." If someone is intent on hurting us, we must defend ourselves. Nevertheless, even though we ask God to break our enemies and humble sinners, this prayer is sensitive to the difference between the essence of a person and the evil that he or she perpetrates. We ask for the evil to be destroyed, not for the person to be destroyed. We believe that every Jew is essentially good. He may get caught up in a lot of negativity, of which he must rid himself, but we do not wish for him to be annihilated. Initially, the theme of this prayer seems to be a request for God to destroy sinners. In actuality, we ask God to rid the sinner of the conceit and arrogance that propel him to evil.

Historical Background

This prayer was not one of the original eighteen prayers of the Shemoneh Esrai instituted by the Great Assembly. However, just as the other eighteen blessings were enunciated by the angels when they witnessed some historical event that revealed an aspect of God, so too was this blessing. When the men of the Great Assembly instituted the prayers, they did not feel it was necessary to include this one, but its historical basis eventually made it worthy of inclusion.

The historical background to this prayer occurred when God punished the Egyptians at the Red Sea. During the preceding 210 terrible years of oppression, the Jews were enslaved and tortured by the Egyptians. There was no sign that God would ever punish the enemies of the Jews. God then took the Jews out of Egypt during the Exodus. The Egyptians subsequently regretted having let them go, and pursued the Jews into the desert, planning to kill or re-enslave them. God made the Red Sea split for the Jews, allowed them to go through unharmed, and returned them to the desert. The Egyptians continued to pursue the Israelites and followed them into the sea, but they drowned in it.[1]

When God punished these Egyptians, the angels became aware that God had noticed how the Jews had suffered under the Egyptians for so many years. By witnessing God's bringing the rebellious Egyptians to justice, the angels understood that sooner or later God metes out justice to the entire world. When the angels saw the destruction of the Egyptians, they exclaimed, "Blessed are You, God, who breaks enemies and humbles rebellious sinners."[2]

Why and How This Prayer Was Added to the Shemoneh Esrai

The Talmud discusses why this prayer became part of the Shemoneh Esrai.[3] The Shemoneh Esrai consists of eighteen blessings. There is an allusion to the significance of the number 18 in Psalm 29, which says that everything in the universe praises God.[4] In that psalm, which refers to the creation of the world and to the sustaining of Creation, God's name is mentioned eighteen times. The eighteen blessings in the Shemoneh Esrai parallel the eighteen times that God's name is mentioned. When we pray, we want to accomplish the goal of recognizing God as the Master of the World. In the Shemoneh Esrai, we recognize God as the Creator of everything in the world and as the Sustainer of all Creation. That recognition is the basis for our requests in the Shemoneh Esrai.

A second opinion says that the eighteen prayers of the Shemoneh Esrai parallel the eighteen times the name of God appears in the Shema.[5] The Shema is the prayer that affirms God's Unity, our belief in Him, and our commitment to do His will. As long as we consider ourselves God's subjects and commit ourselves to doing what He wants us to do, we can ask Him to provide us with everything we require in order to carry out His mission.

Once the Talmud explains why there are eighteen blessings

in the Shemoneh Esrai, it then says that there are really nineteen blessings. In Psalm 29 there is a nineteenth mention of God's name, albeit a different name. The name that appears eighteen times alludes to God's manifestation in this world through His attribute of compassion; the nineteenth mention of God's name refers to His attribute of justice. Thus the additional Shemoneh Esrai prayer, which asks for God to execute justice on His enemies and rebellious sinners, parallels the attribute that is mentioned the nineteenth time in the Psalm.

There are only eighteen actual mentions of God's name in the Shema. However, the first verse of the Shema reads, "Hear, Israel, the Lord is our God, the Lord is One." The word "One" is seen as a veiled reference to God, making nineteen mentions of God's name in the Shema. This nineteenth mention of God parallels those people who oppose the Jewish people, whom we ask God to destroy in this additional prayer. These sinners do not necessarily try to destroy the entire concept of God, but they do try to destroy His role as being One in the world.

Had there been no parallels to nineteen prayers in these two substantiating sources, our Sages still would have felt the need to add the nineteenth one to the Shemoneh Esrai. The Talmud states that the sources in the Psalms and the Shema further supported the legitimacy of adding the nineteenth prayer.

The Talmud refers to this nineteenth blessing as "the blessing of the Sadducees." It is also known as the blessing against the heretics. Sadducees were people who maintained that the Written Torah was given at Mount Sinai but denied that the Oral Torah was divinely given. They not only believed this for themselves, but they were determined to destroy everyone else's commitment to the Oral Law. They stopped at nothing to accomplish this goal. They even went to the foreign governments in power and informed on Jews who believed in the Oral Law. The result of their informing was that many believing Jews were killed.

The prayer against heretics was instituted in the city of Yavneh at the time of Rabbi Gamliel II, after the destruction of the Second Temple. Rabbi Gamliel recognized that the Sadducees' informing on the believing Jews was becoming intolerable and that it was necessary for the Jews to pray to God to take these heretics out of their midst. Constant vigilance against their threats, arguing to prove them wrong, and countering their influences had become an unending endeavor, leaving little time to refocus the believers' attention to where it needed to be.

The Talmud says, "The eighteen blessings of the Amidah were brought before Rabbi Gamliel in Yavneh. He said, 'Is there no one who is of the requisite spiritual caliber, who can compose the blessing which will be efficacious against the Sadducees?' "[6] Obviously, there were many people who wished to do it, but Rabbi Gamliel was searching for someone who was spiritually connected in such a way that he would compose the prayer just as it needed to be worded. Rabbi Gamliel understood that such a prayer was necessary, and he knew the historical background of the angels blessing God for punishing the Egyptians. However, he did not know the exact content of the angels' blessing, and he searched for the person to whom the prayer would be revealed in its entirety.

It was Shmuel HaKatan (Samuel the Small), so named because he was extremely modest and considered himself to be of "small" importance, who created the structure of the nineteenth prayer.

The Talmud says that the following year the words of the prayer were forgotten. Shmuel then spent two or three hours and recalled its entire text. During the several hours that he was the emissary leading the public prayer, he stood in front of the rabbis, and was not taken away. (Normally, if the emissary for the congregation errs in reciting the prayers, he is replaced by another prayer leader. In Shmuel's case, they let him remain as their emissary until the words came back to him.)[7]

The Chidah, a commentator on the Talmud, explains this story. He says that every person can sin by doing what shouldn't be done, and by not doing what should be done. These sins affect all of the different nurturings that God brings into this world. We can ruin our access to God's ability to give to us, or we can cause the giving to be mischanneled. When the Great Assembly instituted the Amidah, it was not designed to be a shopping list of things that people need. It was constructed in such a way that when any Jew says it, anywhere, it "fixes" the nurturing that God sends into the world. It "heals" the nurturing that God destines for the world but that we damage.

The only prayer that the Great Assembly did not institute was one to correct the nurturing that comes from the highest source. This source of nurturing is kabbalistically referred to as *ketter*, meaning "crown," or the Highest One. The reason they did not institute such a prayer was that they didn't believe people could ever do enough negative things to reach and corrupt this highest source of blessing. Thus there was no necessity for the men of the Great Assembly to create a correction for *ketter*.[8]

Rabbi Gamliel saw the impact of the Sadducees' rejection of the Oral Law. He saw their willingness to have Jews murdered in order to legitimize their heretical beliefs. In his wisdom he understood that these actions reached into, and destroyed, the highest realms of nurturing that God bestows onto the world. It was thus necessary that a prayer be created to correct this situation. Rabbi Gamliel realized that a defect was being created in the energy source with which God nurtures the world. He also realized that he was not equal to the task of creating a remedy for it. He therefore appealed to anyone who would know how to destroy the heretics, as well as know how to remove the negativity that they created, which corrupted the flow of nurturing from God to man.

Shmuel HaKatan was someone of such spiritual caliber that he was personally worthy of having the Divine Presence rest upon him. He therefore understood the flaw that was created by the heretics, as well as how to reconstruct that which was destroyed.

When Shmuel HaKatan originally recited the prayer against heretics, it was not said three times a day, as were the regular Shemoneh Esrai prayers. It was said only on the fast days, because on those days Jews prayed not only for personal redemption but for national redemption as well. If the Jews could say it only on days of national correction, that was to be preferred. Unfortunately, by the second year the rabbis realized that the extent of the heretics' damage was so great that daily prayer was required in order to rectify the situation.

Thus, the second time that Shmuel was required to compose the prayer, it needed to be done in a form that would effect the needed correction. Because it had to be a strong prayer, Shmuel needed three hours to compose it. He first had to make his own spiritual connection with God, and this involved meditating for three hours. Only then was he able to reconstruct the prayer so that it would have the necessary strength to become part of the Amidah as well as to affect the world in the desired manner.

Historically, the unique situation with the Sadducees died out after a number of years, and they are not a real force in contemporary times. Nevertheless, Rabbi Eibeshutz says that although the Sadducees died, the threat they posed takes different forms in each period of Jewish history. At one time the force came from Jews who converted to Catholicism. At another time it came from "Enlightened" Jews. Today that threat comes from "Messianic Jews," "Jews for Jesus," and the like. Unfortunately, the continuation of threats from within the Jewish people will never allow this nineteenth blessing to become obsolete until the time of the Messiah.[9]

Meaning of the Words

"Rebellious Sinners"

The term "rebellious sinners" refers to people who come from knowledgeable Jewish backgrounds, are well educated in Jewish law and philosophy, and then turn against their heritage. They are referred to as *zedim* in Hebrew. "The enemies of God" are people who try to eradicate the concept of God and spiritual values. "Rebellious sinners" and "enemies of God" are not necessarily synonymous.

Jews today who sin because of lack of knowledge about, or lack of background in, traditional Judaism are considered to be Jews who sin inadvertently. Many of the sins of people who are removed from their Jewish roots through no fault of their own, are considered acts for which they are not to be held culpable.

Rebellious sinners frequently need to be uprooted from their sources of strength and need to be broken. The intent of breaking such people is not simply to overpower them. Rather, it is to lead them to the humility whose absence led them to negativity. Unfortunately, we have only one recourse for someone who is not simply rebellious but is truly an enemy of God and who hates the Jewish people. That option is for the person to be totally cut off.

We normally pray for wicked people to repent, not be destroyed. We constantly ask God to enlighten people who don't truly appreciate the importance of loving God and doing His commandments. We pray that He will help them attain a true Jewish identity. However, some Jews from knowledgeable and observant Jewish backgrounds are so far removed from their spiritual roots and goals that they become connected to rebellious sins. Their premeditated rebellion can reach such a point that they need to be broken. Without the humility of being broken, there is no chance that they will come back to Judaism.

"Uproot, and Smash, and Break . . ."

Some Jews choose to return to Judaism, whereas others need to be forced to return. This latter group are those about whom we pray, "You should uproot, and smash, and break, and humble quickly." People who have built many barriers between themselves and God feel no need for Him in their lives. Such people believe in themselves so much that they have no room for awareness of God. They become aware of God only when they are forced to confront the limitations of their own power.

This is one type of rebellious Jew. There is another type, whose goal is to destroy the framework and fabric of Judaism. He does not believe in "live and let live." He believes that he is right, and until he proves to everybody else the veracity of his beliefs, which stand in opposition to Judaism, he will not rest. The "Jews for Jesus" are a contemporary example of this type. The goal of these people is to spiritually murder Jews.

In any legal system, murderers forfeit their rights to exist. We hope that such people regret what they do and that they become humble, but as long as they are busy murdering, we do not stand by idly. We don't wring our hands while hoping that murderers will change. The enemies of God who try to destroy Judaism must be dealt with in a similar manner. Enemies can be destructive to a point where we have no recourse but to ask God to take such people out of our midst.

Barriers to God's Giving

When we pray for the destruction of heretics, we simultaneously ask for the destruction of the barriers that prevent God's spiritual energies from reaching us. We are not interested in being vindictive, but we do need to destroy negative things that prevent positive energies from coming down to this world in their correct manner. This is both a national and a personal concern.

Rabbi Eibeshutz says that we must ask ourselves, "How many things have I done that don't allow God's nurturing energies to come to me?" Each of us must determine how much we destroy our own spiritual potentials. When we say the prayer against heretics, we must realize the harm we create by our own negative actions, speech, and thoughts. This is a personal as well as a national agenda.

It is easy for people to complain that God is not giving. God is giving, but the states of negativity that we create don't allow us fully to absorb the giving. In this prayer we ask God to help us get rid of the negativity which bars us from experiencing the fullness of whatever God wishes to grant us.

Rabbi Eibeshutz says that the real problem for the rabbis was that the national leaders were so busy countering the heretics' arguments that they could not address the spiritual concerns of the entire nation. This meant that the Jews' strongest feelings, which could have drawn down God's nurturing, could not be utilized appropriately.

We need to be aware of how far we can, and should, go in uprooting the negativity that keeps us away from God. Then we need to channel our energies into the positive things that allow God's intended goodness to reach us.

Implications of Heretics for Human Relationships

This prayer asks that heretics be completely eradicated. It implies that as soon as people become aware that outside influences are interfering in their lives, they must immediately put a complete stop to them. Doing this may include, for example, keeping out people who attempt to meddle in one's marriage or family, even if the meddlers are parents or in-laws. People who are likely to destroy a couple's relationship must not be tolerated.

This idea also suggests that heresy within a relationship not be countenanced. A marriage can become rocky simply because one or both spouses don't believe that it can work. When people become heretics about their marriage, their thoughts can lead to self-fulfilling prophecies. People doom their marriages when they enter them with thoughts about what will happen when their marriage ends. Such people balk at really committing themselves to the marriage at its inception. When each partner puts 50 percent into a marriage, he or she takes out 50 percent. It is only when each is committed 100 percent that the couple ends up with a complete marriage.

Harboring deep reservations that result in not fully committing oneself to a marriage will erode its very fiber. Heretical thoughts about one's marriage have no place once one is already married and wishes to maintain a healthy relationship.

Notes

1. Exodus 14:26–29.
2. *Shebolei Leket*, chapter 18.
3. Talmud *Bavli*, *Megillah* 17b.
4. Talmud *Bavli*, *Berakhot* 28b.
5. Talmud *Bavli*, *Berakhot* 28b.
6. Talmud *Bavli*, *Megillah* 17b.
7. Talmud *Bavli*, *Megillah* 17b.
8. Commentary on *Aggadot HaShas*.
9. Yaarot Devash on Shemoneh Esrai.

CHAPTER 16

Mainstay of the Righteous

עַל הַצַּדִּיקִים וְעַל הַחֲסִידִים, וְעַל זִקְנֵי עַמְּךָ בֵּית יִשְׂרָאֵל,
וְעַל פְּלֵיטַת סוֹפְרֵיהֶם, וְעַל גֵּרֵי הַצֶּדֶק וְעָלֵינוּ, יֶהֱמוּ נָא
רַחֲמֶיךָ יהוה אֱלֹהֵינוּ, וְתֵן שָׂכָר טוֹב לְכָל הַבּוֹטְחִים בְּשִׁמְךָ
בֶּאֱמֶת, וְשִׂים חֶלְקֵנוּ עִמָּהֶם לְעוֹלָם, וְלֹא נֵבוֹשׁ כִּי בְךָ
בָטָחְנוּ. בָּרוּךְ אַתָּה יהוה, מִשְׁעָן וּמִבְטָח לַצַּדִּיקִים.

On the righteous, and on the devout, and on the elders of
    Your nation, the house of Israel, and on the remnant of
their scholars, and on the righteous converts, and on us, please
bestow Your compassion, Lord our God, and give a good
reward to all those who trust in Your Name in truth. And put
our portion together with them forever, and we will not be
embarrassed, because we have trusted in You. Blessed are You,
God, Mainstay of, and Assurer to, the righteous.

Theme of the Prayer

In this prayer we single out the contribution that is made to the Jewish nation by each of five types of people. After singling them out, we ask for God to be compassionate to them and reward them appropriately for their trust in Him. We then ask God to also reward us in their merit, even if we don't personally fall into one of the five categories.

Rabbi Yonasan Eibeshutz says that people should pray for the welfare of the righteous and the devout because all of the good that we enjoy comes in their merit. "As long as there are righteous people in the world, there is good, and there is blessing, and there is life in this world."[1]

This is a unique prayer insofar as we recognize five groups as being critical components of the Jewish people. In the other prayers of the Shemoneh Esrai, we ask for things for ourselves as well as for the collective good of the Jewish people. Here we focus on five specific groups of people and ask that we be blessed together with them.

Historical Background

Jacob was 130 years old when he discovered that his son Joseph was alive in Egypt. He decided to see Joseph before he died. As he traveled down to Egypt, Jacob became very apprehensive about leaving the Holy Land. He was afraid because he realized that he was beginning the exile of the Jewish people.

Jacob had been very sad the entire time that he had thought Joseph was dead, and his state of sadness prevented the Divine Presence from visiting him. When he had misgivings about leaving Israel, God appeared to him for the first time in many years. The Almighty reassured him and urged him not to be afraid to go down to Egypt. "I will be with you when you go down, and I promise you that you will come up from Egypt, and Joseph will place his hands upon your eyes." This was an assurance from God that Joseph would tend to Jacob's last needs.[2]

Jacob had lived for many years thinking that Joseph had predeceased him. God told Jacob that not only weren't his fears true, but that Joseph would even be with him on his deathbed. In fact, when Jacob actually passed away, Joseph closed his father's eyes for the last time. This act inspired the angels to say, "Blessed are You, God, the Mainstay and Assurance of the Righteous." Jacob had trusted that God's promise to him would come true. When it did, the angels praised God.[3]

The Zohar explains this episode.[4] It says that at the moment of death, every person sees God for at least an instant before he passes away from this world. Were a person's eyes to remain open after this moment, they might see something after seeing the Divine Presence. We don't want this to happen. The sight of the Divine Presence is the greatest gift the soul can have, because meeting its Creator allows it more easily to make the transition between this world and the next. Once someone sees the greatest possible spiritual revelation, we don't want him or her to see anything else. Therefore, we close the eyes of the deceased immediately after death. It is considered especially meritorious for the deceased if his own children close his eyes. This act reflects on the parent's values that his or her children were concerned enough to preserve the greatest possible spiritual vision.

As long as Jacob thought that Joseph was dead, he believed that the leadership qualities of his son would be forever lost to the Jewish nation. Joseph represented everything that Jacob wanted for the continuity of the Jewish people. On the other hand, God had promised Jacob that all of the elements that were required to forge the Jewish nation would never be lost. God had earlier guaranteed Jacob that there would be an army of Jews who would represent Him in the world. Nevertheless, Jacob was concerned that the Jewish leader of the army was dead, even before the battles had begun.

When the situation unfolded in its entirety, Jacob realized that his son was physically alive. Nevertheless he was still concerned that Joseph might be spiritually dead from having lived with the Egyptians for many years. Therefore, Jacob did not completely stop mourning when he discovered that Joseph was alive. He needed to see that Joseph still had the leadership qualities that would enable the Jewish people to carry out their mission, which was to reveal God's presence to the world.

When Jacob began his trip to Egypt, God reassured him that Joseph still had his unique spiritual qualities. The greatest proof of that fact would be shown by Joseph's concern that Jacob not be exposed to anything other than the exalted vision of God when he passed away. Joseph's caring that Jacob's vision of God not be diminished on his deathbed would show that he had elevated himself above the depravity of Egypt and had maintained his spirituality.

When the angels witnessed this, they praised God with the blessing that He is the "Mainstay and the Assurance of the righteous." It was evident to the angels that the forces necessary to form the Jewish people were always kept alive. They realized that the promise made by God to the righteous Jacob had been kept.

This incident demonstrated that no matter how things appear, God always comes through with what we need as a people. We might live in all kinds of "Egyptian" societies, thinking that our requisite spiritual leaders are dead and feeling that the Jews don't have the spiritual wherewithal to remain a nation. Nevertheless, this episode says that the Jewish people will always be physically and spiritually alive. Therefore, anyone who supports our Jewish leaders can be assured that his or her energies will be productive in the end.

Relationship to the Previous Prayer

Unfortunately, there are individuals within the Jewish people who are our enemies and who are devoted to destroying

Judaism. The previous prayer refers to them. This prayer refers to those who suffer most from the destructive among us—the righteous, the elders, and so on. Their contributions to the Jewish nation are undermined by the "sinners" in the previous prayer. As soon as the sinners—the heretics—are put in their proper place, and their influence is diminished, the righteous can immediately take over. Their influence can then nurture the Jewish people in the way that it should.

Every Jew should feel responsible for living up to his or her individual potential. In addition, we should feel obligated to make the Jewish nation what it is supposed to be. A Jew cannot be righteous only for himself, unconcerned about the development of the entire Jewish nation. We must do whatever is necessary to nurture the health of the nation as a whole, even when doing so includes rooting out negative individuals such as heretics. We must be concerned with our personal development, but also with the people who act as our spokesmen and representatives. One of the most important things to God is the spiritual health of the Jewish people. If we care about God, then we must also care about that which concerns Him, that is, the climate of the Jews as a nation.

In this prayer we acknowledge that we may individually fall short of our potential but we are nonetheless concerned with the nation as a whole. We pray for the spiritual health of those who carry the banner of Judaism, and think of ourselves as being connected to a greater whole. When we support and protect our leaders, we make statements about where we belong. If we believe in what they strive to accomplish, then we have a responsibility to fight for them and to protect them.

The Five Types of People We Pray For

We identify five groups of Jews in this prayer. "The righteous" (*tzaddikim*) are those who are meticulous in performing all of God's expectations of them and who carefully observe all of the commandments (mitzvot). According to certain commentators, these individuals are people who have never sinned.[5]

"The devout" (chassidim*) are those who are meticulous in their own personal observances and also do good deeds on behalf of others. They go above and beyond the call of duty. "Chassidim" are on a higher spiritual level than tzaddikim.

According to another interpretation, the word chassidim refers to baalei teshuvah, people who have sinned and then repented.[†] This interpretation is derived from a psalm of King David, which he composed after sinning with Batsheva. In that psalm, he asks God to guard his soul and make sure that it would not be disconnected from its source of holiness, "because I am a chassid."[6] When people sin and then repent, they often have to do more than is required by the law in order to rectify their spiritual state and to reinstate their relationship with God. Here we pray for tzaddikim, who never did anything wrong, as well as for chassidim, who sinned and repented. Both of these groups are integral parts of the Jewish people.

"The elders" are the Jewish sages who make decisions that mold the quality and direction of the Jewish people. They are the same people who are referred to in the prayer for the restoration of justice.

"The remnants of scholars" refers to the scholars who develop the Torah's wisdom with the intensity with which it was given at Mount Sinai. Their wisdom comes from exhaustively studying the text of the Torah, without violating its integrity. They are described as "remnants" because they remain a very small group.

Another interpretation of "the remnants of the scholars" is that they are those who teach Torah to young children. We invest our children with the hopes and goals that we want to come to fruition in the next generation.[7]

---

* The term chassidim in this prayer is not to be confused with the modern term Chassidim. The colloquial term refers to followers of the Baal Shem Tov, or to members of Chassidic sects who follow his teachings.
† The term baal teshuvah is not to be confused with the colloquial usage of this term, which denotes someone from a nonobservant Jewish background who becomes observant.

"The righteous converts to Judaism" were not originally included in the prayer composed by the men of the Great Assembly but were mentioned later by Rabbi Gamliel the Elder. He lived at a time when the Jews suffered tremendously from the persecutions meted out by the nations of the world. Paradoxically, there was a rush of sincere converts to Judaism at that time. Rabbi Gamliel felt that these converts had made a magnificent statement about truth. They deserved, therefore, to be prayed for so that they wouldn't buckle under the pressure of everything negative going on around them.[8] There is a special commandment in the Torah that requires us to "love the convert to Judaism," and we should make every effort to uphold this mitzvah.

Rabbi Eibeshutz, who lived several centuries ago, said that when we say this prayer for the righteous, we should particularly pray for the welfare of the righteous converts to Judaism. We should love them as we love ourselves. He wrote: "This is especially so in our time, when we are trampled upon by so many nations of the world, and they try to make us bite the dust. We have almost no more moral strength left, and the wicked people are on top of the world. The convert, who, in spite of everything, is willing to recognize the real truth, acts like our forefather Abraham did in his time. We are required to love this person and to kiss the earth on which he walks, and to pray very earnestly for his welfare. Let not the challenge of his turning to Judaism be too difficult for him, lest he turn back (to whence he came). The purpose of the Jews' exile all over the world is so that they will bring back those who belong in the fold of the Jewish people."[9]

The convert is a person who leaves what the majority of the world believes in and rewards, in order to join a group that is a tiny minority. This person is especially precious to us because he or she is such a special role model. He or she testifies that regardless of the spiritual darkness which pervades the world, regardless of the "Egypts" that rule the world, truth still shines out. Every righteous convert bears testimony to the fact that regardless of the insignificance of our numbers as Jews, the message we bring to the world will never die out.

Meaning of the Words

"And Give a Good Reward to All Those Who Trust in Your Name in Truth"

The Seder HaYom says that we are not as meticulous or perfect in our actions as are the five groups of people mentioned in this prayer, but our hopes and spirits are in the right places. The five groups of people deserve reward because both their hearts and their actions are in the right places. Since our hearts are in the right places with them, and we strive to emulate them, we deserve to share in God's response to them.[10]

Other commentators interpret this verse to mean that the people who really trust God are those in the five categories just enumerated. They should be rewarded in the hereafter for their efforts.[11]

Some commentators object to this interpretation. They maintain that it is not fitting for Jews to pray that righteous people should be rewarded in the next world for their actions in this world. Their reward is not our concern. We have faith that God is trustworthy and honest, and we believe that He will recompense the righteous even without our prayers. According to these commentators, this verse means that those who trust God should be rewarded so that they will not seem foolish to the rest of the world because of their belief in God. We pray that someone who trusts God during a crisis, and refuses to let it overwhelm him, should be rewarded by God's coming through for him in the crisis. We want to demonstrate visibly to the rest of the world that if we trust God, we won't be shown to be fools.[12]

Another interpretation states that the five special groups of Jews deserve reward for their piety and spiritual endeavors. In addition to this reward, we ask God to give them an additional reward for their unflagging trust in Him. It is one thing for people to ask God for what they need and for God to give it to them because they truly need it. God gives a secondary reward, above and beyond what is necessary, when people trust Him enough to ask Him for things rather than trying to get them through other sources. The act of trust, in and of itself, carries with it a separate, special reward.

"And Put Our Portion Together with Them Forever"

We always want to be together with the righteous. We never want to leave them, even though our behavior may not be on the same spiritual plane as is theirs.

Another explanation of this verse has to do with the effects of being erratic in our spiritual behavior. We create spiritual reservoirs within us when we observe the commandments and develop our spirituality. However, if our spiritual behavior is inconsistent, these spiritual reservoirs become trapped. We have no access to them because our inappropriate actions close off the "pipelines" that connect us to these reservoirs. When we ask God for "our portion to be together with them," we ask Him to give these five righteous groups the portion of spirituality that we have built but cannot access. These righteous individuals who love us will always be able to access these spiritual wells, and they will give this untapped spirituality back to us in ways that will benefit us.[13]

This occurred when the Jews received the Torah. The Midrash says that the people promised God that they would observe the commandments of the Torah and would then learn how to do them in detail (*naaseh venishma*). In reward for their commitment, they were given golden crowns as symbols of their spiritual greatness. Forty days later they made the Golden Calf, and God took away their crowns. The Zohar says that when the crowns were taken away from the Jewish people, they were given to Moses. This meant that Moses, through his inspirational teaching of all of the Jews, would give them back all of their "crowns" (spiritual greatness).[14]

"And We Will Not Be Embarrassed"

Prior to reciting the Shema (Affirmation of God's Unity), we say, "Let us never be ashamed forever because we have trusted in Your holy and great Name." The Vilna Gaon says that we might be embarrassed insofar as we know what truth is but our actions don't totally correspond to it. Our inconsistencies might subject us to ridicule. Nevertheless, whenever we believe the truth, even though our actions might not totally correspond to what we know is right, we can ask God not to shame us and to redeem us from exile. We merit God's bringing us out of exile in a way that we won't be embarrassed, simply by trusting in a Torah way of life and in what its leaders represent.

The Dover Shalom suggests a second explanation of this verse. He says that there is a certain lack of dignity in being dependent on another human being. Most people want to feel that whatever they have accomplished, they have done on their own. This verse says that we will never feel ashamed for our trust in and dependence on God. It is our privilege to know that we can throw all of our problems onto God and that He can shoulder them. We don't feel embarrassed by this.[15]

Rabbi Yonasan Eibeshutz says that this verse is our plea to God that we should not be embarrassed when we leave this world.[16] This concept of embarrassment is discussed in the Zohar. True shame results from something being identified as part of a person when it really is not. (This is not the same type of embarrassment that a person feels when he or she is caught doing something wrong). In this world, we want people to perceive us in a certain way, and we feel embarrassed when they don't see us that way. In the next world, where we see absolute truth, we don't want to be embarrassed to ourselves. When we leave this world, we don't want to be exposed for having been far off the mark of reality.

When we leave this world, we will each meet the souls of our relatives from earlier generations, and they will ask us questions such as: "How could you have done such and such a thing?" "How could you have acted in such a way? Your actions were not becoming of your pedigree, and you strayed away from the heritage of your ancestors who brought you into the earthly world."

As hard as some Jews might try to tear themselves away from earlier generations and "inherited" spiritual values, every Jew eventually has to face the awesome reality that he or she is part of a chain. We can never ultimately escape confronting who we really are and who we really should have been. Somewhere along the line, each of us will meet up with a saintly ancestor who will ask, "Are you truly my grandson?" or "Are you truly my great-granddaughter?"

In this prayer, we say that since we support the five groups

of saintly people, we ask not to be embarrassed when we leave
this world. We want to feel comfortable when we confront our
ancestors and face up to who we were and who we should
have been.

God as Mainstay of the Righteous

We conclude this prayer by saying, "Blessed are You, God,
Mainstay of, and Assurer to, the righteous." When we say that
God is a "Mainstay" of the righteous, we mean that whenever
things are dismal, the righteous person can always lean on
God. These people can know that He will ultimately come
through for them. As long as the righteous person fights for
God's goals, God will not desert His troops.

The Suffering of the Righteous

This prayer addresses a theological difficulty of many Jews.
When Jacob led his family into Egypt, he was afraid that their
spiritual purity would be lost, both through their living in an
impure land with depraved people, and through the suffering
they would endure. The Jews have been in exile for over 1,900
years, during which time they have been very oppressed by
the nations of the world. Over the past centuries some of
Jacob's descendants have had two erroneous attitudes about
being in exile: Some people have thought that the Jews' suffering was evidence that their beliefs were false and that they
should have switched their allegiances and beliefs. Others have
thought that even though the Jews' beliefs were correct, God
had given up on them and on the Jewish people.

Many people believe that if they hold the right beliefs, they
should never suffer. The Jew's appropriate response to national
suffering is to say, "I don't know exactly why we are suffering,
but I will never lose my faith that the Torah values are those to
which I should adhere." This enduring faith is the reason why
we should be included with those who are greater than we are,
and why we merit being redeemed from exile with them.

When we ask in this prayer not to be embarrassed, we mean
that we don't want the humiliation we would feel if we and our

leaders were not redeemed from the spiritual darkness that often rules the world. Even when we suffer, we have faith that God will redeem us just as He redeemed Joseph by not abandoning him when he was in Egypt. In the merit of our overriding trust in God's ultimate plan for our redemption, and by our identifying with those who devote their lives to doing God's will, we can join in the reward of the righteous.

Implications of the Righteous for Human Relationships

When a person sees an admirable quality in a spouse or other partner, the person should not feel threatened by it. Rather, he or she should praise, encourage, strengthen and want to connect with that quality. In this way, the one who lacks that specific quality can unite with it.

This prayer suggests that if someone has qualities of excellence and distinction that are lacking in someone else—for example, one's spouse—the latter can still reap the benefits of those qualities. By having the emotional maturity to adore a spouse's assets, one may strengthen the marital relationship.

Notes

1. Yaarot Devash on Shemoneh Esrai.
2. Genesis 46:4.
3. *Shebolei Leket*, chapter 18.
4. Gesher HaChaim.
5. Avudraham, Commentary on *Tefillah*.
6. Psalms 86:2.
7. Etz Yosef in *Otsar HaTefillot*.
8. Yaarot Devash on Shemoneh Esrai.
9. Yaarot Devash on Shemoneh Esrai.
10. Seder HaYom, Commentary on *Tefillah*.
11. Etz Yosef in *Otsar HaTefillot*.
12. Iyun Tefillah in *Otsar HaTefillot*.
13. Etz Yosef, quoting Naggid U'Mitzvah.
14. *Pre Zaddik Shekalim*.
15. *Otsar HaTefillot*.
16. Yaarot Devash on Shemoneh Esrai.

CHAPTER 17

The One Who Rebuilds Jerusalem

וְלִירוּשָׁלַיִם עִירְךָ בְּרַחֲמִים תָּשׁוּב, וְתִשְׁכּוֹן בְּתוֹכָהּ כַּאֲשֶׁר
דִּבַּרְתָּ, וּבְנֵה אוֹתָהּ בְּקָרוֹב בְּיָמֵינוּ בִּנְיַן עוֹלָם,
וְכִסֵּא דָוִד מְהֵרָה לְתוֹכָהּ תָּכִין. בָּרוּךְ אַתָּה יהוה, בּוֹנֵה
יְרוּשָׁלַיִם.

❦❦❦❦❦❦❦❦❦❦❦❦❦

And to Jerusalem Your city You should return with compassion, and You should dwell there as You have told us You would. And build it (the Temple within Jerusalem) very soon, and in our days, as an everlasting building. And may You speedily establish the throne of David within it. Blessed are You, God, who builds Jerusalem.

Theme of the Prayer

God's greatest presence is not to be found in a particular, fixed place. Paradoxically, He is to be found most easily where people feel anguish over His absence. This is so because the people who feel anguished that God's presence is in hiding are those who are most open to a total relationship with God. Wherever Jews are dispersed throughout the Diaspora and are anguished over the lack of God's presence, God is present with them.

This is what is meant by the concept that God is in exile with the Jewish people. This doesn't mean that God has physically relocated Himself; it means that He is conceptually in exile for the Jewish people. He no longer has the same significance or importance to them that He had when He was able to manifest Himself in the Temple in Jerusalem. Thus, in contemporary times, God is wherever people yearn for Him and appreciate His importance.

Historical Background

When King Solomon finished building the First Temple, the angels exclaimed, "Blessed are You, God, who builds Jerusalem."[1] This event reinforced the idea that people have the ability to heighten the reality of God for themselves through the building of the Temple. The angels marveled at this concept. Intellectually, we can appreciate the concept that God is a reality. But when human beings, through their dedication, determination, and resourcefulness, allow the presence of God to be sensed more in one place than in another, this is a remarkable thing. People need to feel the reality of God in their lives. When Solomon made the presence of God tangible to people by causing the Temple to be built, the angels thanked

223

God for allowing a place to be built where people could experience an extra "dose" of the reality of His existence.

It is interesting that the angels said this blessing when Solomon erected the Temple. We say it now that the Temple has been destroyed. The Sfat Emet, a commentator, explains that when this prayer was said in Temple times, it was a request for God to allow the Temple's continued existence. The Jews didn't take for granted that the Temple would always exist. They understood that it was a gift that had to be constantly appreciated. Since the Temple's destruction, we have been saying this blessing as a request for it to be rebuilt. Inasmuch as we were once worthy of having a Temple, this is not a "pie-in-the-sky" request. Now we ask God to return something to us that was once ours. Thus this blessing has meant different things at different times in Jewish history.[2]

Relationship to the Previous Prayer

This is the fourteenth prayer of the Shemoneh Esrai. The fact that it begins with the conjunction "and" tells us that it is conceptually connected to the previous prayer. One explanation of this connection is advanced by the Levush.[3] The prayer for Jerusalem immediately follows the prayer for the righteous because they are interrelated. God takes care of the righteous because they stand for something glorious. We ask that they receive the honor and respect to which they are entitled, since they dedicate themselves to contributing to the world. Once they are properly appreciated, they should have the influence that emanates from that appreciation and respect.

The concept of "Jerusalem" parallels this idea. "Jerusalem" is not simply a geographical location. It signifies that there is a place in the world where God is recognized. Just as we pray for the recognition of those who fight for the realization of God, we also pray for the place from which the reality of God should radiate. Jerusalem is the place that publicizes the greatness and respect due to God.

When the prophets speak about the honor of Jerusalem, they also speak about the honor of its inhabitants, and vice versa. They are inseparable. When people proclaim God, the place in which they live also proclaims God. When there are righteous people in the world, they teach people how to have appropriate respect for God. When Jerusalem stands in its glory, the place stands as a monument to the proper respect that people should have for God.

According to another commentator, the Iyun Tefillah, there is a different connection between the prayer for the righteous and the prayer for Jerusalem. As long as a *tzaddik* (righteous person) is not respected and is trampled upon, he is in anguish. As long as he suffers, God says that He has no comfort in being in Jerusalem. His place is to be with those who are in pain. If there is a *tzaddik* in anguish anywhere in the world, God doesn't want to go to His home (Jerusalem). He wants to be with the *tzaddik*, to give him the necessary strength and support so that he will not be crushed by the disrespect that he endures. Only after we have ensured the welfare of the righteous through our prayers can we then ask God to return to Jerusalem.[4]

Meaning of the Words

"Return with Compassion, and . . . Dwell There"

In this prayer, we ask God to return to Jerusalem in His compassion, and to live there, in its present state of destruction. The Vilna Gaon interprets this idea as follows: Even though Jerusalem and the Temple have been destroyed, God says that the holiness that He dedicated to Jerusalem remains there. In this prayer, we ask God to return to Jerusalem in such a way that His immanence will be felt. Even if we are not worthy of His making His presence felt in the same way as He formerly did, we ask Him to dwell there in the midst of its desolation in some capacity.

When God destroyed the Temple, He did not make a total and final departure from the land of Israel. We ask God to keep His holiness in Jerusalem so that we can yearn for His complete presence. Were His entire presence to disappear from Jerusalem, we would no longer retain any means by which we could relate to Him. If we couldn't relate to Him, then we certainly wouldn't yearn for Him. His maintaining some part of His holiness there allows our souls to feel the reality that was once part and parcel of the Jews' daily life in Jerusalem. When we feel that holiness, we can yearn for it to return to our lives.[5]

We thus have an interesting combination of God manifesting his reality in Israel, while not doing so in the way that we would like. The reality of His presence is so strong that the experience of being in the land of Israel has a tremendous impact on almost any Jew who goes there. A Jew in Israel has the capacity to realize that the Jewish people today are not what we were, while at the same time feeling a very strong presence of God.

"And Build It Very Soon . . . as an Everlasting Building"

Both the First and Second Temples were built by Jews who had certain spiritual deficiencies, and they were therefore built with certain human limitations. That is why they were capable of eventually being destroyed. The Third Temple will be built at a time when Jews will have reached such spiritual heights that we say that God Himself will build that Temple. At that time, Jews will have a relationship with God that transcends the laws of nature. Although people will build the Third Temple, it will not have the limitations of human endeavors and will never be destroyed.

The First and Second Temples were built with human and earthly materials. On the other hand, we say that the Third Temple will be built with *chomat aish*—"walls of fire." This refers not only to heavenly fire, but also to the fires within us. The levels of spirituality at that time will be all-consuming, made of a burning desire to draw close to God. The devotion to, and love of God will be so intense, they will build a Temple that will be impervious to physical destruction.

"Who Builds Jerusalem"

This concluding phrase is in the present tense, even though it seems to refer to God's rebuilding Jerusalem in the future. The Vilna Gaon explains that when blessings say that God does something in the present, they mean that we see some aspect of that behavior in the present, even if the major part of the act will not be apparent until the future.

For example, the second prayer of the Shemoneh Esrai ends with the words, "Blessed are You, God, who resurrects the dead." That blessing refers to something that partially occurs in the present, although its fullest manifestation will be in the future. The Talmud says that there are four groups of people who lack certain opportunities which prevent them from being fully alive: the blind, those who are so poor that they can dedicate themselves only to sheer survival, lepers who are socially excommunicated, and those who have no children.[6] God can help bring a higher dimension to these people's lives while they are alive, even though in one respect they are missing a fundamental ability to live fully. There is an ongoing resurrection that God provides to these four groups of people.

The seventh blessing of the Shemoneh Esrai is, "Blessed are You, God, Redeemer of Israel" (*Goel Yisrael*). This refers to redemption that occurs on a constant basis, when God provides people with challenges, crises, and tragedies which bring out qualities that had been locked away as mere potentials. The difficult situations make these important qualities come out of captivity. In addition, God is a redeemer in assisting us in redeeming these qualities.

In similar fashion, when we say, "Blessed are You, God, who builds Jerusalem," we may not know how that building occurs on a spiritual level. However, we do know that from every sad event and difficulty that we experience, and from every spiritual challenge that we undergo, individually and collectively, some spiritual contribution is made to the rebuilding of Jerusalem. This indirect form of building contributes to the "walls of fire" which will form the basis of the everlasting Third Temple.

The Talmud says that any generation who does not merit the rebuilding of the Temple is considered to have destroyed it. This idea is difficult to reconcile with the fact that many generations had tremendously righteous people in their midsts. How can we blame these righteous individuals and say that they were partly responsible for the lack of the Temple's being rebuilt? Furthermore, is it conceivable that as we go further away from the time of the Temple, people will be more meritorious and righteous than our ancestors? We don't believe that any future generation would have such merit that they alone would be worthy of rebuilding a Temple that would be everlasting.

The Sfat Emet offers a deeper insight into the idea that Jerusalem is constantly being rebuilt. This idea is based on the above talmudic statement.[7] He explains that the Temple is constantly being rebuilt through the merit of every commandment that is observed, through every good deed that is done, and through every spiritual thought that is contributed by the Jews in exile over thousands of years.[8] Every Jew contributes to the rebuilding of the Temple, and we are constantly progressing toward that goal. Every prayer, every act of dedication to God, and every good deed we do is a spiritual brick in the foundation of the Third Temple. When the Temple is rebuilt, it will be because it has already been built. The spiritual "walls of fire" will have already been dedicated through the spiritual contributions of generations of Jews throughout their exile.

When the Talmud says that any generation who does not see the Temple rebuilt is viewed as having destroyed it, it means that any generation that doesn't contribute its "spiritual bricks" to the Temple's reconstruction is seen as having destroyed it. The future Temple requires everybody's bricks. If any generation does not contribute its share, the Temple will be lacking a certain spiritual foundation. Thus every single Jew has a portion to contribute to the rebuilding of the Temple.

This idea explains why the future Temple is referred to as a *binyan olam*. This can be translated as either "an eternal building" or as a "building of the entire world." This building will be a collective effort of all Jews over all generations, in their glorious times and in their tragedies. During the tragedies, every cry to God, every tear that was shed, every groan that was made in an effort to find God contributed to the rebuilding of Jerusalem. From the day the first tears were shed over the destruction of the Second Temple, the next Temple was already in the process of being built.

Throne of King David

In this prayer we intertwine the concepts of the rebuilding of Jerusalem with the resurrection of the Davidic dynasty. Just as the First Temple was established through the values for which King David stood, so will the final Temple be built by virtue of his values.

The First Temple was built because King David felt that it was inappropriate for him to live in a house built of cedar trees while the Tablets of the Covenant and God's Presence dwelled in a tent. He very much wanted to build a special place where God would reside. Thus, the initiation of the building of the Temple emanated from David's heart. However, God told David that he could not build the Temple because he had "spilled much blood" in many wars. God was pleased by these wars, because David fought them only so that God's will could be practiced in a greater way. Nevertheless, David was forbidden to build the Temple.

The Midrash says that another reason David was denied the ability to build the Temple was that had he done so, the Temple would have stood forever.[9] An everlasting Temple at that time would not have been to the ultimate benefit of the Jewish people. God foresaw that the Jews would sin so greatly in the future that they would not be worthy of the Temple. In those times, they would deserve to die, and God would need to destroy the Temple in order to spare the Jewish people. This idea indicates that the spiritual level of David was greater than that of his son Solomon, since the Temple of Solomon was eventually destroyed. Had David built it, the Temple would have existed forever—but the Jewish people would, God forbid, have been destroyed.

The Midrash says that King David was allowed to build the foundations of the Temple, but not the Temple proper.[10] The spiritual energy that David generated through his tremendous yearning to build the Temple was not ignored or lost. It became etched into time and remains a spiritual entity which helps the Jews yearn, throughout their exiles, for the rebuilding of the Third Temple.

Thus, the foundations of the Temple can be understood to be the Jews' yearnings for God to dwell in their midst in an intimate and glorified manner. Whenever Jews say the Psalms, written by King David, it creates a yearning in their hearts that connects them to King David's yearnings to build God a Temple. As a result, the Temple that David would have built is that which we build every day by virtue of our actions and feelings. David couldn't build an eternal Temple because the Jews weren't ready for one. Nevertheless, David contributed to the world—and to the soul of the Jewish people—that quality that is capable of building an eternal Temple—and will do so.

This prayer doesn't speak about the "Temple of David," but refers to the "throne" of David. It did not make sense to David that he resided in a house of cedar while God resided in a tent. David understood that his royalty and kingdom drew all of their strength from the fact that he represented God in this world. Thus it seemed illogical that God's representative lived in a better residence than the Source itself. Everything that David's royalty represented—glory, honor, splendor, power— were really nothing more than reflections of these attributes as they pertained to God. The "throne of David" is a representation of the honor due to God.

In this prayer we ask God to bring back a royalty that will have David's understanding that its sole function is to help the Jewish nation, and the world, realize God. We cannot ask for a rebuilding of the Temple without also asking for royalty that will bring the realization of God to the people.

The essence of this prayer is that we yearn for redemption and for the spirituality that is our mission to bring to the world. The yearning itself is a spiritual creation that will eventually bear fruit.

Implications of Jerusalem for Human Relationships

Jerusalem symbolizes a home in which God dwells, where His reality is obvious. This is a critical component of human relationships. There should be an obvious presence of God in any home we build. We must make our homes places in which God also feels "comfortable" dwelling.

Notes

1. *Shebolei Leket*, chapter 18.
2. *Siddur Likutei Yehuda*.

3. *Otsar HaTefillot.*
4. *Otsar HaTefillot.*
5. *Siddur HaGra.*
6. Talmud *Bavli, Nedarim* 54b.
7. *Siddur Likutei Yehuda.*
8. *Siddur Likutei Yehuda, Se'ach Yitzchak* (*Siddur HaGra*).
9. *Midrash Shocher Tov* 62:4.
10. Talmud *Bavli, Succah* 53a.

CHAPTER 18

He Who Makes the Glory of Salvation Flourish

אֶת צֶמַח דָּוִד עַבְדְּךָ מְהֵרָה תַצְמִיחַ, וְקַרְנוֹ תָּרוּם
בִּישׁוּעָתֶךָ, כִּי לִישׁוּעָתְךָ קִוִּינוּ כָּל הַיּוֹם. בָּרוּךְ אַתָּה
יהוה, מַצְמִיחַ קֶרֶן יְשׁוּעָה.

Make the offspring of David, Your servant, sprout forth
quickly, and raise his glory in Your salvation, because
we hope for Your salvation all day. Blessed are You, God, who
makes the glory of salvation flourish.

Historical Background

At the time of the Exodus, the Israelites left Egypt and journeyed into the desert. A short time later, Pharaoh regretted having let them go. He summoned his soldiers and they pursued the Israelites, hoping to reconquer them and bring them back to slavery. With the Egyptians in pursuit, the Israelites came to the Red Sea, which formed a barrier in front of them. They were completely entrapped between the sea in front of them, and the Egyptians behind them. At that point God miraculously made the Red Sea split, allowing the Israelites to cross safely on dry land. The Egyptians, in hot pursuit, crossed the sea after them, and God drowned them. When the Israelites saw that their assailants had been killed, they praised God with the Song of the Sea.[1] While they sang God's praises, the angels simultaneously sang, "Blessed are You, God, who makes the glory of salvation flourish."[2]

By the time the Israelites and the angels sang these praises to God, the acts they acclaimed were already finished. It would be understandable for the angels to exclaim that God makes salvation sprout while they were seeing the redemption develop. In this situation, however, the angels were in essence looking back with hindsight when they exclaimed that God makes salvation grow (into future redemption). In order to understand this blessing, we must first understand the meaning of the song that the Jews sang at the Red Sea.

The Song of the Red Sea

The Midrash says that until the Jews sang praises to God at the Red Sea, no one had ever praised God with song.[3] This is baffling, since there were many people prior to this event who were miraculously saved. One such person was Abraham, who was rescued from the fiery furnace of Nimrod. It is inconceivable that these people had not praised God for their personal salvation.

Another midrash says that the song the Jews sang at that time came out of wisdom (*chochmah*).[4] This also seems problematic. If an entire nation were pursued by murderers and the people were miraculously saved, it wouldn't take too much wisdom to be thankful afterwards. What does it mean to say that this act required wisdom?

A third midrash comments on the first word of the Song of the Red Sea, "*Then* (Moses will sing)" (Az *yashir Moshe*). When Moses first went to Pharaoh to plead on behalf of the Jewish people, things subsequently became worse for the Israelites. Moses then complained to God, "From the time that I came to Pharaoh, things have become worse for the Jews" ("*Me'az bati el Paroh* . . ."). Moses started his complaint with the word *az*. He wasn't punished for what he said, because he spoke out of pain for his Jewish brethren. Nevertheless, his manner of complaint was somewhat inappropriate. Therefore, when Moses finally saw the salvation of God, he used the same word, *az*, to praise God in the Song of the Sea, as a corrective for his earlier inappropriate complaint.[5]

When the Israelites went into the desert, the Red Sea was ahead of them and the Egyptians behind them. The reason they didn't flee to the right or to the left, as they normally would have done, was because God brought ferocious animals on either side of them on that specific day. The Midrash says that the Jews at that time were compared to a dove that is stuck in the crevices of a cave. If it leaves the crevices, it will be devoured by a hawk, and it it withdraws into the cave, it will find serpents within.[6] The Jews' task was to realize that God created this situation for a distinct spiritual purpose: When people are saved from a crisis, they normally feel grateful to God. The Israelites could have said to God, "You want us to thank You for saving us? You are the one who created this crisis altogether. You are the one who brought in animals on both of our sides, thereby preventing our escape." When confronted with their situation, the Israelites were not quite sure what their reactions should have been. By using their wisdom, they understood that God's actions had a purpose. They were intended to show the world that God is the Master and Controller of everything that happens. He created the crisis in order to manifest Himself in this way and to demonstrate that when people are in danger, God will help them if they will only turn to Him.

When the Jews realized this, they thanked God for having designated them for their unique mission: Demonstrating God's presence and power in the lives of human beings. This was the message of the Song of the Sea; and this is why we thank God for allowing us to be the people who are endowed with the mission of revealing Him to the world. Our recognition of this mission will help us to survive hard times and crises. But when the Midrash says that prior to the Song of the Sea, no one had ever praised God, it doesn't mean that Adam and all the Patriarchs and Matriarchs never thanked God for saving them. It means that the Israelites had to use their wisdom to understand why God had created the crisis at the Red Sea. They were the first people to thank God for being chosen to proclaim God's presence and power to the world. The Song is a praise to God for their having been selected for this role. It is also a statement of the Jews' gratitude upon realizing their purpose in this world. The Song emanated from a feeling of joy in having all doubt removed as to what their goals in life were to be. When they clearly saw the direction that their lives were supposed to take, they felt exhilarated and thankful.

This concept clarifies why Moses began the Song with the word, *az*. When he first complained to God that the oppression of the Jews was getting worse and worse, he did so because their tribulations seemed to have no direction. When he saw their salvation at the Red Sea, he understood that there was a purpose behind all of their suffering, namely, to create a greater proclamation of God's existence. When Moses sang the Song, he did so not only for that specific salvation, but for all of the troubles that had befallen the Jews—troubles for which he could then see a higher purpose.

The more someone suffers, the greater is the revelation of God that follows it. Jews do not sing praise to God only for being saved. We sing for the entire process of salvation, including that which was painful, because it ultimately reveals God's involvement in the world.

When God allowed Pharaoh's tremendous power to be seen by all, it made people think that there was no power in the world greater than Pharaoh's. Had Pharaoh's power not seemed so absolute, God's vanquishing him and rescuing the Israelites would not have been so impressive. When God drowned Pharaoh and his hosts, it became evident to the world that God is greater than even the greatest of human beings and that He ultimately controls the world.

It is only in retrospect that we truly understand the meaning of why we must go through certain difficulties. At that point, we can praise God for both our salvation and our troubles. Since the Jews at the Red Sea sang a song not only for their salvation but for all of the preceding crises, the angels exclaimed that God caused salvation to grow slowly over time. The event at the Red Sea was only a culmination of this long process of salvation.

Meaning of the Words

"The Offspring of David"

The essence of King David's soul allowed him to generate an abiding faith from all of the crises through which he lived. This faith was that a budding salvation would eventually emanate from it all. The Psalms that David wrote are an expression of this faith. This is why King David is associated with the idea of salvation, so that we say, "the offspring of David" should soon flourish.

According to some commentators, the word *tzemach* should not be translated as "offspring." Rather they view it as the name of the Messiah. The prophet Zechariah said, "Behold, a man by the name of Tzemach will come, and from him will sprout forth and rebuild the Temple."[7] Therefore, *tzemach* could mean the same thing in the prayer for redemption, and this prayer could also be translated, "The Messiah, descendant of David (Your servant), should soon sprout forth."

"Sprout Forth Quickly"

In this prayer we ask for the offspring of David to "sprout forth quickly"—for the Davidic dynasty to sprout and then develop and flourish. But it will not appear suddenly; rather, it will grow through a slow process. Nevertheless, we pray for this to happen quickly. How are these two ideas to be reconciled?

The redemption of the Jewish people is a lengthy process. It is called "sprouting" because the process happens as gradually as a plant grows. One who continually watches a plant grow will not notice the plant changing, yet over time it is obvious that the plant grew. We cannot see how each period of Jewish history contributed to the process of redemption any better than a person can watch a plant grow. The process of redemption is a growth process because that is the best way for us to absorb it. Were redemption to occur suddenly one day, we wouldn't be able to appreciate it. In this prayer, we realize that we must grow into a state of readiness for redemption. Nevertheless, we ask God to make the growth process happen as quickly as possible—like a fast-growing plant, not like a slow-growing one.

"Because We Hope for Your Salvation All Day"

When we refer in this prayer to "Your salvation," we don't mean that God needs to be saved. We mean that, for the sake of the world, we don't want the idea of God to disappear. The salvation of the world requires a growth process, but we worry that the longer crises continue, the more God's reality becomes removed from the world. Our major concern as a people is that the world should not forget the reality of God.

The major exhilaration of the Israelites at the Red Sea was that people would no longer be able to deny the reality and power of God. It was of less concern to them that they personally had been saved. In this prayer, we ask God for the same opportunity that our ancestors appreciated at the Red Sea.

"Raise His Glory (Horn)"

The word *karno* is usually translated as "his horn." In this prayer it is translated as "his glory," referring to the anointing

of kings. Jewish kings used to be anointed with oil poured
from a horn. Since kings embody glory, the symbol of a horn
alludes to glory.

The Talmud refers to our blowing the shofar on Rosh Hashanah (the Jewish New Year). We recite verses that refer to
God as a king and as a God who remembers mankind, and
"we do this all with a shofar."[8] The commentators explain that
we blow the shofar to help us accept God's dominion over us.
The Ritva, a commentator, says that we do this with a ram's
horn because a Jewish king was always anointed using a shofar.
Since we demonstrate the authority of a mortal king by blowing
the shofar, so too do we show on Rosh Hashanah that God is
our King and the director of our lives. Just as a king has his
coronation, we have a similar ceremony for God.[9]

Rabbi Hutner explains further that the function of the shofar
was not simply to make noise, after which people exclaim,
"Long live the king." Every day of the week has a special Psalm
recited on it, and the one for Friday says, "God became King
(on the sixth day)."[10] Man was created on the sixth day and
was immediately able to accept God as his King. The phenomenon of royalty began when man was created, when "God
blew into man's nostrils a soul of life (from God's very own
essence),"[11] making it possible for man to proclaim and to
mirror God's royalty. Because the first moment of royalty was
when God blew His essence into man, the blowing of the
shofar will forever be that which brings royalty into the world.

The Jews' greatest yearning is for the world to realize God's
Kingship over it. This is why we say, "And raise his glory in
Your salvation." The royalty that the soul brings into this world
manifests the existence of God. We ask God to make it illumi-
nate the world so that His salvation will be obvious.

When we blow the ram's horn, we do so with a part of
ourselves that has within it the essence of God. We yearn for
God's salvation and for the reinstitution of His royalty, because
some part of us identifies with and appreciates His realization
by the world.

Rabbi Yonasan Eibeshutz comments on this and the previous
blessing. He says that yearning itself is a spiritual creation.
There are times when we have no other merit apart from our

yearning, and at those times the yearning, by itself, creates our merit. He says:

> A Jew should shed tears without restraint when he recites the prayers for the rebuilding of Jerusalem, and the Temple within it, and for the Davidic dynasty. In so doing, he sheds tears over the exalted state that man has within himself, by virtue of his soul. If we don't have Jerusalem, and the reign of David's dynasty, then we don't have life in its fullest sense.
>
> If the angels above (who realize that one can never take anything away from God) cry out and weep for the destruction of the Temple, shouldn't we? (We are affected by destruction and crisis, and we question the existence of God when we don't see His supremacy in the world.) Shouldn't we cry out over what, from our viewpoints, seems to be the disgrace of God?
>
> Every person is obliged to say in his heart, "Behold, I am prepared to give my life to sanctify Your Name." If, in my lifetime, I am not worthy of seeing the erection of the Temple, and the restoration of Jerusalem and the Davidic dynasty, let me die for the sake of bringing it closer. My eyes want to see nothing but a greater realization of God in Jerusalem, with the Davidic dynasty, because my entire being yearns for the sanctification of Your Name.
>
> Please have compassion on Your shamed children, who are willing to tolerate so much for Your Oneness and supremacy. They are prepared to sanctify Your Name in public, even if they are ridiculed for doing it.[12]

Implications of Royalty for Human Relationships

Royalty is the reward for self-control. No relationship can flourish without standards, self-discipline, and respect for the dignity of oneself and one's partner. The royalty of a relationship comes from mutual respect for each other, and from the self-discipline of living in a way that demonstrates such respect.

Notes

1. Exodus 15:11.
2. *Shebolei Leket*, chapter 18.

3. *Shemot Rabbah* 23:4.
4. *Shemot Rabbah* 23:4.
5. *Shemot Rabbah* 23:5.
6. *Shir HaShirim Rabbah* 2:2.
7. Zechariah 6:12.
8. Talmud *Bavli, Rosh Hashanah* 16a.
9. Talmud *Bavli, Rosh Hashanah* 16a, Ritva.
10. Psalms 93.
11. Genesis 2:7.
12. Yaarot Devash on the siddur.

CHAPTER 19

The One Who Hears
Our Prayers

שְׁמַע קוֹלֵנוּ יהוה אֱלֹהֵינוּ, חוּס וְרַחֵם עָלֵינוּ, וְקַבֵּל בְּרַחֲמִים וּבְרָצוֹן אֶת תְּפִלָּתֵנוּ, כִּי אֵל שׁוֹמֵעַ תְּפִלּוֹת וְתַחֲנוּנִים אָתָּה. וּמִלְּפָנֶיךָ מַלְכֵּנוּ רֵיקָם אַל תְּשִׁיבֵנוּ, כִּי אַתָּה שׁוֹמֵעַ תְּפִלַּת עַמְּךָ יִשְׂרָאֵל בְּרַחֲמִים. בָּרוּךְ אַתָּה יהוה, שׁוֹמֵעַ תְּפִלָּה.

❮❖❮❖❮❖❮❖❮❖❮❖❮❖❮❖❮❖❮❖❮❖❮❖❮❖

Hear our voice, Lord our God, have pity and be compassionate to us, and accept our prayers with compassion and willingness, because You are a God who listens to prayer and supplication. And from before You, King, do not turn us away empty-handed, because You listen with compassion to the prayers of Your people. Blessed are You, God, who hears prayer.

Historical Background

After being oppressed for 210 years in Egypt, the Jews cried out to God for help. The Torah says that God heard their cries, understood their plight, and connected Himself to them as the beginning of the process of their redemption.[1] The angels became exhilarated when they saw that God heard the cries of the Jews, and they exclaimed, "Blessed are You, God, who hears prayer."[2]

What excited the angels so much that they praised God for hearing the Jews' prayers at the beginning of the process of redemption? There were still many trials and tribulations ahead, and the redemption from Egypt would not even occur for another year. Why didn't the angels wait until the actual deliverance before saying their blessing?

There are three forms of prayer. In the first, the supplicant doesn't articulate what bothers him but merely calls out to God. A person may feel pain and may not even be able to crystallize what the problem is. He calls out to God with nothing more than a voice. When someone sobs out of such anguish, the result is this first type of prayer.

The second type of prayer has neither a voice nor sounds. The person knows in his heart or mind that he needs something, and he turns to God with that need.

The third type of prayer occurs when the need for a global salvation is expressed. For instance, if Jews are downtrodden, they may not have a particular need in mind but they are aware that things cannot continue as they are. They pray for God's help to rectify the situation.

After being enslaved for 210 years, the Jews in Egypt no longer knew exactly what to ask for in their prayers. They knew that the way in which they were living was unacceptable and undesirable. Their major prayer at that point was simply to ask God to "hear our voices." They wanted God to hear voices that were searching for Him, that were yearning to come closer to Him.

They also had a specific need, which was for God to rescue them from slavery. God listened to their prayers even though they were not eloquent and did not articulate a specific need. The Jews were capable only of calling out for help. There was a voice deep inside them that knew their physical and spiritual situation was not good. The fact that God paid attention to the Israelites' voices, without their even being able to articulate their needs, is what excited the angels. God is so eager to form a connection with the Jew that He listens to a yearning voice as much as He listens to the actual requests. The "voice of prayer" is the Jewish soul trying to come closer to God.

When we pray in Hebrew, especially if we can't fully understand the words, we know deep in our hearts that the prayers contain secrets and treasures which bypass us. Therefore, at the end of all of the personal requests of the Shemoneh Esrai, we say to God, "We don't know a fraction of what this all means, at its deepest level, but that doesn't really matter. Listen to the fact that there are voices calling out to You. It's not so critical that we don't know the deepest meanings of every word of the prayers. The bottom line is, it's our voice, and we are searching for You. Even if we don't know exactly what to ask for, hear our voice."[3]

The Berditchever Rebbe always managed to find merit and greatness in the behavior of the Jews, no matter what they did. Some of the Rebbe's congregants once complained that other congregants simply babbled their way through the prayer services. The Rebbe replied, "Bring over a 2-year-old child."

They did, and the child began to talk. The child's father understood every word that he said, but no one else was able to understand the boy.

The Rebbe commented: "See, the father knows what the child says. This is also true in our relationship to God. The sounds that we make sound like babbling to us, but the Father of the Jewish people understands our requests."

Sometimes people get lost when they try to be sophisticated instead of realizing the simple beauty of the connection between ourselves and God.

In every other request in the Shemoneh Esrai, we ask for something specific—wisdom, health, livelihood, and so on. Once we finish making our personal requests, we turn to God and tell Him that we have one more request, but it is non-specific. We simply want to have a bridge between ourselves and God, so that He will hear our voices. Once He does so, we will be able to feel close to Him. Afterwards He will be compassionate and give us those things that we've already requested, as well as other things that He knows we need.

Sometimes when children ask their parents for something, they don't really want the item. They simply want to see that their parents love them enough to give it to them. The item is simply a vehicle by which their parents can demonstrate this love. Similarly, in our relationship with God, we don't want only the items that we request. We first want to know that there is a connection with Him and that He loves us. Then we want Him to be compassionate and give us what we need.

This concept explains why the angels blessed God for simply hearing the voices of the Jews in Egypt. When the Jews cried out to God, they didn't know what they wanted or needed, but their recognition that God was willing to form a connection with them was the beginning of their process of redemption. When we cry out to God, we need never feel alone.

Relationship to the Previous Prayer

The theme of the previous prayer is the establishment of the Davidic dynasty in Jerusalem. The commentators explain that a unique level of prayer will be realized when the Davidic dynasty is reinstated. King David's primary method of growth was through prayer. The Psalms that he wrote were the spiritual habitat in which he grew to the highest levels of his spiritual capabilities. When David's dynasty is reestablished, it will bring the Temple in its wake, and with those two situations, a new level of prayer will be created. This idea is based on the verse, "And they shall be brought to My holy mountain, and they will be made happy in My house of prayer."[4] First the Temple will be rebuilt, and then a higher level of prayer will be possible. This Amidah prayer refers to that level of worship.

Meaning of the Words

The Vilna Gaon says that there are times when we pray the three types of prayers simultaneously. This occurs in this prayer of the Shemoneh Esrai.[5]

"Hear Our Voice"

This phrase describes the first type of prayer. A voice (kol) has no words or speech. We ask God simply to hear our cries, without our knowing exactly what it is we need or want. In this part of the prayer, the need is not enunciated. Similarly, when we say, "Lord our God," we are asking that He listen to us because He is our God.

"Have Pity and Be Compassionate to Us"

In these words we ask God to give us what we recognize we need, as well as those things we don't know we need but that God knows we need. This is the second type of prayer, in which the person simply knows that he needs something.

"And Accept Our Prayers with Compassion and Willingness"

This is the third type of prayer. Here we ask for general help and salvation. We ask God to help the Jewish people and the world arrive at the spiritual level at which they should be.

Pity, Compassion, and Willingness

In this prayer we say, "Have pity and be compassionate to us, and accept our prayers with compassion and willingness." "Pity" (chus) means the removal of pain. If a person sees a situation that is very distressing, the anguish the person feels about the situation is "pity." For instance, if a bystander sees a person lose money in a business deal, the bystander may feel bad for the victim and want the situation to end.

Pity can be felt even for inanimate objects; for instance, someone can feel bad that a tree was cut down.[6] When a witness to a situation feels pity, the sufferer or victim does not necessarily have sufficient personal merit to make him worthy of that pity or worthy of having the pain removed. The amelioration of the sufferer's situation by the witness—who cannot bear to see suffering—depends upon the latter's feeling of pity. Thus we acknowledge to God that we may not be personally worthy of having our anguish removed, but that—since God is all-good—we know that it "pains" Him to watch us suffer. Therefore, we ask that He have pity on us in His merit rather than in ours.

"Compassion" (rachamim) occurs when God actually feels the pain of the victim who is suffering. Pity occurs when God knows that the situation is not good and He feels anguish over it, but there is not true empathy with the victim. With compassion, however, He does feel empathy with the victim. When we ask God to hear our prayers with pity and compassion, we are saying that sometimes we don't deserve empathy, but He should ameliorate the situation anyway. At other times, we do deserve His empathy.

The commentators on the prayers say that if someone prays without giving much thought to his words, then he asks for God's compassion.[7] We ask God to empathize with us even if we aren't able to communicate meaningfully with Him. On the other hand, if we are able to pray in an intense manner, then we ask God to hear our prayers with "willingness" (biratzon).

Thus this prayer expresses the recognition that we have limitations in our abilities to pray and to understand prayer. This fact notwithstanding, we turn to God and say, "This was the same situation that occurred with our forefathers in Egypt, yet you listened to them. Please listen to us now."

Listening to the Voice

The Vilna Gaon says that the Hebrew word for voice (kol) usually refers to a request that is not justifiable.[8] For example, Abraham had two sons, the older one from his concubine Hagar, and the younger one from his wife, Sarah. Sarah was afraid that the concubine's son, Ishmael, was corrupting her son, Isaac. She told Abraham to send Ishmael away, but Abraham didn't want to do so. He thought that the influence of the household would refine Ishmael. God said to Abraham, "Everything that Sarah tells you, listen to her voice."[9] Even if what Sarah said didn't make any sense to Abraham and her request seemed illegitimate, he had to pay attention to her.

A second example of this was when God promised Abraham that his children would have merit through him, because he "listened to God's voice."[10] Abraham obeyed God's voice even when the directives didn't make any sense to him, such as when Abraham was told to bring Isaac as a sacrifice to God.

A third example was when the Jews went to war in the time of Joshua. Joshua told God that he wanted the entire war to be over in one day, something that was a military impossibility. But, God listened to Joshua and made the sun and the moon stand still for a certain number of hours. The book of Joshua says, "There was no day like this before, nor will there be such a time after today, that God listened to the voice of man, because God fought for the Israelites."[11] God considered the request inappropriate because there were many ways in which He could have conquered the enemy. Nevertheless, He did what Joshua requested, changing the laws of nature to make the sun and moon stand still.

The Vilna Gaon says that our forefathers followed the voice of God even when they didn't understand God's reasons for wanting them to do something. Likewise, every Jew is expected to follow the voice of God even when it doesn't seem to make sense. For instance, there is an entire corpus of Jewish laws, termed *chukim*, for which there are no rational explanations. Just as we accede to God's requests, even when they don't seem rational, we ask God in this prayer to "listen to our voice," even when our requests are neither completely sensible nor necessary.

When someone listens to God's voice, even when it seems to make no sense, the person recognizes that it is of paramount importance to do God's will. Understanding the nature of His requests is of secondary importance. Sensitivity to God's will, rather than to reason, motivates the person's obedience. Every Jew has inherited the ability to be sensitive to God's will, even when it seems to make no sense. When we ask God to listen to our voice, we recognize that we may not make sense to Him but we ask Him to be sensitive to our desires. Even when we do not personally merit having God do what we request, we ask Him to be sensitive to the fact that our forefathers cared about nothing more than doing His will.

Prayer and Supplication

Another phrase in this prayer is, "Because You are a God who listens to prayer and supplication." Prayers (*tefillot*) are what we say when we are worthy of being heard. "Supplications" (*tachanunim*) are prayers that we say when we are not worthy of it. *Tachanunim* comes from the Hebrew word *chinom*, meaning "for free" or "at no cost."

We also say, "And from before You, King, do not turn us away empty-handed." The Vilna Gaon says that when we pray, angels bring our prayers into the heavenly courts.[12] The heavenly courts can judge us and decide that we are not worthy of having our requests heard. This can occur only when our prayers go through the court system. When they go directly "before You," it is impossible for You, as a Father, to let all of Your children's prayers go unanswered.

What Prayer Accomplishes

We don't change God when we ask Him to respond to our prayers. God's decisions about whether or not to give us something are made with wisdom and with full knowledge that what He does is right. How, then, can we persuade God to change His mind when we pray?

Prayer is supposed to change us, not change God. We are supposed to undergo a transformation when we bring ourselves before God. Through this process during prayer, we realize that we are not the source of our own well-being. God is the source. Through this process, we come "before You."

Rabbi Chaim Volozhin said that once a person makes a close connection with God and bonds with Him, blessing inevitably follows.[13] This is so because when we connect ourselves to God, we become different. Our recognition that God is part of our lives automatically changes something within us. The connection itself allows God's blessing to flow.

Prayer doesn't persuade God to change His mind. When we bring ourselves one iota closer to recognizing God and striving toward Him, one iota closer to raising our voices in prayer, a new bond is created between heaven and earth. Blessing is inherent in any connection with God and is absent in the lack of connection. God is the source of all blessing, and He always makes His blessing available. How much we receive depends upon how much we connect ourselves to the Source. This prayer tells us that once we stand before God, we cannot go away from that experience empty-handed.

It is easy for us to ask God for a certain object and, when the request is denied, to think that our prayers were wasted. Prayer is much deeper than a sophisticated means of taking care of our shopping list. The greatest outcome of prayer comes through the process of simply being connected to God.

We may begin this prayer with the feeling that it is audacious to think we are worthy of having an audience with God. However, once we stand in God's presence and have brought ourselves to talk to Him, whether we are worthy or not, we ask God not to send us away humiliated. We don't want to feel that we don't belong in a close relationship with God. The whole purpose of this prayer is for us to try to form a connection with Him.

Uniqueness of This Prayer

Because this is the last of the personal requests in the Shemoneh Esrai, it has certain unique features.

In all of the other prayers of the Shemoneh Esrai, we make only private requests that match the theme of that prayer. For instance, when we ask for livelihood, we do not insert private prayers for health, although we could insert private requests for our own livelihood. When we ask for health, we can insert a private prayer for the health of an ill person, but we don't ask for wisdom. In this prayer, however, we can ask for anything we wish, because "Hear our voice . . ." encompasses everything.

The Zohar says that if a person sinned on a certain day and wishes to confess while saying the Shemoneh Esrai, then the proper place to do so is in this prayer.[14] Technically, the person could confess in the earlier prayer that asks for forgiveness. The reason we ask for it here is that when we do something wrong, we frequently feel unworthy afterward. We feel that we have forfeited our right to talk to God. This prayer stresses that even if we are unworthy, God will hear our voices. When we confess here, we acknowledge to God that we are unworthy but we ask Him to listen to us nevertheless:

> The way of God is to do good to all of His creations, and in particular to those who supplicate Him with humility and with earnestness, and especially to those who shed tears (during this prayer of "Hear our voice . . ."). Even a person who is full of sins can know that God will listen because the gates that are open to tears never close. A person will never be turned back empty-handed from those gates.[15]

Rabbi Yonasan Eibeshutz says that this prayer is a message to every Jew that there is nothing about which we shouldn't feel comfortable talking to God.[16] Whether it is something relatively minor or something of major importance, we should share all aspects of our lives with God. We should talk to God the same way that we speak to our best friend. We should open up to Him in every possible way, coming to Him not only when we have "important" things to discuss. This prayer is all-encompassing which means that God wants to hear everything about our lives.

This aspect of prayer makes it very personal. If we cannot personally relate to the other twelve requests in the Shemoneh Esrai, this prayer allows us to relate to whatever is of current concern to us. For example, if a man feels frustrated because he has been trying to buy a suit for a month and hasn't been able to find one, then he can use this concern to connect himself to God. He may not be able to relate to the restoration of the Davidic dynasty, but he can relate to not being able to buy the clothes that he wants. There are certain fundamental things for which we have to develop an appreciation, and these things form the first twelve requests of the Shemoneh Esrai.

In the thirteenth request, we can tell God everything that is in our hearts and say anything that is personally relevant to us. Being able to do this ensures that the supplicant will really concentrate during this prayer. People can say the rest of the Shemoneh Esrai with their minds on other matters if they don't find the other prayers relevant, but it is impossible for them to ask for those things that they really want without their thinking about them.

This prayer facilitates the major purpose of prayer: Tying ourselves to God through something that we find relevant to us. We can bond ourselves to God only through needs that we feel, and it is only in this prayer that we unequivocally say that we will not return empty-handed. We can't be sure that we can relate to the themes in the standardized, regimented prayers. This is the only prayer in which we are sure that we can authentically build a bond with God, because we do it through what is important to us.

The second accomplishment of this prayer is that we develop deeper trust in God by relating to Him about something relevant to us. If we believe that we can accomplish all of the "small" things ourselves and turn to God only when there are crises, we live in two worlds. We live as if God has a place in our lives only when we deem it appropriate. That approach contradicts the whole idea of trust in God. In this prayer, we develop a true and lasting trust that God has a place in our lives in both "minor" and "major" areas.

The third accomplishment of this prayer is that once we deliver ourselves to God, we have a much deeper commitment to use correctly that which He gives us through His sensitivity to our requests. Imagine that a person asks God for a marriage partner in this prayer, and God responds by giving the person what he requests. Can that individual then behave with his fiancée in a way that is contrary to God's will?

We need to realize that everything we have comes from God, and that we do not accomplish things on our own. When we don't compartmentalize our lives into parts in which God plays a role and parts from which He is excluded, we feel less entitled to use what we have in a way that violates God's will. Once we realize that everything we have is a gift from God, we have to reappraise ourselves constantly to see if we are using these gifts in the best way possible.

Implications of Hearing Prayer for Human Relationships

It is critical that people be sensitive to the "voice" behind their partner's words. A spouse should want to hear the unexpressed feelings of a loved one and should be sensitive to them. While it is preferable that a person be able to express his or her feelings clearly, it is not always possible to do so. A caring spouse should want to know even the unarticulated feelings, desires, and needs of his or her partner.

Notes

1. Exodus 2:24–25.
2. *Shebolei Leket*, chapter 18.
3. *Se'ach Yitzchak (Siddur HaGra)*.
4. Isaiah 56:7.
5. *Se'ach Yitzchak (Siddur HaGra)*.
6. *Se'ach Yitzchak (Siddur HaGra)*.
7. Etz Yosef in *Otsar HaTefillot*.
8. *Siddur HaGra*.
9. Genesis 21:12.
10. Genesis 22:18.
11. Joshua 10:14.
12. *Siddur HaGra*.
13. *Nefesh HaChaim*, Shaar 2.
14. Seder HaYom, quoting Zohar.
15. Seder HaYom, quoting Zohar.
16. Yaarot Devash on Shemoneh Esrai.

CHAPTER 20

Restoration of the Divine Presence to Zion

רְצֵה יהוה אֱלֹהֵינוּ בְּעַמְּךָ יִשְׂרָאֵל וּבִתְפִלָּתָם, וְהָשֵׁב אֶת הָעֲבוֹדָה לִדְבִיר בֵּיתֶךָ. וְאִשֵּׁי יִשְׂרָאֵל וּתְפִלָּתָם בְּאַהֲבָה תְקַבֵּל בְּרָצוֹן, וּתְהִי לְרָצוֹן תָּמִיד עֲבוֹדַת יִשְׂרָאֵל עַמֶּךָ. וְתֶחֱזֶינָה עֵינֵינוּ בְּשׁוּבְךָ לְצִיּוֹן בְּרַחֲמִים. בָּרוּךְ אַתָּה יהוה, הַמַּחֲזִיר שְׁכִינָתוֹ לְצִיּוֹן.

Be pleased, Lord our God, with Your people, Israel, and with their prayers, and reinstate the service to the Holy of Holies in Your house, and (also restore the) sacrifices of Israel. And accept their prayers with love and willingness, and may the service of Your people, Israel, always be pleasing (to You). And our eyes should see Your return to Zion with compassion. Blessed are You, God, who returns His divine presence to Zion.

257

Theme of the Prayer

This is the seventeenth prayer of the Shemoneh Esrai. It is also the first of the three paragraphs of thanks that we offer at the conclusion of the Shemoneh Esrai.

The Talmud says, "A person who prays should always first recognize everything for which God should be praised. Afterwards, he should ask for the things which he needs. Following that, he should give thanks for that which he received, like a servant who comes before his master. He first says the king's praise, then he asks his master for the things which he needs, and then he thanks the king for being good enough to listen to him."[1]

In the Shemoneh Esrai, the first three prayers represent God's praises, the thirteen middle requests are for our particular needs, and the last three prayers thank God for what He has already provided and for what we hope He will provide in the future.

Two difficulties are raised by this prayer. The first is that the blessing at the end doesn't quite fit the theme of the rest of the prayer. The theme is that we ask God to be pleased with our prayers, but we end with a request for God to return to Zion. This is a Messianic plea that seems to go far beyond the main theme.

The other difficulty raised here is that we already asked God to listen to us in the previous prayer. What does the present prayer add that wasn't included in the previous one?

Historical Background

The Jews received the Torah seven weeks after their Exodus from Egypt, and a mere forty days afterward they made a golden calf. On the Day of Atonement, eighty days later, Moses came down from Mount Sinai where he had propitiated God, and he told the Jews that God had forgiven them. The following day, on the eleventh day of the month of Tishrei, God commanded the Jews to build a Tabernacle so that His presence could reside there among them.

Six months later, on the first day of the month of Nissan, the Tabernacle was erected as a permanent structure. At that time, the Jews offered the sacrifices as God had commanded. God responded to their actions by sending down His holy fire as a symbol that He resided in the Tabernacle.[2] When the angels saw this, they exclaimed, "Blessed are You, God, who returns His divine presence to Zion."[3]

The commentator Nachmanides asks why the story of the Tabernacle appears in the book of Exodus, whose main theme is redemption, when it should appear in the book of Leviticus, whose main theme is sacrifices. He says the reason is that the divine presence really resided in the homes of our forefathers and foremothers. Their homes were tabernacles. When their descendants went into 210 years of exile in Egypt, the divine presence disappeared from the homes of the Jews. They were not truly redeemed until the divine presence once again permeated their homes. Until God dwelled among them, they had not actualized or freed their greatest spiritual potentials.

The greatest accomplishment of any Jew is to be able to bring the divine presence into his or her home. Therefore, when the angels voiced their blessing, they referred to God as "returning" to Zion in the same way that He had been with the forefathers and foremothers. They understood that God had been in this world long before the Tabernacle was built and that His absence during the Jewish exile in Egypt had been a temporary separation.[4]

This prayer, then, expresses our desire to have the relationship with God that existed in the homes of our Matriarchs and Patriarchs. We ask God to reveal Himself to us in the same way that He revealed Himself to the Jews in the time of the Tabernacle.

Returning to Our Source

A primary function of prayer is to help us recognize that God is the source of everything that we need in life. When we ask God to provide for us, we ascend to tremendous spiritual heights. The thirteen requests in the Amidah provide the structure within which we do this.

There are a lot of elements in us that make us resist merging with the Source that created us. We sometimes want to be totally independent of Him. Sacrifice symbolizes to us that we have inherent deficiencies which make us unable to exist independently of God.

Now that we no longer have animal sacrifices, we have prayer in its place. Prayer enables us to recognize that what we need comes from God while being a vehicle that returns us to our Source. The morning and afternoon prayer services are in lieu of the daily morning and afternoon sacrifices, and the evening service takes the place of those sacrifices that burned throughout the night.

When we say that the home of God used to be in the homes of our ancestors, we mean that they saw God as the Source of their existence in every facet of their daily lives. They didn't interact with God only in the synagogue and later enjoy themselves at home without being encumbered by "religiosity." When we pray, we realize that our homes should not be places that are independent of God. Our entire existence has meaning only when we fully return to our Source, not when we compartmentalize our lives into "spiritual" and "secular" areas.

It is for this reason that our forefathers are referred to as *Merkavah LeShechinah*, "the chariot for God's Presence." They created a place for God in this world because they didn't exclude God from parts of their lives. They understood that their greatness would be commensurate with how much they tied their existences to their Source.

In this prayer we say that God "returns His divine presence" to this world. This happens when we realize that our existences are meaningless unless we tie ourselves to God. When we sin, as when the Israelites sinned in the desert, we make a statement that we want God to be excluded from parts of our lives. When the Israelites realized that sinning made them lose rather than gain something, they wanted to bring God back into every facet of their lives. They did so by building a Tabernacle so that He could dwell within them.

Rabbi Yonasan Eibeshutz says,[5] "When a person says this prayer, he should be ready to dedicate his life to the service of God." A person should give his life over to God, just as a person who loves another is ready to give over his life for the person he loves. The person should recognize that he has no meaningful existence without God pervading every facet of his life.

Rabbi Yonasan Eibeshutz continues: "And he should pray that the service should be restored to the Temple, because that is where all of the spiritual accomplishments of the world are rooted." This means that the Temple is the one place in the world where God connects Himself to that which He has created.

Rabbi Eibeshutz also says, "If a person wants to be a sacrifice, it is necessary that he have no blemish within himself," just as an animal sacrifice wasn't allowed to have any physical blemish. "Blemishes" are created when a person reserves parts of his life for God and excludes Him from other parts. A blemished sacrifice meant that part of the animal was missing. Since prayer is a substitute for sacrifice, if it is blemished, the sacrifice is invalidated. This prayer in the Amidah is the dedication of bringing one's whole self in front of God.

The mind-set of being a sacrifice to God requires one to inspect his entire spiritual being and ask if he is bringing something before God that is not whole. In the words of Rabbi Eibeshutz: "Before a person brought a sacrifice he or she was required to repent. Therefore, all prayer requires that the person repent and correct himself prior to praying." Only when one repents can one truly bring his entire self back to God.

In this prayer, we ask God to find favor with His people and with their prayers, and to help us yearn to return to our Creator. The previous prayer referred to prayer as a vehicle through which we can receive what we need. In that prayer (as well as in the previous twelve requests) we focus on receiving. In the present prayer we focus on returning to God, because that is the best possible place to be. We conclude this prayer by referring to God's return to Zion because when we invite God's presence back into the world, it begins the process of ushering in the Messianic era.

This prayer of the Amidah is not considered to be a request because it reflects the general thrust of humanity. The theme is that all humanity must come to realize that life is nothing without God and that we want to come as close as possible to the Source that created us. The greatest thanks we can give to God is to want to come back to Him. The truest praise we can give God is to say that we ultimately cannot be without Him. In order to do this in the best possible way, we need a restoration of the Temple with its sacrifices.

Meaning of the Words

"Be Pleased, Lord Our God, with Your People, Israel, and with Their Prayers"

In no other Amidah prayer do we refer to ourselves in the third person. Elsewhere we ask for things for ourselves in the first person. This prayer addresses our returning to our Creator, and we don't have the audacity to believe that we have enough merit to be worthy of doing that as individuals. We merit returning to our Source only because, collectively, we are "Your people." We might individually merit benefiting from any of the thirteen requests ourselves, but we can merit returning to God only by being part of His representatives in this world. We could never generate sufficient spiritual merit to deserve it individually.[6]

Another reason for referring to ourselves as "Your" people is that when we are on good terms with someone and see him as being like us, we want to listen to what he has to say. When we dislike someone and see him as being alien to us, it is difficult to listen to him no matter how much sense he might make. In this prayer we ask God to see us not as independent beings, but as part of Himself. Since we want to become part of God, we ask Him to be pleased with us as if we were part of Him. Once He does so, He will listen to our prayers.

"The Sacrifices of Israel"

There is a difference of opinion as to how to punctuate this prayer. Some commentators (the Rishonim) say that we ask

God to "reinstate the service to the Holy of Holies. And the sacrifices of Israel, and their prayers, should be accepted with love and willingness."[7] The Vilna Gaon says that it should read, "reinstate the service to the Holy of Holies, and (also reinstate) the sacrifices of Israel. And accept their prayers lovingly and willingly."[8] According to the Vilna Gaon's approach, we ask God to accept our prayers and sacrifices when the Temple is restored. According to the Rishonim, we ask God to accept our sacrifices and prayers today. Since we have no sacrifices today, to what could this possibly refer?

Prayer originates from the act of *karban* (usually translated as "sacrifice"). What *karban* really means is "to come close." The Maharal (a commentator) says that the function of an animal sacrifice was to return a created being to the source of its creation. An innate quality of created beings is that they have an affinity with the source from which they came. This desire is naturally embedded within us. In Temple times, when a person went through the process of sacrificing an animal, he returned the animal back to God, and through this process the person returned himself back to God as well.

God has no need of animals per se. He designated animals as vehicles through which people could effect a total return to God. Through the process of making an animal sacrifice, people became aware that existence unconnected to God felt empty. By offering sacrifices, people could realize that they wanted to be as close as possible to the Source that created them, and they were able to return to this Source.

The Midrash says that there is an angel called *Sar HaGadol*, the "great general in heaven."[9] He is also called the "high priest of the holy abodes above, who offers up the souls of the righteous." These are the "sacrifices" that are mentioned in this Amidah prayer. This is not a request for God to take the souls of the righteous out of this world as offerings for us. Rather, as the Arizal (a renowned mystic) explains, this refers to souls of the righteous who have already left this world.[10] We ask that their souls come into a total union with God, which is the ultimate bliss with which a soul can be rewarded. The greatest pleasure a soul can experience after leaving this world is to be offered as a *karban* on God's altar. No one can comprehend the pleasure that the soul experiences from this. Thus, according to the Rishonim, we pray that God will hear our prayers now as well as draw close the souls of the righteous who are already in heaven.

"And Our Eyes Should See Your Return to Zion with Compassion"

The Yaarot Devash says that our eyes will be able to see that which we gain by our own merit when we return to God. We will not be able to see those things that we do not merit, although we will have a share in them.[11]

As an example of this, Lot's wife was rescued from the city of Sodom in the merit of Abraham. That is why she was told not to look back at the destruction that befell the city.[12] Since she truly deserved to be destroyed with the other inhabitants of Sodom, she wasn't worthy of seeing them die. We conclude the present prayer by asking God that we be worthy of seeing His return to Zion.

The Yaarot Devash continues: "By what merit can we be worthy of seeing God when He returns to Zion? In the merit of shouldering the burden of the bitter exile, and accepting that it comes out of God's love; by believing in God's Oneness (rather than believing that there are other forces that control this world); and by hoping for salvation." If we have these elements, then we can say to God, "We have a right to ask that we be able to see Your return to Zion." Since our eyes saw everything else, our eyes deserve to see the return of the divine presence to Zion as well.

Implications of Being Pleased for Human Relationships

In this prayer, we ask God to find us and our actions desirable. It is important that if we and a partner feel distant from each other, we must be able to narrow our gap by conveying a sense of true desire for one another. In order to do this, we must build our partner's confidence that we find pleasure in him or her. It is destructive to bear grudges against someone who is close to us, and it is equally damaging for either person in such a relationship to retain a sense that he or she is unworthy of regaining the other's love.

If we care about making a relationship work, we must make our partner feel good about his or her efforts to draw us close and please us, while making it clear, when there has been tension, that we will let bygones be bygones. We need to communicate with each other, to show our pleasure in each other's company, in order to reinstate each other's confidence in the relationship when tensions have interrupted its closeness.

One way that we solidify our relationships is by helping each other recall positive memories, and not allowing our shared pleasures to be forgotten. We must also be willing to let go of memories of our loved ones' negative behavior so that these don't destroy the enjoyable feelings we try to build together. The more we re-evoke positive memories, the more we can attempt to recreate similar feelings in the present and the future. We should never feel that our pleasurable experiences with our partner are irrevocably lost.

This prayer underscores the idea that we do not only want to perform correct actions so that God can reward us or refrain from punishing us. We want our relationship with Him to be paramount, which in turn motivates us to want to do what pleases Him.

Similarly, people should not "keep score" of each other's good and bad points, so that we are primarily focused on how many assets we have and how many deficiencies the other person has. When people do this, they become so consumed with being right that they lose sight of simply finding pleasure with each other.

When we are pleased with our partner, we should make every effort to show our pleasure so that he or she can feel truly accepted. When we do this, especially after we have become distanced from each other, we must do so consistently. Otherwise, if our efforts to reinforce our partner's solid footing with us are erratic, we destroy our credibility in building a secure foundation for the relationship.

Notes

1. Talmud *Bavli, Berakhot* 34a.
2. Leviticus 9:24.
3. *Shebolei Leket*, chapter 18.
4. Nachmanides, Introduction to the Book of Exodus.
5. Yaarot Devash on Shemoneh Esrai.
6. *Se'ach Yitzchak (Siddur HaGra)*.
7. Tosafot on Talmud *Bavli, Menahot* 110a.
8. Beur HaGra, *Shulchan Aruch, Or HaChaim*, chapter 120.
9. Etz Yosef in *Otsar HaTefillot*; Talmud *Bavli, Menahot* 110a; see also Tosafot on *Menahot* 110a.
10. Etz Yosef in *Otsar HaTefillot*.
11. Yaarot Devash on Shemoneh Esrai.
12. Genesis 19:17.

CHAPTER 21

Prayer of Thanksgiving

מוֹדִים אֲנַחְנוּ לָךְ שָׁאַתָּה הוּא יהוה אֱלֹהֵינוּ וֵאלֹהֵי
אֲבוֹתֵינוּ לְעוֹלָם וָעֶד. צוּר חַיֵּינוּ, מָגֵן יִשְׁעֵנוּ אַתָּה
הוּא לְדוֹר וָדוֹר. נוֹדֶה לְךָ וּנְסַפֵּר תְּהִלָּתֶךָ עַל חַיֵּינוּ
הַמְּסוּרִים בְּיָדֶךָ, וְעַל נִשְׁמוֹתֵינוּ הַפְּקוּדוֹת לָךְ, וְעַל נִסֶּיךָ
שֶׁבְּכָל יוֹם עִמָּנוּ, וְעַל נִפְלְאוֹתֶיךָ וְטוֹבוֹתֶיךָ שֶׁבְּכָל עֵת, עֶרֶב
וָבֹקֶר וְצָהֳרָיִם. הַטּוֹב כִּי לֹא כָלוּ רַחֲמֶיךָ, וְהַמְרַחֵם כִּי לֹא
תַמּוּ חֲסָדֶיךָ, מֵעוֹלָם קִוִּינוּ לָךְ. וְעַל כֻּלָּם יִתְבָּרַךְ וְיִתְרוֹמַם
שִׁמְךָ מַלְכֵּנוּ תָּמִיד לְעוֹלָם וָעֶד. וְכֹל הַחַיִּים יוֹדוּךָ סֶּלָה,
וִיהַלְלוּ אֶת שִׁמְךָ בֶּאֱמֶת, הָאֵל יְשׁוּעָתֵנוּ וְעֶזְרָתֵנוּ סֶלָה. בָּרוּךְ
אַתָּה יהוה, הַטּוֹב שִׁמְךָ וּלְךָ נָאֶה לְהוֹדוֹת.

We thank You, that You are the Lord our God, and the God of
our fathers, forever and ever. You are the Rock of our lives,
the Shield of our salvation, in every generation. We will thank
You and tell Your praise, for our lives which are given over into
Your hand, and for our souls which are in safekeeping with
You, and for Your miracles which are with us every day, and
for Your wonders and goodnesses that (occur) at all times—
evening, and in the morning, and in the afternoon. You are
good, for You have not stopped Your compassion, and (You
are) the Merciful One, for Your lovingkindness has not ceased.

We have always hoped in You. And for all of these may Your Name be blessed and exalted, our King, constantly, forever and ever. And all of the living shall thank You forever, and praise Your Name with truth, the God who is our salvation and our help forever. Blessed are You, God, whose name is Good, and to You it is fitting to give thanks.

Theme of the Prayer

This is the eighteenth prayer of the Amidah, and the second one that expresses thanks to God. It is known as the prayer of thanksgiving, and in it we thank God for the many good things that He has done for us. This prayer is also known as the Modim prayer.

Historical Background

The Talmud relates the following story[1]: God did not want King David to build the Temple. David said to God, "Master of the World, forgive me for the sin I had with Batsheva."

After David went through an intensive process of repentance, God told him, "You are forgiven."

David continued, "Make a sign for me in my lifetime that I am truly forgiven."

God replied, "I will not agree to make a sign for you in your lifetime, but I will do so in the lifetime of your son Solomon."

When King Solomon finished building the Temple, he wanted to bring the holy ark, with the Ten Commandments inside it, into the Holy of Holies, where they belonged. When he tried to do so, however, the doors of the Holy of Holies slammed closed. King Solomon prayed to God in twenty-four different ways, and yet the doors did not open. Then Solomon said, "Gates, lift up your heads, and let the gates of the world open up, and let the King of Honor enter."

When Solomon said, "King of Honor," he was referring to the Ten Commandments, which represented God's Word, but the gates didn't understand this. The gates wanted to suck up King Solomon for what they thought was an allusion to himself as the "King of Honor." The gates said to Solomon, "Who are you referring to when you say, 'King of Honor'?"

Solomon replied, "To God, who is great and mighty." He then rephrased his request, saying: "Who is the King of Honor? The Lord of Hosts is the King of Honor."

The gates still didn't open. Finally Solomon said, "Lord, God, do not turn away the face of Your anointed one in shame, and remember the lovingkindness of Your servant, David." He was answered immediately, and the gates opened.

The Talmud says that at that moment, the faces of all those who had ridiculed David, and who had said that he would never be forgiven, turned black with shame.[2]

Another midrash says that King Solomon actually brought David's coffin into the Temple and told the gates to open out of respect for the one who was in the coffin.[3] When that happened, the gates opened up. David stood up and saw the gates of the Holy of Holies part for him. That was a clear indication that God had forgiven David.

David alludes to this incident in one of his Psalms: "You have preserved me from the grave, You have made me come alive from those who descend into the pit."[4] The literal translation of this verse is that David was given life in the World to Come; the midrashic explanation is that David was raised from his grave so that he could witness the doors of the Holy of Holies open in his merit.

When the doors finally opened, the angels exclaimed, "Blessed are You, God, that Your Name is good, and it is fitting to give thanks to You."[5] What was it about this episode, more than any other in Jewish history, that made the angels feel that God's Name is good and that He is worthy of thanks?

Solomon was incredibly dedicated to building the Temple. When he reached the step that was the culmination of the process, the doors of the Holy of Holies slammed in his face. The Midrash says that the doors didn't open up for him because he was too self-confident.[6] He believed that the Temple was sanctified even without the Ten Commandments being in the Holy of Holies, since the Temple had been built with so much spiritual energy. Solomon's belief that the Temple was holy in the absence of the Ten Commandments resulted in the Temple doors closing, as if God were saying to Solomon: "You believe that the Temple is already holy, so have it your way.

Who needs the Ten Commandments inside if it is already holy?" As long as Solomon maintained his position, he was unable to get the doors to open.

The Temple doors yielded only when Solomon invoked the yearning of King David. David wanted to build the Temple his entire life. His humility in yearning to have a symbol that he had been forgiven for his mistake with Batsheva was what finally forced the gates to open. David's heartbreak over sinning, and over losing the opportunity to personally build a "residence" for God's divine presence, was what allowed the Temple to open its doors.

The angels said the blessing that God is good and that it is fitting to thank Him when they saw God's sensitivity to David's desire to have a sign that he had been forgiven. The angels blessed God when they recognized that His goodness opens up new vistas, new areas of spirituality that people close off to themselves. The angels exclaimed that the goodness that comes into this world is not really something of which we are worthy, but that it flows from God's goodness.

The Concept of Bowing

Adam, the First Man, was created in the image of God and put into the Garden of Eden.[7] God told Adam that he could eat any fruits in the garden except for the fruit of the tree of Knowledge of Good and Evil. At that time, Adam's nature was to be totally good. The inclination to do something wrong (the *yetzer hara*) existed only outside of him.

The snake then enticed Eve to eat of the forbidden fruit, and Adam also ate some of it. His actions showed that inherent in his initial nature was the option to do that which was right or that which was wrong. However, by going against God's command, Adam internalized the inclination to do wrong things, by which he created a mixture of good and bad.

As a result of Adam's choice, people are spiritually devoted one moment and are interested in sinning the next. Our mission is consequently to try to discriminate right from wrong to the best of our abilities and to pursue what is positive and dismiss what is negative.

The concept of thanking God, and bowing to Him, is related to distinguishing between what is right and what is wrong. Adam introduced the negative force into himself because he wanted to be like God. His arrogance made him not want to accept that God's command was for his ultimate benefit. He thereby created a perception of reality in which good and bad became mixed. God told Adam to listen to Him, whereas Adam "stood up" to God and decided to listen to himself.

When we bow, we show that we subjugate our will to God and acknowledge His will as being supreme. We demonstrate that God has ultimate wisdom and goodness and is the ultimate Director of our lives. Every time we bow, we break our resistance to allowing ourselves to be dominated by God's will. We demonstrate physically that we want to break our "stiff-necked" approach that denies that what God commands is good for us.

When we bow, energy is allowed to flow through our spines that otherwise cannot. It's almost as if there were a blockage, and breaking open the vertebrae of the spine allows our true life force to flow through us. This idea stands in contradistinction to the belief that the more independent we are, the more life energy we will be able to create and sustain. Some people believe that the more they subjugate themselves, the less life energy they will retain. When we stand up arrogantly in front of God, we create a *klipah*, a shell which surrounds our access to life. When we bow, we shatter the shell that confines us, and we allow our life energy to nourish us.

When we bow, we should focus on breaking our stubbornness and unwillingness to listen to God, who is the One who knows what is ultimately good for us. We are then supposed to straighten up gradually and be standing totally upright when we say God's name in the blessing that follows. This is done because bowing breaks our "shells" and allows our life energies to come through. As we straighten up, we then have the ability to face God. This process is known as "the revelation of the energy of the One who is the Source of all life."[8]

According to the Talmud, there are four places where we bow in the Amidah.[9] We bow at the beginning and at the end of the *Avot* prayer (the first prayer of the Amidah), and we bow at the beginning and at the end of the present (the Modim) prayer. The Talmud says, "He who does not bow in the Modim prayer, his spine will turn into a snake at the end of seventy years (the normal age at which someone dies)."[10] This statement refers to the following mystical concept and is not to be understood literally.

When someone is unwilling to bend to the will of God, his spine becomes like the snake in the Garden of Eden. That snake symbolizes the evil inclination that persuaded Adam to stray from God. In other words, "his spine shall turn into a snake" means that the person's life force becomes controlled by the inclination to do what is wrong. If someone is not willing to break his arrogance, then his life force becomes "sold" to the negative inclination.

When a person bows in the Amidah, he is supposed to bow deeply enough so that all eighteen vertebrae in his spine protrude. The connection between this prayer and the idea of eighteen vertebrae is that this prayer is the eighteenth one in the Shemoneh Esrai. The significance of bowing until all of the vertebrae protrude is that it is not sufficient to bow to God in only some areas of our lives. We must show our deference to God in all areas. To the extent that we are willing to bow to God in all areas of our lives, our spines can become pipelines for positive life energy.

The Concept of Thanksgiving

The Hebrew word for thanksgiving is *hodaah*. This word also means "to admit" or "to acknowledge." Rabbi Hutner said that every expression of thanks that one person gives to another is really a form of admitting.[11] People sometimes have difficulty saying "thank you" to another person because it implies that the first person needed the second. People who are very arrogant don't want to admit that they need something from someone else. Thus, thanking someone is related to the idea of admitting something. In the Modim prayer, we admit that we need God and that we appreciate everything He gives us. It is much easier for us to believe that we independently accomplish and provide everything we have, rather than it is to give credit to God.

The first place in the Torah where the Hebrew word for "thanks" appears is when Leah gave birth to her fourth son, Judah. She said, "This time I will thank God."[12] Rashi comments that Leah felt grateful to God for her having had *each* of her children. However, her husband, Jacob, had three other wives. Since they all knew that Jacob was destined to have twelve sons, they initially assumed that each wife would have three sons. When Leah had Judah, she recognized that she had been granted more sons than was her portion. Upon the birth of her fourth son, she admitted to God that she had been given something that was beyond her fair share.

As long as people get what they feel entitled to have, they find it hard to thank the benefactor for these gifts. They feel that they are only getting what is rightfully theirs. True thanksgiving occurs when people feel they have been given more than they deserve.

In the Modim prayer we say that God is the source of all goodness and that is why we have received from Him. We are not so arrogant as to say that we have received because we deserved to receive.

Relationship to the Previous Prayer

In the previous prayer we ask God to restore the Temple service. The priestly blessing follows the present prayer. It would seem logical for the priestly blessing to follow the previous prayer, since Solomon blessed the people when he finished offering sacrifices while dedicating the Temple. The reason the Modim prayer separates the previous prayer from the priestly blessing is that the worship of God and the admission that God is the source of everything we have in our lives form one unified concept. This means that the closer we come to God through sacrifices and prayers, the more we realize that everything we have was given to us by God. Moreover, we realize that we aren't given things because we deserve them; rather, God gives them out of His goodness.

Even though our spiritual attainments fall short of God's

greatness, God still gives to us. We develop a feeling toward God of, "You're so good, and You give us so much." This is such an essential feeling that gratitude is one of the major motivations behind our listening to God.[13]

Meaning of the Words

"We Thank You . . . Forever"

This prayer begins, "We thank You, that You are the Lord our God, and the God of our fathers, forever." The Hebrew word *modim* (translated here as "thank") can have three different meanings. It can mean that we admit that God is our God. It can also mean that we are thankful that God selected us, that we can turn to Him, and that He has never switched us for another people. It can also mean that we bow to God. Thus, the beginning of this prayer can mean that we will forever admit our recognition of God, forever thank Him, and forever bow to Him in acknowledgement that He is our God and that we have had a long-standing relationship with Him through our ancestors.

"Rock of Our Lives"

This phrase refers to our souls which are hewn from beneath God's throne of Glory. We are a chunk of the gold mine of spiritual essence, which is God. Our real lifeline comes from that part within us that is mined out of the very existence of God.

"The Shield of Our Salvation in Every Generation"

According to one interpretation, the phrase "in every generation" refers back to our thanking God.[14] Thus the prayer begins, "We will thank You, bow to You, or admit to You . . . in every generation." According to another interpretation, this phrase should be connected to the verse that follows it. According to this version it reads, "In every generation we will admit to You and tell Your praise."[15]

"For Our Lives . . ."

"For our lives which are given over into Your hand" means that every moment of life is ours only because You give it to us.

We normally take our existence for granted. Thus, with these words we admit to God that every moment of our lives is a gift that He has granted to us.

"For Our Souls . . ."

Next we thank God "for our souls which are in safekeeping with You." With these words we thank God not only for the fact of our existence, but also for the quality of our existence. The quality of our lives is due to the fact that we each have a soul. It is not enough to "admit" our thanks to God for having a soul. When we think about the tremendous quality of having a soul, we must sing God's praises: "And tell Your praise . . . for our souls."

The Hebrew word for safekeeping is *pikadon*, which really means "collateral." The soul of a human being is also called a *pikadon*. Some commentators say that the word here refers to the fact that part of our soul rises to heaven when we go to sleep each night, and we are not assured of getting it back the following day. We say that our souls are in safekeeping with God because He returns them to us every day, even though we may not merit His doing so.

Rabbi Yose HaGalili said: "This sign should always be in your hand. As long as a person is alive, his soul is in the hand of his Creator."[16] This means that God designates a tremendous amount of soul for each person, but each of us must draw it into ourselves. God sets up the situation, but it is up to each of us to do what we must to release the soul from its root into ourselves. Each of us has within us only a fraction of what our souls contain. God evaluates what we do with what we have, and if we merit it, He sends more of our souls into us.

In this Modim prayer, we thank God for giving us life. We also thank Him for designating so much potential spirituality to us, should we only wish to make use of it.

Levels of Appreciation: Three Kinds of "Thank You"

There are gradations in how we admit things to God, and in how we sing His praises. We need to have different levels of appreciation according to what we receive from God. We must express this appreciation differently and try to reciprocate it according to the magnitude of each separate gift. It is not appropriate to group all of the gifts of life together and express a generic thanks for them, or to reciprocate with a generic response. Just as a gift is not meaningful unless it is appreciated for its unique contribution, our saying "thank you" to God— one example of how we reciprocate His gifts—also requires discrimination.

God gives different things to different people. He might give one person $100 through the winning of a sweepstakes, and give a second person $1,000. The first person is required to give a tithe of $10, whereas the second person is required to give $100. If the latter gives only $90 while the former gives his required $10, the one who gave $90 can't compare himself with the former and feel good that he gave so much more. We are always required to appreciate and reciprocate in measure for what God gives us.

This requirement to be appreciative in appropriate measure can be illustrated in the following way. Insofar as both Jews and gentiles are alive, they each have the same things for which to be thankful. Nevertheless, Jews must also be appreciative of what we get as a people that is different from what any other people receive. In addition to expressing appreciation for what we have personally and individually been granted, we must express special appreciation for having been singled out for special gifts from God.

For this reason, we are required to give three types of "thank you" to God: One is for those gifts that we have received as living beings. A second is for those gifts that we have received as Jews. The third is for what we have received as individuals. If we address only one or two of these three, then we are derelict in our reciprocating to God what He has given us. If we don't thank God for what He has specifically given us, then we have not really appreciated God's unique relationship with us as individuals.

The Vilna Gaon says that thanking God "for our lives which are given over into Your hand" is a general "thank you" which we give God for simply being alive. "And for the souls which are in safekeeping with You" is a second thanks for making us Jews. "And for Your miracles which are with us every day" is the third type of thanks, for the specific gifts that God gives us individually.[17]

"Your Miracles . . . Your Wonders"

"Your miracles" (*neesecha*) are those things that are obvious to us, whereas "Your Wonders" (*neefliotecha*) are God's hidden miracles.

You Are Good . . . We Have Always Hoped in You"

In this passage we say that there is no end to God's compassion and that God extends Himself to human beings in limitless ways, because He is Omnipotent. When we say, "We have always hoped in You," we mean that God has repeatedly demonstrated His goodness to us. (On Purim and Chanukah there is a special prayer inserted at this place in the Modim prayer, because there are things for which we are especially thankful on these two holidays.)

"And For All of These (Things) May Your Name Be Blessed"

Having thanked God for all of the wonderful things that He does for us, we now praise Him. Many people feel that what they have is meaningless if they don't get everything they want in exactly the way they want it. They make themselves miserable when their exact desires aren't gratified. We, on the other hand, express our delight with all of the goodness that God has bestowed on us.

"All the Living Shall Thank You Forever . . . Our Salvation Forever"

We say here that as long as we are alive, we have opportunities and challenges and hope. We have reasons to be thankful for simply being alive. We then refer to God as "our salvation and our help forever." "Salvation" occurs whenever God helps us when we have no way of helping ourselves. At those times when we are capable of doing something on our own, we don't appreciate someone else taking over. Therefore, when we can help ourselves, God helps along with our own efforts. God thereby helps us in different ways, depending upon whether we are totally overwhelmed by the task at hand or need only some assistance.

"Blessed Are You, God, Whose Name Is Good"

With these final words of the prayer we say we recognize that the various opportunities and gifts of our lives come from God's goodness. Therefore, it is appropriate to give praise and thanks to God: "To You it is fitting to give thanks."

The "Rabbinical" Modim Prayer

The rabbis of the talmudic period determined that the congregation should say a second Modim prayer when the representative of the congregation (*Shaliach Tzibur*) repeats this prayer. This is known as the *Modim DeRabbanan*, the Modim prayer that was instituted by the rabbis, hundreds of years after the corpus of the Amidah was redacted by the men of the Great Assembly.

The reason a second Modim prayer is recited is to enable the congregants to thank God once again, along with their emissary. Were the congregants to sit silently while the *Shaliach Tzibur* thanked God, one might think that they had exhausted their thanks to God in their silent prayers. In order to demonstrate that we can never thank God enough, we repeat a Modim prayer along with the recitation of the original by the *Shaliach Tzibur*.[18]

Implications of Thanksgiving for Human Relationships

In this prayer we recognize that everything that God does for us is significant. A spouse should always seek to appreciate what is positive in a partner rather than being eager to criticize and belittle. The smaller a spouse feels, the less opportunity there is for a relationship.

It is very easy for one spouse's contributions and assets to go unnoticed unless they are verbalized by the other spouse. Once a spouse verbalizes appreciation for the other's qualities, each spouse loves the partner more than if such an "accounting" were not made. The one who expresses appreciation becomes more aware of the partner's special qualities, and the one who is complimented feels greater love toward the other. In this way, the relationship becomes enhanced via spouses' acknowledging the dignity of each other through mutual complimenting.

The more positive things a spouse can find in a partner, and the more he or she can recognize the other's strivings and accomplishments, the stronger the foundation of the relationship becomes.

Thanking a partner demonstrates that a spouse finds him or her worthwhile. All people need to feel that their spouses find something to appreciate in them. Relationships grow from each person's good feelings about themselves and their spouses, not from a sense of being taken for granted or feeling worthless.

One way of developing this type of appreciation is by regularly taking the time to ask oneself what life would be like without the spouse. How many good things would be lacking were it not for this spouse? It is much better to realize these blessings while the spouse is still alive rather than later. Spouses should share what they can while there is still an opportunity to do so.

Notes

1. Talmud *Bavli, Shabbat* 30a.
2. Talmud *Bavli, Shabbat* 30a.
3. Midrash, *Vaera* 8:1.
4. Psalms 30:4.
5. *Shebolei Leket*, chapter 18.
6. Midrash, *Bamidbar* 14:3.

7. Genesis 2:8.
8. Sfat Emet in *Siddur Likutei Yehuda*.
9. Talmud *Bavli, Berakhot* 34a.
10. Talmud *Bavli, Baba Kamma* 16a.
11. Pachad Yitzchak, *Chanukah*.
12. Genesis 29:35.
13. Ibn Pakuda, *Duties of the Heart*, treatise 3.
14. Iyun Tefillah in *Otsar HaTefillot*.
15. Iyun Tefillah in *Otsar HaTefillot*.
16. Sifri, Pinchas.
17. *Se'ach Yitzchak (Siddur HaGra)*.
18. Talmud *Bavli, Sotah* 40a.

CHAPTER 22

The One Who Blesses His People Israel with Peace

שִׂים שָׁלוֹם, טוֹבָה, וּבְרָכָה, חֵן, וָחֶסֶד וְרַחֲמִים עָלֵינוּ וְעַל
כָּל יִשְׂרָאֵל עַמֶּךְ. בָּרְכֵנוּ אָבִינוּ, כֻּלָּנוּ כְּאֶחָד בְּאוֹר
פָּנֶיךָ, כִּי בְאוֹר פָּנֶיךָ נָתַתָּ לָנוּ, יהוה אֱלֹהֵינוּ, תּוֹרַת חַיִּים
וְאַהֲבַת חֶסֶד, וּצְדָקָה, וּבְרָכָה, וְרַחֲמִים, וְחַיִּים, וְשָׁלוֹם.
וְטוֹב בְּעֵינֶיךָ לְבָרֵךְ אֶת עַמְּךָ יִשְׂרָאֵל, בְּכָל עֵת וּבְכָל שָׁעָה
בִּשְׁלוֹמֶךָ. בָּרוּךְ אַתָּה יהוה, הַמְבָרֵךְ אֶת עַמּוֹ יִשְׂרָאֵל
בַּשָּׁלוֹם.

Grant peace, goodness and blessing, graciousness, lovingkindness, and compassion upon us and upon all Israel,
Your nation. Bless us, our Father, together as one, with the
light of Your face, because by the light of Your face You have
given us, Lord our God, a Torah of life, and a love of lovingkindness, and righteousness, and blessing, and compassion,
and life, and peace. It is good in Your eyes to bless Your people
Israel at all times and every hour with Your peace. Blessed are
You, God, who blesses His people Israel with peace.

Theme and Historical Background of This Prayer

This is the nineteenth and final prayer of the Shemoneh Esrai. It continues the theme of thanking God that began in the previous two prayers.

The Israelites entered the land of Israel under the leadership of Joshua. They subsequently spent seven years conquering the land and seven years settling it. God promised to bring peace to the land following these two stages. When the angels saw that people could have a feeling of total peace in this world, they were moved to say, "Blessed are You, God, who blesses His people Israel with peace."[1]

The Priestly Blessing

When the emissary of the congregation repeats the Shemoneh Esrai, the Priestly Blessing is recited immediately prior to this prayer for peace. The Priestly Blessing asks God to bless the Jewish people. It reads, "God should bless you and protect you; God should shine His countenance upon you and be gracious unto you; God should find favor with you and grant you peace."

Meaning of the Words

We ask for six things in this verse—peace, goodness, blessing, graciousness, lovingkindness, and compassion. These parallel the six blessings that the priests gave the Jewish people. This final prayer immediately follows the Priestly Blessing and serves as a sign that God has consummated this blessing to the Jews. An alternative significance of our mentioning these six things is that God blesses the priests with the same things that they invoked upon the Jewish people.

"Bless Us . . . with the Light of Your Face"

When we ask God to bless us "together as one" with the light of His face, we mean that we want Him to give all of us all of the blessings we have asked for with a "pleasant face"— that is, willingly. We ask Him to turn to us with loving attention. There are times when God gives us things simply as a means of keeping us alive in the hope that we will subsequently become worthy of His giving to us in a greater way.

In this prayer we also ask God to feel comfortable enough that the light of His face be directed toward us. We want a relationship with Him, we don't only want the things that He can give us. We want to feel that God gives to us with so much attachment that He wants to talk to us "face to face."

"Because by the Light of Your Face, You Have Given Us . . ."

Here we say that when we come to God with unity ("as one"), we can then ask Him to bless us willingly with certain gifts. These gifts are a Torah that teaches us how to live, a love of doing acts of kindness, and a sense of righteousness, as well as blessing, compassion, and peace.

"Bless Us . . . Together as One"

Some commentators say that we cannot be worthy of seeing God's countenance unless we Jews are as "one."[2] Thus the phrase "Bless us, our Father, together as one" can also be read, "Bless us for we are one." This unity forms the vessel within which God can channel His blessing. When we are not unified, we are not capable of absorbing the blessing that flows from the light of God's "face."

The Nature and Importance of Unity

This is the only prayer in the Shemoneh Esrai in which we ask God for something that depends upon our being united. When we ask for forgiveness or health, for example, we don't do so in the merit of our standing before God "as one." It is only when we ask for God's blessing in the "light of His face" that we need to dip into the wellsprings of unity and ask for peace in that merit.

The Talmud says that Adam was created as a single individual whereas all other creatures were created in masses. We learn many things from the nature of Adam's creation. First, if a person saves one individual, it is as if he saved an entire world. Similarly, if someone does not save a person while having the opportunity to do so, it is as if he destroyed an entire world. The fact that Adam was created alone implies that it was worthwhile for God to create the entire world in the merit of one person.

The second thing we learn from Adam's creation is that no one can say that his family line is better than someone else's. We all come from one father. If many people had been the original progenitors of the human race, certain of their descendants could then claim a superior lineage.

The Talmud continues: "Look at the difference between man and God. Man has a seal and an emblem, and no matter how many different ways he presses down the emblem, the seals that result are always essentially identical. God imprints Himself upon the human being, and every single resulting seal is different. The same way that every person's face differs from another's and no two are exactly alike, so too are their ideas different."[3]

This talmudic quotation emphasizes that human beings are limited in their creativity. God has no limit to His abilities to make billions of people, each different from the next. Had we been created en masse, we would not possess any uniqueness. God created each person as a unique being, and He relates to each person according to his or her uniqueness.

This talmudic passage presents a seeming paradox. On the one hand, it says that no one can lord his uniqueness over another person, because we all ultimately descend from the same forefather. This is a statement of the unity of mankind. On the other hand, it says that God preserves the individuality of every person. Furthermore, each person has to make his or her special contribution to the world and not assume that others will do it for them.

One might think that the combination of many people's

uniqueness would make it impossible for them to unify. It might seem that we could all be truly compatible only if we were all created the same. The Talmud tells us that uniqueness and "oneness" come from the same source. People's true uniqueness is not in their physical appearance or endowment. Each person's uniqueness comes from God blessing each with a soul that has special potentials and abilities. Each soul can accomplish only its unique task. As a result, there are unique contributions that need to be made to the world, and these can be made only by each individual. Were we unique only in our physical endowments, then we would have conflicts between our respective physical desires. Peace comes from the inherent unity of the spiritual endowments of all human beings. Our souls do not have the physical limitations that our bodies have. Since all souls derive their uniqueness from the same Godly source and are not subject to physical limitation, they can all be unified.

King Solomon said that people's pursuit of their physical desires inherently creates separations between people.[4] Since the physical world is limited and fragmented, striving after material things sometimes allows for agreement between people and at other times creates conflict.

The Nature and Importance of Individuality

A person's individuality is most visible in the light that radiates from his or her face. We can very often see someone's personality by looking at his or her face. Before Adam sinned, his uniqueness was very clear. He knew that he had been created in order to relate to the world in a way that only he was capable of doing. He knew that it was "worth it" for God to have created the entire world solely for the unique contribution he would make to it.

Once Adam brought death into the world, it became more difficult for people to believe in their uniqueness. People saw that they died just as did all other living creatures. They realized that just as the world continued without other living creatures, so the world would go on without humans as well. People might remember a deceased person for a short while, but the world seems to continue just the same, without really missing the people who are gone. Thus the phenomenon of death destroys many people's sense of individual uniqueness.

Nevertheless, our sense of spiritual individuality is always preserved because we believe in the continuity of the soul. We don't believe that death is final, and we believe in the future resurrection of the dead. There is something eternal about each one of us.

Before Adam sinned, every part of him proclaimed his individuality. The Midrash says that after Adam sinned, God put His "hand" on him and diminished his spirituality. Yet, there was one part of Adam's body that God did not diminish: his face.[5] The only thing that reminds us of our individuality is the brilliance of the light which radiates differently from every person's face.

When we ask God in this prayer to "Bless us . . . together as one, with the light of Your face," we ask God to help us unify all of our individual potentials and contributions. These gifts reflect His essence. Only when we recognize the "light of Your face," which reflects our true uniqueness, can we unify "together as one."

If we come before God in a state of disharmony with each other, God sees us each looking after our own individual self-interests. There can be disharmony only if people pursue their respective physical desires. God sees disharmony among people as emanating from the body, not from the soul. As long as we are steeped in our physical desires, we can't ask God to grant us spiritual uniqueness from the light of His face. Once we show God that we are interested in unity, He sees that we are interested in spirituality. We can then ask for spiritual individuality.

The Concept of Peace

In our literature, peace is not only the absence of war, but it is something actively positive in itself. In the Torah a man named Zimri, the head of one of the Jewish tribes, had an illicit sexual relationship with a Midianite princess named Cozbi in front of the entire Jewish people. This incident led to the outbreak of an epidemic. At that point, a man named Pinchas zealously executed Zimri and Cozbi, risking his own life in the process. He did this, in part, to stop the epidemic that resulted from Zimri's actions. God rewarded Pinchas for his wonderful act by granting him "My covenant of peace."[6]

A second example of peace being due to a positive act is found in the Priestly Blessing. God instructed the priests to bless the Jews by putting His Name on His people, and He promised that He would consummate their blessing. (An alternative explanation is that God promised to bless the priests themselves for their blessing the Jewish people.) As has been mentioned, the Priestly Blessing appears in the Amidah directly prior to this prayer for peace. This is because the priests blessed their people after the sacrifices were offered in the Temple, and the prayers that accompanied the sacrifices precede this prayer in the Shemoneh Esrai.

The commentators ask, "What kind of blessing does God give the Jewish people, or the priests, via the Priestly Blessing?" The response is that God has only one kind of blessing, and that is a blessing of peace. We know this from the verse, "God will give strength to his people, God will bless His people with peace."[7] This tells us that when God gives a blessing whose nature is not further elucidated, that blessing is one of peace.

We often try to create peace in our own lives, and we fail. For instance, the State of Israel was created in order to foster a feeling of peace for the Jews; yet no matter what has been done to try to preserve this feeling of peace, it has eluded us. This example teaches us that peace is not something we can unilaterally create for ourselves; it is a condition that requires God's involvement. Our ability to have peace with the nations around us reflects the level of internal peace among the Jews themselves. If we have no peace with each other, we will have no peace with our neighbors. The Or HaChaim wrote that there will be times when we will be able to live in the land of Israel, but we will not be able to live there in peace. Internal strife and conflict would make it impossible to experience the benefits of living in the land of Israel.[8]

External peace can be seen as a barometer of our internal

spirituality. To have peace with each other, we therefore need to develop peace within ourselves. When we request peace, we ask God to unify our physical and spiritual selves. We don't want to have separate identities, being in a spiritual mode at certain times and in a physical mode at others. Someone who is at peace with himself integrates his physical and spiritual drives. The Hebrew word for "peace" (*shalom*) derives from the word meaning "complete." We have true peace when we unify our physical and spiritual sides.

When we say that the only blessing God gives is that of peace, we mean that the most essential blessing He can grant is for our physical and spiritual selves to be integrated with each other. Our physical and spiritual parts should not be at war with each other. We cannot find peace when we attend only to our physical uniquenesses and then try to gratify our physical drives. This makes us similar to everyone else in the world. But when we are able to harness our physical drives to serve our spiritual uniquenesses, then we truly feel at peace, and every moment of life is fulfilling. This situation is truly the greatest blessing anyone can have.

God is One and is not fragmented. The more we emulate God, the more we can receive His blessing. When a Jew finds unity internally and a unity in the external world, then he or she is truly blessed.

Pinchas fought against immorality. Immorality is the compartmentalization of a person's physical and spiritual drives. The Zohar says that Zimri, the man whom Pinchas killed, had a tremendous soul. Whatever well-intentioned motivations Zimri may have had when he acted, the other Israelites followed his example in deed, without any redeeming motivations. Pinchas felt that Zimri and the other sinning Israelites were disgracing themselves by relating to their commonality with the rest of the world. Human beings should never lose sight of that which dignifies them and makes them unique. What Pinchas abhorred about Zimri's illicit deed was that it represented a descent from his uniqueness and its balance with his physical being. Because Pinchas couldn't tolerate that, God blessed Pinchas with His covenant of peace. By striving to find his uniqueness, Pinchas demonstrated that he was on the path to inner unity. Focusing on our spiritual uniqueness gives us the wherewithal to develop an inner sense of unity, and thus true and lasting peace.

When the Israelites entered the land of Israel, they had no more conflicts between their spiritual and physical selves, and therefore they had peace. Jews can attain this type of peace only when they live in their own land, with their own government, ruled by the laws of the Torah. As long as Jews are strangers in the Diaspora, they cannot fully integrate their physical lives with their spiritual lives. The real challenge of unifying our two selves occurs when we live in our own land. The more we have from the physical world, the greater is the challenge of integrating our spiritual and physical perspectives.

For example, people who have no money don't get into business arguments, because they have no money to fight about. The more people have, the more they potentially have to fight about, and the greater is the challenge of unifying their two selves. The truest test of inner unity among Jews is how well they interact with each other when they all are sharing the same resources and are living in their own land.

When Jews lack their own land, they lack the greatest challenge to their unity. This is why the angels made their exclamation only after the Jews had conquered and settled the land of Israel and had truly made it their own. When that happened, and they still had internal unity as well as unity with their fellow Jews, it was truly remarkable. The angels were justifiably exhilarated when they exclaimed, "Blessed are You, God, who blesses His people Israel with peace."

God did not make this world a miserable place strewn with insurmountable obstacles. We do have challenges and barriers to overcome, but God created the world in a way that each of us can reach true inner peace. Once the Jews unquestionably possessed their land, the angels recognized God's attribute of granting people the ability to find real peace.

The request for peace is truly a prayer of thanksgiving to God. Our two selves are diametrically opposed, yet there is a way of unifying our spiritual and physical dimensions. We can accomplish this feat only because of God's greatness and goodness. Since God is One and He endows us with a sense of unity, we can strive for our own inner unity and "oneness."

Peace does not come about through compromising one's self. It comes about through finding one's truest essence.

Implications of Peace for Human Relationships

There are two important points we can learn from this prayer. First, when two people get married, it is critical for them to share some kind of spiritual goal in order for unity to be created. When they have no spiritual goal, then by definition they relate to each other as physical beings. This state creates separation, because physical things are separate by nature.

The second point we can learn from this prayer is that after we have done everything humanly possible to nurture our relationships, we still need to ask God to bless us. We should pray for God to bring harmony, wholesomeness, good qualities, and grace into our lives. We should ask God to give us that which is a prerequisite for every relationship to grow and thrive—a sense of inner peace, as well as true peace with our loved ones.

Notes

1. *Shebolei Leket*, chapter 18.
2. Achrit Shalom in *Otsar HaTefillot*.
3. Talmud *Bavli, Sanhedrin* 38a.
4. Proverbs 18:1.
5. *Yalkut Shimoni Tehillim* 830.
6. Numbers 25:12.
7. Psalms 29:11.
8. Or HaChaim on Leviticus 26:5.

Index

About the Author

Yitzchok Kirzner is Rabbi of Congregation Kol Yehuda in Brooklyn, New York, and is Director of the City-Wide Educational Outreach Programs of the Jewish Renaissance Center in New York City. He is the founder of the West Coast Jewish Learning Exchange in Los Angeles, California, and also served as its Director.

《✧《✧《✧《✧《✧《✧《✧《✧《✧《✧《✧《✧

Lisa Aiken received her Ph.D. in clinical psychology from Loyola University of Chicago. A psychologist in private practice, she is also a public speaker and writer on topics of Jewish interest.